C.B.

THE LIFE OF
CHARLES BURGESS FRY

CLIVE ELLIS

J.M. Dent & Sons Ltd
London Melbourne

First published 1984
© Clive Ellis 1984

This book is set in 10/13 point Linotron Aster by
Tradespools Ltd, Frome
Printed in Great Britain by
Richard Clay (The Chaucer Press) plc, Bungay, for
J.M. Dent & Sons Ltd
Aldine House, 33 Welbeck Street, London W1M 8LX

British Library Cataloguing in Publication Data

Ellis, Clive
   'C.B.'.
   1. Fry, C.B.   2. Cricket players—
   England—Biography
   I. Title
   796.35'8'0924   GV915.F7/

   ISBN 0-460-04654-3

Contents

Foreword

For sheer versatility, Charles Burgess Fry was unique. In one man there was a scholar, poet, novelist, journalist, editor, teacher, politician, cricketer, soccer player, rugby player, golfer, angler, athlete, skater, skiier, sculler, diver, tennis player, hunter and boxer. As a physical specimen he could have been plucked straight out of Ancient Greece. He stood 5 feet 10½ inches tall and in his prime as an athlete weighed 12½ stone, and was confidently muscled, lithe, with panther-like speed. He was the product of a bold, adventurous age, though he stood apart from his leisured contemporaries because there was no family wealth behind him. Maybe today, attempts would have been made to programme him as yet another specialist, but I suspect that his independent spirit would not have been tamed. For more than anything he was a tremendous enthusiast.

When I began researching this book I assumed that I would discover a central theme to C.B. Fry's life, but I gradually found that each aspect of his career posed half-a-dozen questions. A startling divergence arose between Fry the thinker and Fry the practitioner. He himself could never quite decide whether he was a tyrant or a rebel and in the absence of certainty he kept a foot in both camps.

He preached that a batsman who was fit and healthy could embark on the first Test Match of his life with the same sangfroid he might be expected to show on the village green. He preached it, but he did not practise it: he was patently wracked with anxiety, for instance, when he was facing the Australians. He preached that fielders should not drop catches if they were fit, balanced and alert. But he himself spilled an inexplicable proportion of the easy catches which came his way (the hard ones he was more than likely to pocket!). He preached that journalists should always be helpful and constructive. Yet he had an irrelevant, snobbish obsession with the basic educational background of most Australian cricketers. He preached discipline and yet apparently exempted himself from its restrictions.

He had the in-bred arrogance of someone who knows that nature has allotted him an undue share of her gifts, yet he could be shy and insecure, his domineering manner being only by way of compensation. There were two distinct sides to Fry's personality, therefore, and he was not always able to choose which face he wore. When, for example, as one of the most famous cricketers in the world, he would be asked for his autograph, it was never certain whether he would treat the request in the wholly flattering light intended or regard it as pure effrontery and dismiss the auto-graph-hunter with a contemptuous gesture.

Fry was quite capable of being alone in a crowd. Towards the end of his life he wrote to the BBC, saying he could 'talk a lot of rot and be listened to', but the listeners tended to grow weary of the self-possessed monologues. It was as if his life never ceased to be a public performance and there was a critical gap in his conscious-ness, where most people accommodate the trivia and mundane domestic matters.

Notwithstanding all this, he was a giant and vital personality with a splendid sense of humour and, it must be admitted, a gift for self-deprecation which forgave much of the adulation for his own qualities. Some people have suggested that he was ultimately a disillusioned failure, but if this was failure I would defy anyone to define success. The only thing he lacked was naked ambition, a doubtful virtue in any case.

Considering all these aspects of C.B. Fry's life and character it is astonishing that no one up to now has written a full biography of him. In 1912 A. Wallis Myers began the job with a book which traced the first forty years of Fry's life, and I make no excuse for quoting liberally from a study which offers valuable insight and is, these days, scarcely to be found. Fry's autobiography, *Life Worth Living*, appeared in 1939, and while it has been justly acclaimed as a most entertaining book, vital gaps were still left for someone to fill: for example, there were the last fifteen years of his life to describe, as well as the need to revive some of the incidents and experiences which he would have preferred to see vanish in the mists of time.

There have been other writings about Fry, but he has not really been well served by those who have presented him as a paragon of excellence. I have tried instead to give a rounded picture of a man who succeeded gloriously, but who also occasionally disappointed himself, his family and friends. I have tried, too, to provide a fresh interpretation of chapters in Fry's life which, in factual terms, have already been well chronicled.

Unfortunately I cannot say that I have been able to call upon help from C.B.'s family, but I am convinced that this does not alter the basic justification for this book. Understandably there are not many people alive today who remember Charles Fry further back than the 1930s, and most of those who wrote about him are now dead. In these cases I have been forced to rely on chronicled references, but this has been a highly selective process, especially in relation to Fry's own voluminous writings, and this line of research has uncovered some previously obscure anecdotal gems. Wherever possible, and relevant, I have sought out primary sources.

I am greatly indebted to the many people who responded enthusiastically on hearing that I was writing a book about Fry. Among the great cricketers of the past I must thank Sir Donald Bradman, Gubby Allen, Abdul Hafeez Kardar and Percy Fender, one of the few surviving cricketers whose career overlapped with Fry's. I was also delighted to receive letters from the well-known commentators on the game, John Arlott and Peter West. E.W. Swanton described a biography of C.B. Fry as 'a daunting task'. He may well have been right, but I hope I have justified that task. I am also grateful to Ronny Aird, former Secretary of the MCC, Stephen Green, curator at Lord's, H.A. Osborne, in charge of the Sussex cricket library at Hove, and Robert Brooke, who kindly answered some statistical inquiries.

John Walker enabled me to trace Fry's triumphant career at Repton School and invited me to relive the sublime pleasure of eating a school lunch! C.S.L. Davies, keeper of the archives at Wadham College in Oxford, was also very helpful, and Oxford Liberal Ivor Davies lent valuable assistance when I was looking into Fry's political exploits. I treasure especially a meeting with Reg Sinfield at Colston's School in Bristol. He is the link between the two most important and enduring things in C.B. Fry's life, cricket and the training ship *Mercury*. Sinfield was a cadet on the *Mercury* and went on to become a professional cricketer, playing once for England just before the Second World War.

Other *Mercury* old boys to whom I am particularly grateful for recollections are Capt. Ron Webb, OBE, Lt. Cdr. Peter Whitlock, MBE, RN, Capt. Jack Cousins, the Rev. Bob Precious, James Darby, Ian Dodd and Rex Mudway. Among those who have lived in Hamble, where the training ship was based, I have to thank Mabel Whitcombe, Violet Chandler, Alan Hooker, Ian Underdown and especially Richard Robinson for helping me to piece together the *Mercury* story.

My journey through the BBC's Written Archives Centre at Caversham Park, Reading, was eased by Gwyniver Jones, herself a confessed fan of C.B. Fry. Sunday Wilshin worked as a producer for the BBC when Fry was a regular contributor and she was able to give me a valuable insight into his relations with the Corporation. She was also one of his lucky dancing partners, the most accomplished of whom was Josephine Bradley, who recalled for me her first meeting with Fry fifty years ago and their subsequent close friendship.

Staff at the British Museum, the Newspaper Library at Colindale and the India Office Library were most helpful and I also received valuable assistance from the Society of Authors, the English-Speaking Union, the Horatian Society, the United Oxford and Cambridge University Club (formerly Oxford and Cambridge University Club) and the Merchant Navy and Airline Officers Association.

Finally, since I have referred so often in this book to the writings of Fry, especially his autobiography, *Life Worth Living*, because he was a man who expressed himself so frequently and so forcibly in print, I must acknowledge the kind permission of Associated Book Publishers Ltd for allowing me this privilege.

Clive Ellis
Essex, 1984

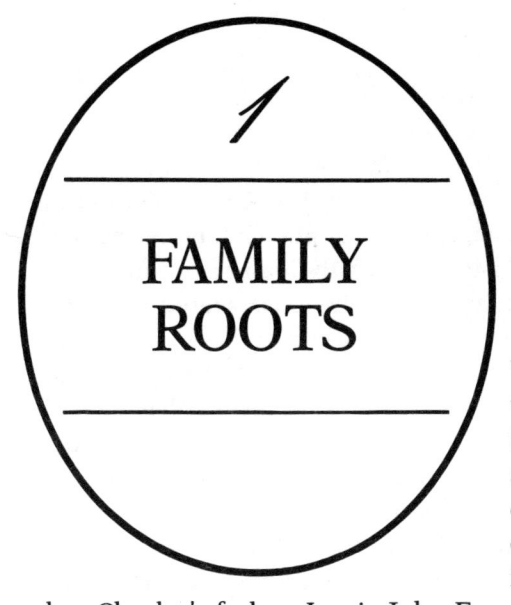

1

FAMILY ROOTS

When Charles Burgess Fry was born in East Croydon, Surrey, on 25 April 1872 it signalled the start of a new era for the family. The roots of the Fry family were firmly embedded in Sussex, but Charles's father, Lewis John Fry, worked in the Civil Service and had to be within easy reach of London during the week. Hence, he and his wife were in Croydon when their first child, Charles, came into the world, although they still retained their Sussex base and regarded the county as home.

Young Charles's early memories of the northern part of Sussex, which had played host to generation after generation of Frys, were too brief for him to have detailed recollections. In his autobiography, *Life Worth Living*, written in 1939, he reflected: 'After all these generations all that I, the eldest son, now possess in the ancient Saxon clearing is a pew in Rotherfield Church.'

His father had the dignified bearing of a military man. He worked at Scotland Yard and concluded his career by controlling the constabulary candidates' department. In his younger days his sporting prowess was limited to rowing – he was a member of the Thames Rowing Club – but in retirement he became fond of golf and shooting. Charles's mother, born Constance Isabella White, showed little athletic ability.

C.B., as he soon became widely known, who was followed into the world by a brother and a sister, wasted no time in revealing a mischievous, independent streak, which gathered momentum when the family moved to Kent, first living in Chislehurst, then Orpington. One sport which took his fancy was bird-stalking: he developed an uncanny facility with a catapult and tried to confine his prey to sparrows and starlings, although he bagged a robin by

1

mistake on one occasion.

He became enchanted with the game of cricket at the age of seven, watching from the top window of the house at Orpington as two of the best local players engaged in net practice. From then on he insisted on getting a closer view of the game, relishing the pleasing sound of willow against leather as he peered over the hedge at the bottom of the garden. His interest was eventually rewarded with an invitation to join in one of these practice sessions and soon C.B. was watching his heroes when they played on the village ground in Orpington. About a year later he was asked to make up the numbers for a game and succeeded in scoring seven, the result of two powerful hits to leg.

It was about the same time that C.B. discovered that he had immense natural spring. A high-jump competition formed part of a Sunday School treat and when C.B. was taken to watch by his nurse he was invited to compete by the organizing curate. He won the event easily and although he did not qualify for the prize he was sufficiently motivated by the experience to rig up a high-jump bar at his home.

His latent ability as a long jumper was revealed in more unorthodox circumstances: there had been cases of hydrophobia in the neighbourhood and when C.B. saw the family's pet fox terrier foaming at the mouth he was understandably panicked. He later recalled the curious incident:

> This sort of thing acts like lightning in a boy's mind, so I ran half a dozen strides, cleared the sloping top of the banks and the high hedge half-way down it, landed in the soft earth, and was up a Victoria plum-tree before Dan, who was looking at me from the top of the bank, knew what was up. He went on champing his mouth, foaming, and wagging his tail, and then came slowly down the steep little path and sat at the bottom of the tree. Presently I saw my father, who had come back from London by the evening train. I shouted to him that Dan was foaming at the mouth. My father, as usual to anything I said, twirled his golden moustaches and shouted, 'Nonsense!' but he came up the garden in his black morning coat and London trousers carrying an overcoat and a pudding-basin of water in the other hand. Shielding his legs with the overcoat,

he presented the water to Dan, who immediately lapped up the lot. So I came down, though Dan was certainly still foaming. While we were looking at him he turned away, went up the bank, and brought back a large toad which he deposited for our admiration. I then went back to see where I had jumped, and I was astonished at the distance I had cleared from the top of the bank over the intermediate hedge.

The active young mind was always seeking new, if solitary diversions, all the while milking the knowledge of people around him. His parents were not particularly inspirational, but an uncle on his father's side had been a fine hurdler, high jumper and tennis player, and there were two interesting characters in his mother's branch of the family. C.B.'s grandfather, Dr Charles White, had been at Cambridge and after being invited to go to St Petersburg as tutor to the Russian Prince, later Czar Alexander II, he returned to England and to more down-to-earth academic pursuits. He started a private school at Brighton and Charles used to be sent to Hove Lodge 'in order to get a bilious attack and be dosed with syrup of Senna by Dr Dill'.

When C.B.'s grandfather died it was his Uncle Percy who introduced pupils at Hove Lodge to the mysteries of Homer and Virgil. Percy White became a fine and prolific novelist and he was also an accomplished enough cricketer to be chosen for the Gentlemen of Sussex. More important, he taught the inquisitive Charles Fry how to shoot with a catapult.

C.B. did not have as much success at trapping birds with bird-lime – he found the ingredients hard to obtain – but he did become a juvenile authority on fishing thanks to *Every Boy's Book*, and he eventually persuaded his father to buy him a fishing rod. He discovered a pond near to Orpington Priory, but these were barren waters and, acting on a tip from his governess, he transferred his attentions to Keston Fishponds. The twelve-mile round trip did not discourage him and even though he faced a long wait before bagging his first roach he walked obsessively to Hayes Common for the 'excitement of watching a float'.

A summer holiday to North Wales had fresh delights and challenges in store, for now there were trout to pursue. The Frys had the best of all possible teachers in a man called Jones, a positive magician at conjuring reluctant fish from the depths. Young Charles marked his debut by catching a trout of pleasing dimensions and, after a lifetime of fishing many of the bounteous waters of the world, he still rated Jones from the Fairy Glen as the best fisherman he had ever seen.

At the age of nine C.B. was despatched to Hornbrook House at Chislehurst and into the fearsome clutches of Mrs Humphrey, who ran the establishment with her husband. Mrs Humphrey was a six-footer who assumed the proportions of a giant for the terrified pupils in her charge. Fry said in *Life Worth Living*: 'The reason I was sent to Hornbrook House in order to be educated by Mr and Mrs Humphrey was that my mother told my father that I was getting out of control; she never knew where I was from morning till night (due to hazel copses and Keston Fishponds); my father met a man in the train who told him that Hornbrook House was the nearest school to Orpington he knew of. So there I went.' It was not an arrangement which met with the young Fry's approval. He detested being a weekly boarder and the memory of the train journey back to the school each Monday morning was a recurring nightmare.

In years to come Fry developed a mature notion of happiness, shaped to a great extent by his own experiences. He was a firm believer that strength of feeling was determined by opposite emotions and sensations, almost in the manic-depressive mould. In *Fry's Magazine* in 1905 he wrote: 'Excepting the children, who have a perfect genius for happiness, as well as an often unrecognized capacity for sorrows whose depths the elders rarely gauge, it seems to me that the happiest folk are those who apparently have the least worldly reasons for being so. It is the people that find life a smooth road who grumble and grizzle, and mope and pule. Happiness is largely a matter of contrast. The old world jogs on the see-saw principle. Time is a pendulum beneath the great dial of eternity; human life is made up of reactions.' He went on to suggest that health, enjoyment of fresh air and basic fitness were other important constituents of happiness and it was in these that Fry found great solace throughout his life. The misery of his early days at Hornbrook House therefore contrasted strongly with his love of the outdoors, his zest for solitary adventure and his quickly developed talent for sports.

C.B. avoided specific criticism of his parents in his later writings, but he was acutely aware of their indifference to his upbringing. They were nothing more than solid middle class, but in those days people even at a modest income level could afford to entrust governesses, tutors and maids with much of the day-to-day trivia involved in raising children. If C.B. learned how to be self-sufficient at an unusually young age, this is not to suggest that he felt internally secure. Far from it: he remained uncertain about other people and could be both exuberant and introspective, depending on his mood. He was not devoid of emotional attachment to his parents—he suffered badly during his mother's serious illness while he was up at Oxford—but the relationship was incomplete, because his parents were keen to hand over the responsibility of looking after such a lively child to institutions.

If one is to believe C.B.'s own account of his time at Hornbrook House he was certainly the victim of considerable injustice. One weekend he decided to walk home so that the sixpence intended for his railway ticket could go towards catapult elastic instead. His mistake, though it was irrelevant to the original crime, was to eat sweet yellow apples from the orchard at his home. He went down with severe stomach-ache and the doctor advised that he should not return to school until the Tuesday. That in itself implied no guilt, but Fry's mother saw fit to write a letter to the school, explaining Charles's absence and owning up to his unscheduled perambulation. The formidable Mrs Humphrey, who never took to C.B., hauled him into the study when he returned and accused him of being first cousin to a thief. It was not discovered that he had purchased catapult elastic, but his alternative explanation of a trip to the toyship in Old Chislehurst scarcely deserved Mrs Humphrey's severe displeasure.

It was unfortunate, then, that Mrs Humphrey took a number of classes when she was not dealing out malevolent punishments. Fry admitted:

She is the only woman I have ever really been afraid of. For some reason she did not like me, hated my inability to do long division of money, and always made me feel that I had no ambition in life except to deceive her; whereas in fact I should never have thought of trying anything so foolish. Once, having done all the examples in addition of money, I virtuously wrote out some sums for myself to do. This was fatal, because I put down figures like 23 shillings and 19 pence. There is no law of nature why a boy should not add up any sets of pounds, shillings and pence that he chooses. But Mrs Humphrey regarded this virtuous effort at industry as an instance of ineffable deceit; I lost her minimum good opinion for ever.

Here, then, were the seeds of independence: a bemused victim of parental indifference, facing a draconian régime at school. Wallis Myers observed in his biography, *C.B. Fry: The Man and his Methods*, that 'His school holidays were spent in comparative loneliness. He never had much aptitude for picking up stray acquaintances. He was in no sense a prig, and as frank and open as any boy in the kingdom; but he was intensely keen and serious about all things, books as well as games, and other boys, less earnest and more prone to slack, were inclined to stand off. Perhaps they were a little resentful of his superiority.'

C.B. later wrote an article in the magazine, *The Captain*, on boys' clubs and remarked how much more complete his own childhood would have been if they had existed where he lived. He admired the initiative of his brother, ten years younger, who formed an organization at Streatham. It was called the Ixion Club, half literary and half conversational, although members also accepted bicycle rides as being within their terms of reference. They sometimes used C.B.'s study for meetings. He was not a member himself, but the Ixion Papers, records of the club's activities, lived in the top right-hand corner of his writing desk.

Charles Fry stood out from his contemporaries, not just because of his budding talent as a sportsman, but because of his rare ability to apportion his time so that no daylight hour was wasted. He was perhaps the archetypal hyperactive child, but only in the literal sense of the term: there was an overriding purpose to everything he did, and both in movement and in speech he gave the impression that he was pumped up, as the Americans would say, and in danger of missing the train.

Despite C.B.'s natural gifts his academic promise was in severe danger of being submerged at Hornbrook House. Apart from the ill-considered teaching methods there was the appalling food, with the porridge succeeding in giving him boils. After his second year, however, there was salvation in the shape of H.V. Pears, who took over Hornbrook House. He was the son of Dr Pears, who had established Repton as a public school of the first rank. The new headmaster was much more enlightened and Hornbrook House took on the personality of a preparatory school, devoted first and foremost to the Classics. C.B. revelled in this switch, and was quickly elevated to the top class. There were no longer weekly boarders, so he only went home during school holidays, but he felt much more secure in the new environment. From this point on the scholar in him developed quickly and, in a year and a half, he was transformed into the star pupil who won an open scholarship to Repton.

Sports were also happily accommodated into the new régime at Hornbrook House, and C.B. was captain of both cricket and football. He remembered one particular cricket match where the father of H.G. Wells was umpiring, and in a moment of ill-advised inattention was struck a resounding blow on the forehead by a powerful legside hit from Charles Fry. He was out cold, though he recovered sufficiently to witness the remainder of C.B.'s innings. The batsman went on to make 27 not out and also took four wickets in the game.

C.B. confirmed his promise as an athlete when the family were on holiday in the West Country. He wrote about it in *The Captain*: 'My first athletic performance was winning a steeplechase at a seaside place in Dorsetshire when I was twelve years old. I beat a policeman, two coastguards, a fisherman, a gardener, and three boys. A bob-tailed sheep dog ran in the race, and actually won, but was disqualified for not having paid an entrance fee. The prize was half-a-sovereign.'

C.B. had a highly developed awareness of the mystical, something which was founded on personal experience. It was during a school holiday when he was at Hornbrook House that he was woken in the early hours of the morning. He heard footsteps coming down the passage towards the door of his bedroom, which was then opened, and sensed a tall figure passing by the end of the bed. He saw a dim silhouette against the grey light outside the window and instinctively took it to be his father checking whether there was any disturbance in the yard below. Then the figure faded, but no one left the room. Young Charles then remembered to his horror that his father was on a walking holiday abroad . . . morning couldn't come soon enough. When he told his mother what had happened she was not in the least surprised or sceptical, for two of the staff had given in their notice on the strength of seeing a female figure in their bedroom.

C.B. later related another ghostly tale to his biographer, Wallis Myers, in which his mother figured. On this occasion her image appeared to him before he had gone off to sleep one evening, but when, the following morning, she apologised for not having followed her usual custom by coming into his room to see that everything was alright, the experience took on a more sinister light.

Charles Fry was an eager participant when the subject of ghosts came up for discussion and he was later to be an enthusiastic proponent in debates at both Repton and Oxford. He also had cause to believe that there was significance in dreams. When he completed the remarkable treble at Oxford as captain of cricket and football and president of athletics a piece of presentiment was recalled. While he was at Repton he had gone to see *Macbeth* and in his dreams that night three weird sisters had appeared, hailing him as captain of 'Varsity soccer, president of 'Varsity athletics, and captain of 'Varsity cricket.

C.B. was thrown towards adulthood when barely into his 'teens. By the time he went to Repton he was already aware that he must largely fend for himself and at the public school he found it easier to cope with term-long absences from home than with the weekend releases which had confused and distressed him so acutely at Hornbrook House. It was not so much a question of deciding that school was superior to life at home as working–and playing– under a consistent régime rather than constantly switching between conflicting ideals at home and at school.

2

SCHOOL DAYS

The modern schoolboy often has an unbalanced conception of work and play, but C.B. Fry was one of a committed breed, equally at home in the classroom, the debating chamber and on the sports field. He admitted that the spirit of competition drove him to excellence—he was never happy coming second. And, indeed, first place rarely eluded him at Repton, except in mathematics, a subject which was always his Achilles heel. However, his results owed much to endeavour: 'I do not believe any boy has ever worked harder,' he later wrote.

It was as an athlete that C.B. first earned a mention in the *Reptonian*. In the spring of 1886, just before his fourteenth birthday, Fry recorded excellent times of 12.0 seconds for the 100 yards and 28.8 seconds for the 220 yards. A year later the magazine reported: 'Fry was *facile princeps* among the Juniors, and carried all before him.' He won the 100 yards in 11.4 seconds, equalling the school record set in 1879, and also won the high jump, hurdles and 800 metres.

In 1888 he took the Second Aggregate, awarded on the strength of perfomances in open events. He was still under sixteen, but he won the senior 100 yards and high jump and, in finishing second in the long jump, leapt 17 feet 5 inches to set an under-16 record.

By 1889 C.B. was jumping just a couple of inches short of 20 feet, benefiting, as he later recalled, from some unusual coaching: 'My house-master, Mr Forman, was the only coach I ever had in athletics, and that on only one occasion. One afternoon he happened to be crossing the School paddock when I was practising the long jump on the rough turf into an elementary pit. He stopped for a few minutes, told me I did not jump high enough, took off his black mackintosh and made a heap of it between the take-off and the pit. The mackintosh frightened me into jumping much higher.' Fry also won the senior hurdles and 100 yards, ducking under 11 seconds, and was rewarded by winning the First Aggregate, just ten points ahead of his great friend and rival, Lionel Palairet.

The following year he was pipped for First Aggregate by the other Palairet brother, Richard, but he was restored to his rightful place at the head of the pack in his final year. His leap of 21 feet was an outstanding school long jump record and lasted well into the twentieth century, finally being surpassed by a future Olympic champion, Harold Abrahams. He also high-jumped 5 feet 6 inches, only an inch less than the Repton best.

He made the same resounding progress as a soccer player. The standard at Repton at this time was particularly high—the school was quite capable of giving a good game to professional sides like Derby County—but C.B. forced his way into the 1st XI defence at the age of fifteen in 1887. A couple of years later he had made such an impression that the *Reptonian* described him as a 'wonderfully promising player, and even now, perhaps, the best back the School has ever had; kicks well with either foot, and is very quick in recovering from a mistake.' By this time C.B. had already played a number of games for the Casuals, the crack amateur side, and he even found himself turning out in an FA Cup tie at the tender age of sixteen. (Both the Casuals and Corinthians, for whom Fry appeared after he started at Oxford, were quick to vet promising public school players.)

In his penultimate season for the school team he was off colour at first, but as the games progressed his judgment improved and he became far more cool under pressure. As skipper of the side in his final year Fry set a tremendous example and the *Reptonian* was moved to match its previous plaudits: 'The most brilliant back the School has ever had. A strong kick from any position, and a very difficult man to pass, as his great pace always enables him to retrieve mistakes. Captained the team with good judgment in the field.'

As for cricket, C.B. won his place in the Repton 1st XI in 1888 and, although he averaged just 13 an innings, a plucky knock of 32 in the big game against Malvern was enough to win him his colours. The *Reptonian*'s reflections on the summer showed that he had some way to go before becoming the complete batsman: 'Keeps his bat straight and is a hard wicket to get; style terribly cramped. Did well at Malvern, and will probably score more freely on fast wickets; covers a lot of ground at mid-on but is apt to drop catches.'

By the following summer he had made a significant advance, playing his shots with more freedom and batting with far greater consistency. He averaged more than 36 and also enjoyed himself in the house matches, carrying his bat through both innings of Forman's game against Hall. He scored 76 out of 138 and 98 out of 130.

His talents as a bowler were not realised or exploited until 1890, but he then started to take a few wickets for the school. His batting, on the other hand, was not quite as consistent as the previous year, but he did make an accomplished 92 against a rival house, Burton. He was also chosen to play for a Public School team against the Gentlemen of Surrey at Richmond and did particularly well, scoring 50 in one innings and taking seven wickets.

Even that, however, could not rank with his heroics in the senior house match final against Priory. Forman's took a first-innings lead of 112, thanks mainly to 87 from C.B., but their advantage appeared to have been nullified overnight when half the team went down with ptomaine poisoning after eating a suspect steak and kidney pie. Luckily Fry had abstained and he made 70 not out in a total of 98 for 5 to see Forman's home, but, as the *Reptonian* pointed out, he was not the only person to emerge with credit: 'It should be mentioned that five of Forman's team were absent indisposed; however, the Priory captain courteously allowed five substitutes to field, and, although we believe it was a totally unprecedented action in an important engagement, he offered to allow them to bat, which offer was accepted by the captain of Forman's and thus set an example in sportsmanlike conduct which it will be well for future generations to follow.'

Chickenpox kept Fry on the sidelines in his final term and he was unable to start playing cricket until the middle of June. However, he made up for lost time with a sparkling 144 against the Old Reptonians and also made 130 not out in the house match final as Forman's repeated their 1890 victory over Priory.

C.B. also shone in less conventional sports. He was no great swimmer, but in his fourth year he finished equal first in the school's open diving competition. His extra spring proved to be invaluable as he won the coveted sack race in 1890, a light-hearted sideline to the athletic events proper. The *Reptonian* said that C.B. 'flew the obstacle that others had tamely to crawl over'.

It is obvious from reports of debating society meetings that Fry was quickly into the thick of things. Personal experience made him a committed seconder of the motion in November 1887 'That in the opinion of this House, a belief in ghosts is tenable.' The *Reptonian* said of the debate: 'Mr Fry, after successfully deciphering his own writing, maintained that ghosts do exist in churchyards. He thought that the widespread belief in them betokened some reason in favour of their existence. Mr Fry answered a remark that, "if a child was kept twenty years in seclusion, it would not know anything of ghosts", by saying that a person in such a condition would probably become an idiot, deaf and blind.'

F.R. D'OMonro, who wrote the *History of Repton Cricket*, said that Fry was a rebel because he took nothing for granted, and this was perfectly illustrated by a debate in February 1891. The motion was 'That in the opinion of this House the custom of fagging is beneficial in every way.' C.B. opposed the motion vehemently and 'declared that fagging was degrading, bad alike for seniors and juniors, led to bullying, and destroyed the proper feelings of equality.' One might think that he was merely stating the obvious, but the fact that the motion was passed by 50 votes to zero shows that he was the sole progressive voice among a horde of hidebound traditionalists.

C.B.'s first few weeks at Repton had been academically shaky, but, as Wallis Myers revealed, once the momentum was going there was no stopping him: 'On arrival he was placed in the Upper Fourth, and came out third at the end of the term. Before a year had passed he was top of the Remove, in July had won the prize of the Lower Fifth, and at Christmas that of the Middle Fifth. Each term he gained promotion. He reached the Upper Fifth before he was fifteen. Continuing along the path of self-support, for which throughout his life he has never diverged, he won a Foundation Scholarship in 1887, and in the same year bore off the Gell Greek Testament Prize. Though he lost the Upper Fifth Prize through a weakness in mathematics, he was first in Classics, and when barely over fifteen was promoted to the Sixth.'

Tangible rewards continued to come his way. In 1888 he carried off the Latin Verse Prize and in 1889 the prizes for Greek Verse and Latin Prose. The following year he held an even greater monopoly of the prizes, winning the Latin and Greek Verse, the Latin Prose, and, to prove that he had some facility with modern languages, he also won the French Prize and was second in German.

At the end of 1890 he was entered for the joint examination to get into Trinity and Wadham Colleges and, much to the delight of both Fry himself and the school, he came out on top of the Wadham list and was awarded their first Classical scholarship.

C.B. was head boy of Forman's, now known as The Cross, from 1888 until his departure in 1891 – an unusually long span. He was, of course, an academic and sporting inspiration to the rest of the house, but he also played a leading role in the readings which were traditionally held on Speech Day. In 1888 Aristophanes' *The Frogs* was performed and on the evidence of his rendition of Molière's *Le Malade Imaginaire* the *Reptonian* wrote, 'Fry is evidently an actor: he discharged his part most efficiently.' This was a simple but critical observation, highly relevant to C.B.'s whole life. He had enormous presence as a person and this physical impact was enhanced by his highly theatrical delivery, which made him such a captivating speaker. He also revealed at Repton that he had a fine singing voice and managed to finish in the top three in a singing competition at the school in 1890.

Despite his Midas touch C.B. was not the subject of much jealousy. The Repton of the 1880s held greater store by success, and more especially effort, than the public schools of today. People who knew Fry only superficially were inclined to say that he was conceited and that he swaggered, but those more familiar with his ways defended him stoutly against such criticism. They saw nothing wrong in someone gaining pleasure from favourable results and they argued that his quick, rolling walk indicated nothing more than intense energy and joy in graceful movement.

Fry's boundless enthusiasm was infectious, but he was appreciative of the efforts of others, even if they were in direct competition to him. He was also quick to recognize the contributions of people who helped him in his pursuit of excellence, although later remarks suggested that he was mostly forced to fall back on self-coaching!

Christopher Hollis's father and uncle were both at Repton at the same time as Fry, his uncle being an exact contemporary. Hollis wrote in *Oxford in the Twenties*: 'My uncle was a man of no particular distinction—whether academic or athletic—but Fry, who was a generous man, liked to have something kindly to say about anyone of his acquaintance. He liked my uncle, but when I asked him for any word of commendation on his achievements all that he could think to say was, "He used to sit at the back of the class and, when the master was not looking, made a noise like a cow." Then he added meditatively, "He was very good at making a noise like a cow." '

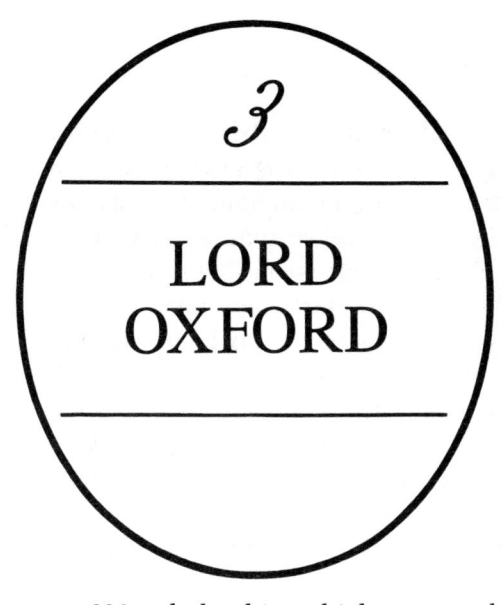

3

LORD
OXFORD

Charles Fry's arrival at Oxford was not one of those cradle-conceived passports to the upper echelons of government. He went up with just £3 in his pocket, no parental allowance and an £80 scholarship which was to be absorbed in college fees. Nevertheless, this unpromising background obliged him to reveal the resourcefulness which would always serve him well when survival was the priority.

Fourth on the scholarship roll headed by Fry was F.E. Smith, a product of Birkenhead School, who enlivened both Oxford and the world of politics with his ingenuity, wit and gift of the gab. The following year saw John Simon's arrival. He was an altogether less flamboyant political animal than Smith, but he, too, went on to achieve senior status in Cabinets before and during the Second World War. These three alone would have been sufficient to elevate Wadham from the status of Oxford minnow to big fish, but there were two others in the supporting cast who, in any other era, would have captured more attention. Adair Roche went on to become a leading judge and a Lord Justice of Appeal, while Francis Hirst promised much as an economist before failing to realise his full potential.

This extraordinary influx of talent at Wadham put an end to derisory comments about the college, like the riddle, popular among undergraduates, which went: 'Why is the Wadham boat like Noah's Ark?' The answer was: 'Because it moves slowly upon the face of the waters and is filled with all manner of beasts.' Wadham was also known as the Nazareth of Oxford colleges because no good thing came out of it. These quaint taunts lost all relevance as Wadham's famous five dominated Oxford life with their remarkable combination of scholarship, athletic prowess and personality. It was a measure of C.B.'s impact that he clearly overshadowed his illustrious contemporaries; indeed Wadham was often named Fry's College during his triumphant four-year stay. There was a saying that Wadham consisted of Fry and small fry. And although C.B. answered to no particular nickname at Oxford he was often referred to as 'Almighty' and received parcels which were simply addressed to Lord Oxford.

Inevitably, the comparisons were still being made long after these three undergraduates had dispersed in search of worldly or spiritual reward. In the biography of F.E. Smith by his son it is said: 'C.B. Fry's brilliant early promise petered out in after years into a somewhat desultory and disappointed career, and, when he looked back upon these days in his autobiography, it is depressing to note the jealousy he had come to feel for his brilliant and more successful friend. The references to F.E. Smith are jaundiced, and the praise grudging.'

This is not a particularly accurate appraisal of Fry's assessment of Smith. In *Life Worth Living* C.B. gave his first impressions of F.E.: 'The moment he opened his mouth he betrayed a Lancashire accent that would rival Gracie Fields. The first indication of his being an uncommon intelligence was that, discovering with characteristic promptness that no sort of provincial accent was an advantage at Oxford, this perceptive youth entirely cured himself in about six weeks, and indeed developed a tendency to precosity.'

C.B. and F.E. were firm friends at Wadham, dominant personalities both, but united by circumstances, a common quest for adventure and a love of sharp conversation. However, they did not always see eye to eye and enjoyed a healthy rivalry which endured well beyond their shared experiences at Oxford. There is no better illustration of this than the often related exchange between Fry and Smith in the *Mercury* rose gardens at Hamble after the First World War, by which time F.E. had become the Earl of Birkenhead. He said: 'This is a lovely place and a fine show, C.B. But for you it has been a backwater.' Fry replied: 'The question remains, whether it is better to be successful or . . . happy.'

That retort failed to capture the essence of the dispute, which was more faithfully explored by Neville Cardus in his *Autobiography*: 'I have been told that if Fry had not "squandered" his talents on games and pursuits diverse and sometimes mutually exclusive, he might have distinguished himself in (1) politics, (2) the theatre, (3) the law, (4) literature. For my part I think there are politicians and KC's and actors enough; there has only been one C.B. Fry.'

The suggestion that while Charles Fry merely made runs F.E. Smith made history is hardly borne out by the collective memory of a nation. Politicians, apart from the obvious importance of their acts and pronouncements, have not, from Fry's day to the present, captured hearts in the same way as sporting heroes. Prime Ministers' names are remembered, but F.E. Smith failed to reach Number 10 and a random poll today would surely find more people recalling the exploits of Fry than Smith.

Maurice Bowra, who had a lengthy spell as Warden of Wadham after the Second World War, wrote this about the achievements of C.B. and his contemporaries in *Memories 1898–1939*: 'He may at moments have felt a twinge of envy for his old friends who had done so much better; but if he did, he did not show it, and what I liked in him was his detachment. He was eager and natural, and though perhaps he lived on a manic curve, of which I never saw the downward trend, he was happier than Simon and lasted much longer than Birkenhead.'

C.B. was decidedly homesick in his first few weeks at Oxford, but he then settled in quite happily, despite walking a precarious tightrope. His instinct for survival and his fierce independence overcame the handicaps of minimal assistance from his parents and constant demands on his time from the multitude of studies and interests with which he insisted on surrounding himself. Fry maintained, however improbably, that he was naturally lazy and he claimed to function best when he was obliged to live on his wits. There was, of course, a dark side to this mode of existence. His mental agility may have been seen to best effect when his back was to the wall, but he also left himself open to severe stress.

The dilemma was illustrated by the variety of factors which led to him getting nothing better than a fourth-class degree in his Final Schools. Two years earlier he had gained an outstanding First in Classical Moderations and it was widely supposed that he would match this achievement in Greats. Here, as in so many happenings in Fry's life, one has to sift through contradictory evidence before arriving at the most acceptable explanation.

I am doubtful of the reasoning which he offered to Maurice Bowra: 'He claimed that it was because he was made to read "a fellow called Mill", whom he could not endure, and that if only he had been told to read F.H. Bradley, he would have done very well. There may have been truth in this. Fry had a keen sense of literature and Bradley's impassioned dialectic would have appealed to him much more than Mill's dry arguments.'

In *Life Worth Living*, Fry said he was happy enough with the course, but financial exigencies meant that he had to devote quite a lot of his vacation time to journalism and tutorials rather than to the concentrated reading which would have guaranteed a better result. (He cut his teeth as a journalist with the university magazine *Isis*, which noted that he was not only an outstanding practician but also a perceptive student of sports. Operating under various pseudonyms he wrote bright pieces on cricket, soccer and rugby.) C.B. was no stranger to the problems of allotting time to various activities; indeed his mental energy was even more remarkable than his physical ability. Wallis Myers seems to have grasped the most plausible reason for C.B.'s exam failure. He revealed that Fry's mother was seriously ill and, according to Myers, concern for his mother, allied to worries about his ways and means, 'placed a severe strain on his sanguine temperament'. This euphemism may be taken to mean that C.B.'s exam disappointment was explained by a nervous breakdown, confirmed by Christopher Hollis. Myers went on: 'In truth he entered the examination room for the Finals an untrained man, having scarcely read a line for weeks. Most candidates, thus handicapped, would have failed ignominiously, but the natural resources of his mind served him well, and he was able to prevent a catastrophe.'

Although it was sporting excellence which made Fry Oxford's most famous son, he also became involved in Wadham's institutions, notably the Debating Society and Literary Society. The latter, when it boasted Fry, Smith, Simon, Roche and Hirst, had enough talent at its disposal to satisfy the Oxford Union itself in a less exalted era, and certainly for Smith and Simon it proved the ideal stepping-stone for stirring words on the larger stage, where Hilaire Belloc, later a contributor to *Fry's Magazine*, was the outstanding personality and speaker. Fry declined F.E. Smith's suggestion that he should join the Union, contenting himself with in-college discussion. He even suffered a rare defeat at the end of October 1892 when opposing Tom McVey's motion 'that Scots had superior national character to English.'

One of the most memorable episodes in Fry's final year at Oxford was his appearance in the Oxford University Dramatic Society's production of *The Merchant of Venice,* in which C.B. played the Prince of Morocco. An enduring spell of freezing weather and accompanying illness, which struck down some of the members of the cast, also restricted the size of the audiences at the New Theatre during the run from 20 to 26 February 1895. Expectations had been high, as the *Oxford Magazine* announced the week before the play opened: 'We hear great things of Mr Fry as the Prince of Morocco.'

The magazine gave the production high marks, saying that 'Fry, as the Prince of Morocco, showed that he had considerable powers of elocution, and certainly looked as though "this aspect of his had feared the valiant".'

One aspect of his performance proved especially memorable. Fry himself recalled: 'I was all right until the first night, when on discovering that I had made a mistake about the casket, I said my lines beginning, "Oh, Hell, what have we here?" with such emphasis and effect that the next night the entire University turned up to hear C.B. say, "Oh, Hell." Not being able to trust my countenance, I had to leave out the swear words for the rest of the run and say, "What–have–we–here?" very slowly.'

According to more than one contemporary source, however, the line remained intact for the whole run, and it was certainly employed on the final night. In *The Oxford Amateurs,* Alan Mackinnon said he received a letter from Fry confirming the above version, but went on: 'I have no wish to dispute Mr Fry's version of this incident, but I am bound to add that other authorities present on the occasion distinctly aver that the famous "Oh, Hell", given with truly profane vigour, was a feature of every performance.' The *Oxford Magazine* concurred with Mr Mackinnon: 'The last performance of the OUDS was productive of the usual enthusiasm and the usual amenities. Mr Fry again "brought the House down" by the vigour of his regret.'

Isis reported: 'Mr Fry's famous ejaculation was breathlessly awaited, and there was a storm of applause, after which, during the second's pause, came in a deep voice from the dresser, a solitary "encore!" which once more brought down the house. The rag at the end was of course the great thing of the evening, and it lasted very nearly till the next day. Bouquets were showered on actors and actresses alike; Mr Fry was presented with a huge "Soccer pill" in a lace bouquet-holder, which embarrassed him not a little.' The gift was, doubtless, by way of comment on C.B.'s fondness for medications and preparations which helped to keep his sporting performances at a high pitch.

Fry's reading of the part did not commend itself to everyone who saw the play. The *Oxford Magazine* published a letter, complaining about the 'strange oaths', the editor preceding it with the observation that they 'must decline to vouch for the facts'. The letter, written by Miss Jemima Pinkerton from The Academy, The Mall, Chiswick, in London, is worth reprinting in full:

Dear Mr Editor,

I trust that you will allow me to lodge the following objection against the insidious manner in which our own Theatre contributes towards the corruption of the young.

I may tell you that in the ordinary course of our curriculum we impart a knowledge of the dramas of the Swan of Avon, and in anticipation of the forthcoming production of *The Merchant of Venice* had directed considerable attention to that work. As a treat, to which our young ladies had long looked forward, on Saturday night we took our academy to the performance. Scarcely had the play commenced when an unfamiliar line struck my ear, while Miss Amelia Sedley (my best pupil), who was following in her school edition, said that she could not find the place. I replied, 'My dear, every good actor has his own reading of his part.' Much succeeded that seemed strange; but the crisis came, when the beautiful Mr Fry, as he opened his casket, shouted, 'O——!' (I cannot write the wicked word). I said, 'Girls, we must go,' and we filed out in indignation. The audience was evidently of our opinion, for they cheered our bold action for some minutes.

Sir, I maintain that with a Rev. Vice-Chancellor and a Right Worshipful Mayor, such language should be impossible. I shudder to think of its effect on all the young men.

This was the beginning and end of Charles Fry's formal acting career–though much later in life he contemplated following the example of C. Aubrey Smith, a fellow Sussex cricketer, who was typecast by Hollywood producers as the perfect English gentleman.

It was shortly before the opening of *The Merchant of Venice* that Fry had revealed another string to his sporting bow. Denied by the icy conditions from playing football and rugby, the logical replacement pastime was skating and C.B., despite having very little experience of the art, devoted himself so wholeheartedly to its mastery that he represented Wadham in the inter-college races on Blenheim Lake and came close to an unofficial Blue as a member of the Oxford team who took on Cambridge on the Fens.

Fry's quickly won fame at Oxford was marked by a visit from Max Beerbohm, the celebrated writer and cartoonist, who had already been at the university long enough to merit the title of eternal student. The fruits of his visit to C.B.'s rooms appeared in the *Idler*. Beerbohm made out that when he arrived at 11 am Fry had only just risen, whereas the subject recalled that the interview took place at teatime as he was emerging invigorated from a cold tub.

Beerbohm offered an interesting description of C.B.'s rooms: 'I stood upon the hearthrug and took a look around. A regular college room it was, rather dark under its low ceiling and beautifully panelled with oak. Engravings of the academic kind–little boys with apples and little girls with pears–mingled with drawings by younger artists and many photographs of the football and cricket teams, and all the other bodies adorned by the gentleman in the next room. It was evident that he was a smoker, for there were pipes all over the room–pipes in racks and pipes in cases and pipes of every description.'

C.B. attempted to steer clear of tobacco when he was playing sport, but he enjoyed cigarettes, cigars and the pipe. He felt that no harm was done if the smoker did not inhale and was of the opinion that there was still satisfaction to be gained under such restriction. He later wrote in *Fry's Magazine*: 'It always seems to me that to smoke a cigarette, if it be of pure and good tobacco, is the surest way to get the solace that smoking brings, without taking in alien unpleasantness such as a foul pipe provides. Mind you, I smoke a pipe as well.'

Fry accused Max Beerbohm of making him coin the phrase, 'Golf is like glorified croquet', complaining: 'Such a phrase was beyond me at that age, and I had never played golf, and Max had never mentioned the subject; but he thereby succeeded in earning me a wide unpopularity.'

It has been written, and doubtless believed, that C.B. began to experiment with golf just before the Second World War, and at the age of 65 astonished a professional at Southampton by outdriving him, but suggestions that he was then a complete novice at the game are patently false. When he was chosen as one of the first Isis Idols in May 1893 it was said that 'He plays a fair game of Golf and thinks he plays a good one, and is fond of practising in the Wadham quad with a tennis ball.'

There was another reference to C.B.'s stuttering attempts at mastering the game when he wrote an open letter to Plum Warner in the *Daily Express* on the eve of the 1903–4 cricket-tour to Australia. He concluded: 'I shall think of you as I dig with my niblick in the furze bushes, and, likely enough, regret that I am not with you hitting at a bigger ball with a simpler instrument.'

There was a great deal of golfing instruction and explanatory photographs in *Fry's Magazine*, indicating the editor's well-developed interest in the game, but posterity has been invited to consider golf as a teasingly untested part of Fry's repertoire. He never quite came to grips with the game, but could, nevertheless, be persuaded to ascribe to a handicap of four or five.

It was through Max Beerbohm that C.B. met Will Rothenstein, later Sir William, who was compiling a set of lithographs of Oxford characters. Fry, who cut a magnificent figure from first to last, was a natural choice for Rothenstein's collection, although he was unhappy that the artist wished to capture him in football gear rather than cricket flannels. Fry's reaction was that 'the result looked like a coal-heaver; but it was a good drawing.'

In true Oxbridge tradition C.B. was not above a little tomfoolery and he had a willing ally in F.E. Smith for some daring escapades. The two undergraduates founded the Wadham Cat Club, a necessarily exclusive group. The qualification for membership was to invade other colleges after hours by perilous journeys over spiked railings, before returning to Wadham by the identical route. The additional prize of dinner at the Clarendon awaited anyone who could compound their boldness by extracting college keys from the porters while they slept.

Within days of his arrival at Wadham, Fry had scraped with authority and he continued to take pleasure from outwitting those who were slower of thought and action than himself. Soon after he had gone up to Oxford a breakfast for new scholars was held in C.B.'s rooms. It developed into a rare drinking session and afterwards Fry was dared into embracing the statue of Dorothy Wadham, the wife of the founder. He was discovered by the sub-warden with his hands around her cold waist.

That incident resulted in nothing more than a ticking-off, but towards the end of his time at Oxford he was faced with a court appearance after another piece of high spirits. On this occasion F.E. Smith tempted him into indiscretion and after appearing before the Oxford City Police Court his case was remitted to the Chancellor's Court on 20 March 1895. The *Oxford Chronicle* reported the case like this:

> Charles Burgess Fry, undergraduate of Wadham College, was summoned for wilfully extinguishing five street lamps in High St on March 15.—He pleaded guilty.—P.C. Higgins said he saw defendant climb two of the lamp posts and extinguish the lights at 11.45. He stopped the defendant and said, 'Mr Fry, I believe.' Defendant replied that that was so. There were three other lamps out further up the street.—Defendant had nothing to say in defence.—The Vice Chancellor said the Bench were very sorry to see a young man of the defendant's ability and youthful promise brought up for these school-boyish tricks. He would be fined 40s and costs 7s 6d or 14 days' imprisonment.

C.B. was also a thorn in the flesh of railway officials at Paddington Station when he was returning home at the end of term or on his way back to Oxford. He developed quite a reputation for kicking over railway lamps and had a knack of escaping before he could be apprehended.

But if Charles Fry basked in his sporting and academic glories, and wept little over his minor indiscretions, a financial spectre always haunted him. The demands on an average undergraduate's pocket were quite considerable, but the sporting commitments to which C.B. was bound throughout his time at Oxford put him under even greater pressure. 'In those days', he wrote, 'one really needed £250 a year at Oxford to be comfortable. It could be done on £200, but few, if any, of the comparatively leisured gentlemen commoners whose company I frequented had allowances of less than £400 a year.'

Fortuitously, of course, the constant, pressing need for money directed Fry towards journalism—and the steady demand for his services as a writer between his departure from Oxford and his adoption of the training ship *Mercury* ensured that the early struggles had not been in vain. This is how Wallis Myers described C.B.'s university career:

> The four years spent at Oxford did not bring Fry unalloyed happiness. It was generally supposed that he had 'a jolly good time', experienced the best of all worlds, and was, like the majority of undergraduates, in receipt of a liberal allowance from home. A good time he had in many ways, but it was not free from nervous strain or anxiety. Let it be stated to Fry's credit that he paid every penny of his Oxford expenses by his own exertions, and out of his own pocket. It was the only way. Property which his father held in the home counties depreciated about this period, and Mr Lewis Fry was not able to give his son the financial assistance that most young men embarking on a University career would expect. C.B., as at Repton, had to help himself. There was no rich benefactor waiting with open cheque book to pay the piper.

Charles Fry's sporting triumphs have been given separate billing. Suffice it to say here that he won Blues in soccer, athletics and cricket while still a freshman; and was president of the athletics team and captain of the football and cricket sides in 1894. He was denied a rugby blue at the end of that year because of injury and he and F.E. Smith even rowed for Wadham in the procession of boats which took place on the Monday before the Eights. It all added up to an astonishing potential, but he was a superior sort of dilettante and no one was sure, least of all Fry, where his future lay. On 22 June 1895 *Isis* did Fry the honour of making him their Isis Idol for the second time, the first hero to make a return appearance:

> In somewhat similar circumstances, the great overgrown spoiled baby, Alexander the Big, was one day found weeping because he had no more worlds to conquer. Charles Fry hasn't got quite so far as that yet, but he wouldn't follow such a poor spirited example if he had. No! he would do what Kepler, and Columbus, and Adams did—discover new worlds. Meanwhile, however, he condescends to pay Alexander the sincerest flattery of the proverb; thus far at least—that, having conquered everything in Europe that is worth conquering (including the natural acerbity of some Wadham Dons, at least one chucker-out, many policemen, and all the ladies who know him) he now intends, like the Macedonian, to attack Asia; for when he has successfully negotiated the I.C.S. Examination this next vac, he will probably waste his sweetness on the desert air of the N.W.P. (North Western Provinces) or the Deccan.

The Indian Civil Service's loss was cricket's gain: he failed the mathematics part of the exam, but was saved from making an instant decision about his alternatives by the invitation to tour South Africa with Lord Hawke's team. Even prior to his departure it was rumoured that he might attempt to make a life for himself in South Africa.

In August 1895 the normally reliable *Sporting Life* reported that C.B. was being taken on as a master at Eton, but it was in fact Charterhouse that secured his services in 1896. This was a compromise for C.B. He wanted to be able to play cricket throughout the English summer, but at least as a teacher he was able to turn out for Sussex from the beginning of July to the end of the season. He rated teaching very highly as a profession, but felt unfulfilled as an assistant classics master at Charterhouse. He was given little opportunity to impose his personality on the school and despite the fact that there was no one else capable of coaching cricket properly at the school Fry's credentials for the job were ignored. After he had left the school in 1898 C.B. was apt to recall the highlight of his two years as almost having taught Greek to William Beveridge!

Although C.B. was capable of wondrous things on the football field his performances did not yet command total confidence. One of his earliest games for Oxford was against Notts County in November 1891. The *Oxford Magazine* reported that 'Fry, though occasionally brilliant, was not at all safe in kicking, and frequently found a forward too good for him.' However, Fry was chosen to play for an England side against the touring Canadians on 19 December 1891, though the team did not actually represent the cream of English soccer and the match, which England won 6–1, was not regarded as an official international. Fry made mistakes and, according to 'The Old Athlete', writing in *Athletic News*, he was 'hardly up to International form yet'. The writer continued: 'Why, the scratch lot which met the Canadians at the Oval on Saturday no more represented the football strength of England than would an eleven if I were in it.'

The Oxford sides in Fry's time were of a high standard, but due to various circumstances they only shared the honours with Cambridge in the four 'Varsity matches between 1892 and 1895. The 1892 game was particularly forgettable for Oxford as they lost by an embarrassing 5–1 margin. According to *The Times* the Oxford defence was 'severely taxed', but they would certainly have scored more than one goal but for the brilliance of the Cambridge 'keeper, L.H. Gay.

Oxford gained a measure of revenge the following year when a goal three minutes from the end by C.D. Hewitt gave them a 3–2 victory. The defences on both sides played well, but C.B. was probably the pick of the bunch. In this match, as in the following two years, Fry's full-back partner was W.J. Oakley, himself an England international and also a fine hurdler.

The 1894 side, with Fry as captain, looked particularly strong. They had G.O. Smith, one of the finest centre forwards in the history of the game, to lead the attack, and G.B. Raikes, another England international, was in goal.

The run-up to the Cambridge match was not without hiccups: on 28 October 1892 Oxford played London Caledonians at Caledonian

Park. There were some unsavoury incidents during the game and the *Scotsman* pointed the finger squarely at C.B., accusing him of rough play, of 'using his might most unmercifully' and of 'singling out for his attentions the lightest and most unoffending man in the team—I mean Peter Hunter.' The report went on to say this of Fry: 'His language was disgusting. To call a man a "pig" is surely coming very low down for a 'Varsity man. To prefix the epithet with a disgusting adjective may be permissible at Oxford, but it is out of place at Caledonian Park. It is only right to say that Fry's comrades were disgusted at his behaviour.'

The accusations were roundly condemned in *Isis*, their reporter writing: 'I have personally interviewed three members of the team, who all of them say that they never heard any such expression used, and that they were disgusted neither at the behaviour nor the language of the Captain, nor of any other member of their own side. I have also seen Mr Fry himself, and he denies most emphatically ever having called a man "a (disgusting adjective) pig". "I am not in the habit," added the "genial Wadham athlete," "of calling people 'pigs' at all. Oxford isn't a board-school." '

Isis suggested that the boot had literally been on the other foot. It was claimed that Fry had been taunted by Hunter, who was encouraged to have a go at C.B. in the hope that the Oxford skipper would lose his appetite for the battle . . . and his temper.

There were no such problems in the 'Varsity match although when the two sides arrived at the Queen's Club in London on 21 February the ground was frost-bound and patently unfit for play. However, Fry was mindful of the fact that both he and Oakley were due to be involved in the 'Varsity athletics match three weeks later and he was reluctant to ask for a postponement. The Cambridge captain was happy enough for the game to go ahead, believing that the tricky conditions would help to neutralize Oxford's more talented players. C.B. thought that his side were too good to lose, whatever the conditions, but Cambridge's heavier side triumphed 3–1. The Oxford captain's performance drew this terse comment from the *Oxford Magazine*: 'Fry, despite some mistakes and an inclination to kick out when he should have kicked to his forwards, worked hard.'

The bonus for Fry in his final year in the Oxford soccer team was the chance to play as a striker, a position which he had always coveted, and the move was endorsed by the *Oxford Magazine*: 'The play of the forwards seems likely to be strengthened by the assistance of Fry. He possesses that most important of all requisites, pace, and has also shown that he is capable of shooting both hard and straight.' Fry's concentration on rugby at the end of 1894 led to some people questioning his right to a place in the soccer team for the 'Varsity match.

However, there was never much doubt that he would be included in the Oxford side, even though he was selected to play in his accustomed position of right full back. Oxford built up a 2–0 lead in the first half and a third goal soon after half-time indicated that it was not to be Cambridge's day. 'Of our backs Fry was the more versatile, but Oakley the sounder,' was the *Oxford Magazine's* verdict, while the *Referee* said, rather uncharitably, that 'probably the better of two fifth-rate teams won.'

C.B. achieved a remarkable feat in 1893 by galvanising a distinctly unpromising hotch-potch of players into a Wadham team which came close to taking the inter-college title. Joseph Wells wrote in his *History of Wadham*: 'Even for the University Fry probably never played more brilliantly than he did for his College in the Final of the Association Cup Tie in 1893, when Wadham nearly wrested the cup from Magdalen. Till within the last quarter of an hour Wadham was ahead, and nothing seemed able to break down the stubborn defence of the two backs, Fry and Lister: but then Magdalen scored twice in ten minutes, and kept the cup by two goals to one.'

The *Oxford Magazine* described Fry as 'a *unus homo*', adding: 'He was brilliant in the first ¾, but ran out of steam towards the end.' Effectively, C.B. had 14 players to choose from, and six of those were either painfully short of ability or totally unfamiliar with the game.' *Isis* reported that Fry played magnificently in both defence and attack and it also praised his splendid coaching.

One of his charges was F.E. Smith, who filled in manfully at centre half, and it was he who could take much of the credit for introducing Fry to rugby. To begin with, C.B.'s efforts as a wing-threequarter were limited to college games, but his explosive pace and try-scoring exploits soon announced him as a potential member of the University team. The added attraction for Fry was that rugger enjoyed much higher status in Oxford's sporting hierarchy than soccer.

'Considerable excitement' was caused by his inclusion in the threequarter line for the University's game with London Scottish on 27 January 1894, but he made a disappointing debut. The *Oxford Magazine* reported: 'He hardly maintained his reputation, as, despite one or two runs, he did not seem at home with the short passing game, and scarcely shone in defence; moreover, a certain punt of his at the finish had rather a disastrous result.' The kick went straight to a London Scottish player, McGregor, who dropped a goal to seal the match in his side's favour.

The rugby highlight of that winter was Wadham's triumph in the inter-college competition. Captained by F.E. Smith, whose combative attitude and fierce tackling took him to the verge of a Blue, the side also included Fry, Simon and Roche; if not the most talented, it was certainly one of the most cerebrally capable fifteens ever put out. Wadham's reward for internal supremacy was a challenge match at Fenner's against Caius College, their Cambridge counterparts, who boasted four Blues and two internationals. Wadham brought off a notable victory, but rather marred their success with some anarchic behaviour on the train back to Oxford, doing their best to destroy the carriage in which they were travelling. F.E. Smith was faced with a hefty bill for the damage.

Fry came of age as an attacking force in rugby at the end of 1894 when he won a regular place in the Oxford side and seemed set for a fourth Blue. Certain aspects of the game were still a mystery to him, the *Oxford Magazine* reporting that he was undecided what to do in a crisis and liable to get too far in front of the play, but his talents as a fleet-footed and elusive runner were enough to guarantee his place in the team. His stirring charges down the wing inspired incipient poetry from friends and Oxford rugby enthusiasts who marvelled at the glorious sight of Fry in full flight. Fry! Fly! Try! greeted his dramatic surges into the game.

No match better illustrated the instant adulation which he could attract in rugby, but was denied to him in his largely defensive role as a soccer player, than the game against the formidable Blackheath side on 10 November 1894. Fry later played some games for the Kent club, but on this occasion he tormented their backs with some compelling runs. He scored two tries, one of them a magnificent effort, and Oxford wound up as 11–6 winners. Plum

Warner, a year Fry's junior at Oxford, recalled years later that the sequel to the match was almost as memorable as the game itself. A large proportion of the crowd, moved to instant hero-worship, followed Fry all the way back to Wadham, cheering ecstatically.

That experience may well have convinced C.B. that there was no game quite as fulfilling as rugby, but a fortnight later the dreams of a fourth Blue lay in ruins. After ten minutes of Oxford's game against the Harlequins he wrenched a muscle in his left leg trying to stop a rush and had to struggle on at full back for the remainder of the game. He was provisionally selected for the Oxford team to play in the 'Varsity match in December, but the captain, W.C. Carey, was reluctant to risk him in such an important game, although Fry had apparently recovered from the injury in time to take his place in the side. However, there were no recriminations from C.B., who said he would have made the same decision if he had been in Carey's shoes.

Fry's rugby career did not endure much beyond his time at Oxford, but, as mentioned, he did play for Blackheath, the nearest major club to his home, and was chosen as reserve for a match between the North and South, effectively an England trial. All this in spite of his inability, or reluctance, to come to terms with the demands of tackling. F.E. Smith said he resembled a fainting schoolgirl when attempting to floor an opponent, but Plum Warner pointed out that Fry's exceptional speed enabled him to get a second bite at a man who had eluded his grasp first time round. C.B. described himself as 'a scrambling tackler' who never learnt the art of falling on the ball to stop a rush nor the art of collaring people round the ankles. 'My tackling consisted chiefly in jumping on my opponent's back and embracing his neck.'

In spite of this deficiency, shared by some of the finest attacking players that rugby has seen, it is intriguing to speculate on the impact Fry might have made if he had played the game more, and at an earlier age. He might well have made an outstanding fly half. He obviously possessed the footballing skill and talent for quick, tricky running that are necessary to succeed in this position; and if he had ever regarded the game as a serious addition to his catalogue of sporting achievement he would, no doubt, have become a fluent passer of the ball and a more reliable tackler. Unfortunately, however, rugby was never a game in which this extraordinary sportsman more than scratched at the surface of his potential.

Charles Fry was quick to show his ability as both a sprinter and a jumper at Oxford. In November 1891 he took four firsts in the Freshmen's Sports, winning the 100 yards, the hurdles, long jump and high jump. His distance in the long jump was 21 ft 5 ins, but within a few months this had been dramatically improved. He showed even greater versatility in the Wadham Sports on 27 November, winning a total of six events. This time he ignored his known speciality, the long jump, but still emerged triumphant in the 100 yards, 440 yards, 120 yards hurdles, high jump, hammer and throwing the weight.

At the same time, he was announcing himself as an automatic choice for the Oxford soccer team, winning his first Blue at the end of February 1892. Just over a month later Fry was back at the Queen's Club as a member of the Oxford athletics team and although Cambridge triumphed overall by five events to four there was much personal satisfaction for C.B. He had sown the seeds of something special with a long jump of 22 ft 7 ins in the Oxford trials and at the Queen's Club he produced a superb leap of 23 ft 5 ins not only to shatter the inter-varsity record, but also to add two inches to the English record. Afterwards Fry recalled that the jump had been a textbook affair, with a smart take-off from the board and a 'neat' flight through the air. He also competed in the high jump, but had to be content with fourth place, jumping 5ft 6½ ins.

An American journalist, clearly suffering from a sketchy knowledge of athletic standards, came to interview C.B. about his prodigious long jump and asked the precise distance he had achieved. Fry replied twenty three five, prompting the American to query whether he was talking in feet or yards. The impish Fry told him yards and maintained that this was the version which found its way into print.

But the athletic achievement which gave Fry an indelible place in the record books came the following year when he equalled the world long-jump record which had been set up by the American C.S. Reber at Detroit in 1891. The setting was Iffley Road in Oxford, where the university's internal sports were held on 4 and 6

March 1893. Long jumping was a perilous business at this stage in the event's development and it put such a severe physical and mental strain on C.B. that his training for the most part consisted of sprinting and high jumping. The upper edge of the take-off board would be flush with the track, but on the pit side of the board was a trench, so if the athlete overstepped the board by more than a fraction he was liable to be jettisoned head-first into the pit. On this particular occasion Fry managed to spike his big toe in practice, so it seemed unlikely that a record leap was imminent.

The first part of his run-up was fluent enough, but everything appeared to go wrong as he approached the board. He put in a short stride and consequently took off well behind the board, failing to get the added momentum that the hard surface is designed to give. However, for some reason which remained a mystery to both athlete and spectators he achieved more spring than usual and gained exceptional height, probably three feet off the ground at the highest point in the leap. He remembered that he did not have the usual problem of struggling for his balance when he landed in an attempt to avoid falling back. He bounced clean out of the pit and landed six feet away on the track. A broad grin gave notice to the enthusiastic crowd that he had done something out of the ordinary and the tape-measure confirmed it.

In his biography of Fry, Wallis Myers said the take-off was from nine inches behind the board, indicating an actual leap of 24 ft 3½ ins instead of 23 ft 6½ ins, but this was probably an exaggeration. A contemporary account in the *Oxford Magazine* gave a more modest assessment of the actual distance, but also described the enormous impact made by Fry in his first eighteen months at the university:

> It came to the spectators (and it is said to himself) as a surprise, for he was shortening his stride before the jump, and seemed uncertain of his take-off. As it was he rose from three or four inches behind the board, a fact which makes his jump better than the equal American record, which was measured, we understand, from the jumper's last toe-mark. The enthusiasm was tremendous, and well it might be, for in Fry we have undoubtedly the best all-round man seen in Oxford for

many years. In these days, when grace and varied power of movement is so much sacrificed for the training of special muscles for over-specialised sports, Fry remains a notable example of what athletes were in the palmiest days of the Greek games.

The final reference could hardly have failed to give C.B. further satisfaction and his performances in the meeting as a whole simply illustrated the wisdom of the magazine's words. He tied with A. Ramsbotham in the 100 yards in 10.4 seconds and these evenly matched sprinters also finished level in the contest with Cambridge two weeks later. In both races Fry, who had a bullet start, took an early lead but was pegged back by Ramsbotham in the latter stages. C.B. finished second in two other events in the Oxford trials, producing a personal best of 5 ft 8½ ins in the high jump and being narrowly beaten by W.J. Oakley, his full-back partner in three 'Varsity football matches, in the hurdles.

There would be no exaggeration in saying that Fry had reached his peak as an athlete before the age of twenty-one. He did manage to jump over 23 feet again in the match with Cambridge in 1893, but his 1894 victory was achieved with a leap of 22 ft 4 ins and in 1895 he was denied a quartet of successes in the event when he was handicapped by injury and only jumped 21 ft 9 ins.

He brought his best legal time for the 100 yards down to 10.2 seconds, although he also recorded a wind-assisted time of ten seconds flat. He represented Oxford in their unique match with the American university Yale in July 1894 and regarded his victory by a foot in the 100 yards as the best run of his life. However, he was short of practice because of cricket commitments and could only manage third place in the long jump, leaping just over 22 feet. He had a nasty accident on the final jump when the take-off board split as he hit it and he was sent careering into the pit.

One can only speculate on the improvements Fry might have made if he had remained involved in athletics after Oxford and on how modern, specialised training might have bettered his performances. It would not be flattering him to suggest that the advent of the hitch-kick technique would have enabled C.B. to jump in excess of 25 feet, a distance which would have put him in line for international vests these days. And on a modern tartan track he might well have been capable of running the 100 metres in 10.6 seconds, again very much in the international class.

Logically, someone with his irresistible combination of basic speed and natural spring should have found the high hurdles a benefit event, but he was unable to cope with its peculiar requirements. He flirted with the hurdles while at Repton, but was never sure how many strides he should take between hurdles. At one stage he adopted the unique technique of taking off and landing on the same foot, a feat comparable with Mike Procter's ability to bowl fast off the wrong foot. It never had any future as far as speedy hurdling was concerned, but illustrated Fry's fundamental athleticism.

Wallis Myers confirmed this, referring to a novel form of indoor training: 'Probably what did him more good than anything was his daily standing jump in his rooms at Wadham. He would take up a position in front of an arm-chair and clear it with one spring; or, more dramatically, would sometimes face the mantelpiece, crouch down, take a leap upwards, turn in the air and bow to the "gallery" with his feet planted on the shelf.' Ben Travers in *94 Declared* said that it was a feat which Fry offered to repeat in the library at Lord's when well into his seventies.

His reputation as a standing jumper brought the odd challenge. During the lunch interval of a match between Lancashire and Sussex the Lancashire fast bowler, Walter Brearley, said that Fry should have no problem leaping over the table. C.B. replied that it was just about impossible, but Brearley maintained that half-a-dozen of the Lancashire players would be capable of making the leap. Fry bet him £5 that no one from 'this lot' could do it and was amazed to see Brearley himself take up the bet and succeed!

Another story which comes to mind is when Percy Chapman first saw C.B., at a cricket match played in the grounds of a country house. Chapman recalled that Fry chivalrously offered to bring tea out for the ladies. He attempted to hurdle a low fence while carrying a tray laden with cups of tea, but misjudged the height of the obstacle and fell flat on his face to his own considerable embarrassment.

C.B. was generally intent on replacing past triumphs with new ambitions and challenges, but he was clearly disappointed not to have been able to carry his athletic abilities through to full potential. However, there were not the clubs that there are today and any athletic achievements outside Oxbridge had to result from individual resolve. Fry was not simply interested in competition— he also wanted the comradeship which the University club had in abundance, but which was sadly lacking elsewhere.

He contented himself with varying accounts of his world record leap—he was never one to miss the opportunity for decorating stories with increasingly implausible flourishes. The revised version has it that he had eaten a hearty lunch before strolling across to Iffley Road and was puffing on a cigar between leaps! It was said that he placed the cigar carefully on the ground before making the record jump and when he returned to pick up the cigar the ash was still unbroken. It seems churlish to challenge the veracity of this romantic tale, but C.B. was not in the habit of mixing business with pleasure and his customary abstinence when faced with any physical challenge suggests that he would have been unlikely to threaten his performance in this way.

An equally improbable angle on the jump was related by the critic James Agate in *Ego*. He and Fry were having dinner with Clifford Bax in December 1938–'Fry, alluding to man's universal desire to shine at something else, said: "I always wanted to be a minor poet. I remember when I did my record long jump saying to myself when I was in the air half-way, 'This may be pretty good jumping. It's dashed poor minor poetry'." '

Among the crowd on that momentous day had been the famous writer Compton Mackenzie, then a small boy. Fry later got to know him quite well and when he and Denzil Batchelor were invited to tea with Mackenzie, C.B. presented him with a photograph of the scene on that memorable day in 1893, with the young Mackenzie visible in the crowd.

For some reason the longevity of Fry's records has been rather confused, and it has often been suggested that his share of the world record remained intact for twenty-one years. In fact, it was the university record which lasted for that length of time, the Cambridge man H.S.O. Ashington adding three-quarters of an inch to the distance in 1913. The world record survived for rather less than ten years and when the American Alvin Kraenzlein won the Olympic title at Paris in 1900 he jumped a fraction of an inch further than C.B.'s record.

In the following year there was an astonishing breakthrough by Irishman Peter O'Connor, who jumped 24 ft 11¾ ins in Dublin to set a formidable world record which was not surpassed for almost twenty years. However, no Englishman exceeded Fry's distance until the 1920s.

C.B.'s entry into the jumping record books threw up an interesting psychological sideline which has fair relevance today. Fry's leap established new horizons for other promising jumpers who had been challenging his supremacy at Oxford. Suddenly they all added a foot to their best distance, as if Fry had extended the bounds of possibility. (However, the theory of excellence breeding excellence was not endorsed by the events which followed Bob Beamon's earth-shattering leap at altitude in Mexico in 1968, when he added almost 22 inches to the world record with a jump of 29 ft 2½ ins. On the contrary, it had a depressive effect on the world of long jumping and even the standards which had been achieved prior to Beamon's prodigious effort were not maintained. It is only in the past few years that the outstanding American, Carl Lewis, has truly filled the void. Contemporary jumpers have now passed the 28 foot barrier and Lewis, who shares the explosive sprinting talent of Jesse Owens and to a lesser extent Charles Fry, seems to have the potential to challenge Beamon's mark, if not lift it above the magical target of 30 feet.)

By the time he went up to Oxford, Fry's career as a Surrey player had already ended. He qualified for the county by virtue of having been born in Croydon, but Surrey's subsequent indifference to his talent must have made him glad that he had a residential qualification to play for Sussex.

He had made a promising 65 for Surrey 2nd XI against their Nottinghamshire counterparts and his chance appeared to have come when he was asked to play for the county champions against Warwickshire at the end of the 1891 season. Fry was taking part in a holiday match at Lynton in Devon when the telegraph arrived via Minehead Post Office. He greeted the news with a thunderous hit to leg, almost decapitating Lynton's square leg, who happened to be Sir George Newnes, a key figure in Fry's future as a journalist and the man who brought *Fry's Magazine* into being thirteen years later.

'Surrey put a weak eleven into the field', said *Wisden* of Fry's debut on 24 August. Warwickshire were not classed as a first-class county at the time and they capitulated in less than two days, Surrey winning by ten wickets. Fry went in second wicket down in Surrey's first innings and was highly relieved when he got off the mark, but he was yorked by W.A.J. West when he had made only three. (West, better known as an umpire, later followed Jim Phillips' example by no-balling Fry for throwing.)

Warwickshire were dismissed for 54 and 135, Bill Lockwood taking four wickets in four balls, and Surrey required just five to win. Fry was sent in with W. Brockwell to finish the job, but had still to get off the mark when the winning hit was made.

Great things were expected of Fry at Oxford on the strength of his solid apprenticeship at Repton, but a prodigious all-round performance in the first trial game proved to be rather misleading. Playing for Lionel Palairet's side he scored 118 in the first innings, including 13 fours, but survived two easy chances. It was his knock of 53 out of 66 in forty minutes in the second innings, made in dull light, which raised more eyebrows. There were no plaudits for his bowling, despite a match return of 10 for 103. The *Oxford Magazine* concurred with many other sound sources of opinion in writing: 'Of his bowling we are inclined to speak with reservation: it is but charitable to suspend one's judgment; but, certainly, from the pavilion it looked first cousin to a throw.' Similar verdicts were to haunt Fry for the next ten years until persistent criticism, on and off the field, as good as ended his bowling career.

Another century in the final trial not only booked Fry's place in the Oxford side for 1892, but also suggested that they might have a highly reliable run-maker in their midst. It was not to be: he was out for a duck in each of his first three games for the University and but for a fine century against Somerset would have averaged a few points less than his eventual mark of just over 19. The high scores which became a hall-mark of his play for Sussex and Hampshire were elusive at Oxford. At this stage he had a tendency to play rash shots early in his innings and frequently paid the penalty. At least he made some impression in the 'Varsity Match, scoring 44 in the first innings and 27 in the second as Oxford won by six wickets. Nevertheless, his efforts were overshadowed by a brilliant partnership in Oxford's first innings between M.R. Jardine (140) and V.T. Hill (114), who put on 178. (Jardine was father of the more famous Douglas.)

The Lord's match was also notable for some classic eccentricity from Gerry Weigall, who, although nominally playing for Cambridge, did almost as much as any Oxford man to decide the outcome. Weigall, who, like Fry, took to demonstrating the finer points of batsmanship with an umbrella later in life, managed to run out two of his colleagues, including the captain, Stanley Jackson, who was supposed to have been greeted with these immortal words as the two met in mid-wicket: 'Go back, Jacker, I'm set.' Weigall did make top score for Cambridge with 65, but afterwards made a greater name for himself with shameless buffoonery, both on and off the field.

Wisden summed up the disappointment of Fry's first season for Oxford by saying, 'He scarcely justified the very high opinions formed of him.' They also had unequivocal things to say about his highly individual version of the art of bowling: 'He was made very little use of at Lord's, this being probably due to some stringent remarks that were made as to the character of his delivery. His style of bowling was anything but pleasing to the eye, as he loses all the advantage of his height by dropping almost on to his knees as he lets the ball go out of his hand, and more than that his action is so unfair that he will certainly have to alter it.'

There was no great improvement to report in Fry's batting form the following summer. He was a little more consistent than he had been in 1892, but only managed two half-centuries, against the Gentlemen and Sussex, giving his future county a taste of his true potential. He took 4 for 17 in the first match, against Lancashire, but his bowling was not in great demand. 'As a bowler', *Wisden* said, 'he evidently tried very hard to get out of the objectionable style he developed in the previous year, but he never was particularly deadly.'

The 'Varsity Match was a disaster for Oxford, beaten by 266 runs, but at least Fry had the muted satisfaction of top-scoring with 31 as Oxford were shot out for 64 in their second innings. However, there were other factors which made the match significant. Taking his place in the Cambridge side was Ranji—Kumar Shri Ranjitsinhji—with whom Fry was to form a close and enduring friendship.

The game also exposed the absurdities of an outdated law on declarations and proved that acts of gamesmanship are not confined to the present day. The law at the time was that sides trailing by more than 80 on first innings were obliged to follow on. Oxford were in danger of falling behind Cambridge's total by more than the prescribed figure and the last two batsmen decided that it would be no bad thing if they were obliged to go straight back in. Conversely, the Cambridge bowler, C.M. Wells, who had earlier dismissed Fry for seven, realised that the Oxford batsmen were determined to play carelessly and wanted to pre-empt their plan with deliberately wayward bowling. He started with a no-ball which went to the boundary, then after the Oxford batsman Brain had exerted himself considerably to prevent four wides off the next delivery, he was powerless to intercept the following ball, which did go for four wides, thus averting the follow-on.

In response to this curious incident the follow-on law was changed in 1894 so that teams were only obliged to bat again if they trailed by more than 120 runs on first innings. This alteration was undermined by the 1896 University Match, with a virtually identical scenario to the 1893 game, and finally in 1900 the modern system of optional follow-on after a deficit of 150 runs was adopted.

Ranji's *Jubilee Book of Cricket*, which came out in 1897, had some earnest observations to make about the ethics of these occurrences:

'It is for the historian rather to point out that these events were really effects of a general cause at work in recent cricket – the growing keenness of the competition, which is slowly changing a pleasant game into a serious business. The Oxford and Cambridge match was at first, perhaps, too much of the former: it is now tending in the direction of the latter.

'No human institution is perfect: it will always tend to excess or defect. But how nearly perfect in its own way is cricket, and especially Oxford and Cambridge cricket! It is a game which keeps boys out of mischief. It is a training of youth for a manly life. It lays up a store of strength and health against old age.

Could this have been part of Fry's contribution to the book?

Directly after the University Match in 1893 Fry and Ranji had their first taste of the big time when they were chosen for the Gentlemen against the Players at the Oval. The game itself was exciting enough, the Players shading it by eight runs, but Fry made a negligible impact. He was dismissed for eight and 22 and was given just seven overs in the Players' second innings.

In 1894 Fry succeeded Lionel Palairet as captain of the Oxford team. This completed a unique treble as he had been president of the athletic club and skipper of the soccer team already that year. He lacked Palairet's experience, but the *Oxford Magazine* felt he might 'reasonably be expected to make up in keenness what he lacks in the knowledge of the game'.

The Oxford side were not one of the best to represent the university and they had a dismal run in matches leading up to the clash with Cambridge, but the Light Blues, if anything, had even more pronounced weaknesses, particularly in their bowling attack. Fry himself began the season well, making 75 in Oxford's first innings against Somerset, but he was overshadowed by Lionel Palairet, who delighted in making 181 for his adopted county against his old university. Palairet was widely regarded as the most graceful batsman of the era and although Fry said a few years later that he was incapable of bringing the same elegance to his batting, he had amended his opinion by the time *Life Worth Living* came out in 1939. He said there: 'I evolved such cricket as I achieved from watching Lionel Palairet play, and from my own inner nature. Mostly the latter, because I was a driver with a full swing, and not a modulated lunger in the stylish manner of Palairet.'

Fry's batting average for Oxford in 1894 crept over 30, but bearing in mind that his tally of 454 runs included two centuries and two other scores of 70 or more it was hardly cause for round-the-clock celebration. He lamented that opposing sides were getting the better of rain-affected wickets and although he was playing well in the nets he could not carry the same form with him to the middle. Less than a fortnight before the match with

Cambridge, Fry was given a new bat to try out. It appeared to be too heavy, but it certainly did the trick when Oxford went down to Brighton to play Sussex. He made 119 in the second innings and, although he did not make many runs in the next match against the MCC, he had the considerable consolation of performing the hat-trick—and his victims included Andrew Stoddart.

It was typical of the reception accorded to Fry throughout his life that his success in the 1894 'Varsity Match should be equally praised and resented. His undefeated 100 should have been enough to gag his critics, some of whom had suggested that he should drop himself after his early-season struggles with the bat. However, the Cambridge attack were described in some circles as the worst ever put out by the university. Fry took half-an-hour to get off the mark and his early tameness drew barracking from the crowd. When the wicket-keeper, R.P. Lewis, came in at the fall of the ninth wicket, Fry was on 83, and although Lewis managed to play out the remainder of the over, Fry sensed that he would have to hit out if he was to reach his century before his partner succumbed. He slammed three fours, a three and a two, then watched as Lewis was predictably dismissed. Naturally, Fry's detractors suggested that he should have spared them the earlier tedium by taking aggressive measures in the first part of his innings. The fact that Oxford went on to win by eight wickets seemed to vindicate his caution.

More than forty years later Sir Home Gordon, a seasoned student of the game, offered a historical perspective on Fry's innings. Speaking at a dinner, which C.B. also happened to be attending, he assured those present that Fry's innings in 1894 was undoubtedly the worst century he had seen in over fifty years of watching tussles between the rival universities. Fry concurred with the judgment quite happily, but *Wisden* took a more chari-table view: 'For Fry the match was a great triumph. He scored 100 not out, his fielding at slip was most brilliant, and he managed his side with admirable judgment'—and went so far as to announce him as one of their cricketers of the year, although they were actually young cricketers of the year. The choice was somewhat charitable and based more on potential than actual achievement. In Oxford itself there were few doubters. Joseph Wells, in his *History of Wadham*, described the 'Varsity Match as the 'crowning success of the most brilliant athletic year which has ever fallen to the lot of an undergraduate.'

In his final year he was able to play just nine innings for Oxford, but contrived to make quite an impression with both bat and ball. He was out for 99 against Kent, also taking five wickets in the first innings, and scored his second century against his county colleagues in a rain-drenched match at Hove.

Oxford have rarely had a more formidable batting side than the one which lined up in 1895. Plum Warner opened with C.B. and after them there was Harry Foster, G.J. Mordaunt, Henry Leveson-Gower and the legendary footballer G.O. Smith. Sussex were quite content with their total of 487, but Oxford topped that with ease, scoring 651. Mordaunt hit an unbeaten 264, but although Charles Fry lent valuable support with 125 he was excessively restrained, showing the sort of attrition which left eager critics scratching their heads in amazement. How could someone with such remarkable athletic gifts as C.B. resort to unrelieved stonewalling? The match itself created a record for run aggregate in a game in England.

Fry split a finger in the MCC game at Lord's yet almost did the hat-trick again. He took two wickets in two balls, but the umpire decided that his next delivery rebounded against the stumps from the wicket-keeper's pads, although it was the opinion of bowler and fielders that the ball had struck the stumps direct.

The injury wasn't severe enough to keep him out of his fourth University Match, but unfortunately the much-vaunted Oxford batting failed to respond to the occasion and Cambridge won by 134 runs. C.B. had a miserable match as a batsman, scoring nought and one, but did have the satisfaction of taking 6 for 78 in Cambridge's first innings. Oxford would have lost by a much greater margin if it had not been for a brilliant hundred by Harry Foster in their second innings.

C.B. played in two Gentlemen v Players games immediately after going down from Oxford and made his mark in both. At Lord's he made a hard-hitting 60 on a fiery wicket in the second innings, adding 72 for the last wicket with Ernest Smith, but the amateurs lost by 32 runs. At the Oval he appeared as the true all-rounder. Cast in the unlikely role of main strike bowler he took 5 for 90 and 3 for 89, numbering Bobby Abel and Tom Hayward among his victims. This, allied to an invaluable knock of 77 in the Gentlemen's first innings, was largely responsible for a large defeat being translated into an honourable draw.

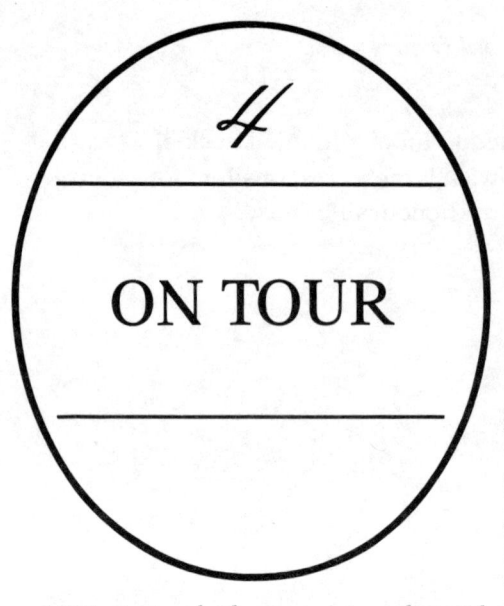

4

ON TOUR

There were no United Nations blacklists for Charles Fry to worry about when he accepted the invitation to join Lord Hawke's touring party on its four-month trip to South Africa at the end of 1895. Instead, there was ample evidence of the mounting tension between the British and the Boers. Not content with experiencing this charged atmosphere at close quarters the touring cricketers took it upon themselves to create their own adventure.

C.B. had only played a handful of matches for Sussex, with limited success, so it was potential more than anything else which made Ranji recommend his 23-year-old county colleague to Lord Hawke. Fry would not have merited a place in the England side for a home series at this stage, but a number of top players were not available for the tour and it was a justifiable gamble to choose a promising young cricketer like Fry.

The bulk of the party gathered at London's Waterloo Station on 30 November before travelling down to Southampton and setting sail on the Union steamship *Guelph*. Lord Hawke and his right-hand man, Sir Timothy O'Brien, left a week later on the speedier Royal Mail steamer *Moor*. There was an enthusiastic welcoming party at Cape Town as *Guelph* reached port on 22 December. Christmas Day was spent in a vain attempt to climb the Table Mountain and on Boxing Day the cricket programme began with a match against the fifteen players representing Western Province. C.B. did nothing of note with the bat, but finished with match figures of 10 for 82 to suggest that he would be a useful all-round presence.

The local side won the game and were so pleased with themselves that they arranged another one-day fixture, in which they were again triumphant, but attention was diverted from the cricket by the abortive Jameson Raid, in which Dr L. Storr Jameson, an administrator in the British South Africa Company, led a force of 470 men towards Johannesburg in the hope of provoking a revolt among the Uitlanders and overthrowing the government of Paul Kruger.

C.B. had scored an excellent 148 against a Cape Colony side and en route to Johannesburg the touring party got an early taste of the lavish hospitality of Douglas Logan, the benevolent Scotsman who had both helped to organise the tour and agreed to finance it.

The team's first scheduled game in Johannesburg was called off and they were out of action until 13 January. This game was approaching a conclusion when a loud explosion nearby brought it to an abrupt halt. The feeling in the magazine *Cricket* was that these little diplomatic incidents should not be allowed to interfere with the great game: 'As a rule, the chief enemy to the success of a tour is the clerk of the weather, and battles and sieges are conspicuous by their absence.'

The team's nervy train journey to Johannesburg was recalled by Fry in his magazine ten years later. The train had ground to a halt within range of the Transvaal border and the passengers were joined by a dozen Free Staters, one of whom went into the English team's carriage. 'We entered into conversation, and tried to find out what the commandoes were doing there; but he was very close, and wanted to know who we were. We explained our mission, and suggested a cricket match on the veldt, as the train seemed well fixed for hours. He was not taking our chaff at all. "No," he said, taking off his hat and showing his close-cropped curly yellow hair— he was tall, with a bronzed fair complexion, and a little sun-blacked moustache, and he was dressed in grey cords like a superior gamekeeper—"no, we don't play cricket, but we shoot." I can hear the cool sarcasm in his round voice now. He was quite serious that ten of us should step out and shoot off a match at five hundred yards.'

By way of alternative sport it was suggested that C.B., as the fastest sprinter in the team, would act as moving target on a real-life rifle range. The Free Staters were to pay £100 if they missed their man and if they succeeded they would receive a modest £20. Fry was relieved that the train moved off before this diversion could be pursued!

Sammy Woods, a vastly entertaining anglicized Australian, recalled a conversation that he and C.B. heard between two of their faint-hearted colleagues on the way to Johannesburg. 'Why are we going to this confounded place? Most likely when we get there they (the Boers) will fire at us on the cricket field.' 'Well,' said the other, 'I am in the Militia. Still, I don't and never did, want to go into action, and I do hope it won't be so. If it does and gets to the papers what will dear mother say?'

At Pietermaritzburg Fry made his second big century of the tour, this time 153, proving that he had adapted to the matting wickets as well as anyone. He was also part of the team of cricketers who took on their hosts, the 7th Hussars, in a novel form of polo. It was actually like a mixture of polo and hockey because six cricketers on foot competed with four Hussars on horseback. The result was an unexpected 2–1 victory for the tourists, who were grateful that their opponents managed to avoid physical contact between ponies and humans.

Flushed by their success the cricketers agreed to take on the local pony club, with the small matter of a £100 bet resting on the outcome, but this time their sense of adventure backfired. After the third chukka the score was 1–1 and with the locals calling for fresh ponies Lord Hawke felt it was time to call the contest off. This time the cricketers had taken a fearful battering from the ponies and in one collision C.B. had been sent flying ten yards. There was more cricket to be played and it was doubtful if anyone would be left to play if the carnage was allowed to continue.

The English team had become accustomed to the problems of making runs against 15-man teams in South Africa, but these difficulties assumed nightmare proportions at the end of January and beginning of February 1896 when the English played three successive matches against sides boasting 22 players. The premium on short singles was all the greater and Fry said he and Sammy Woods decided on the calculated, though mostly successful, risk of attempting runs when the ball trickled to short slip!

But if the batsmen found themselves competing against unsporting odds, the bowlers had nothing to complain about and no one enjoyed himself more than George Lohmann, a superb medium-pacer, who managed to return the unusual figures of 11 for 54 in the second innings of the match with Graham's Town. Lohmann was also the major difference between the two sides in the three Test Matches which were very much dominated by the ball.

The First Test was played at Port Elizabeth in the middle of February, by which time Charles Fry's batting form had largely deserted him. Nevertheless, he managed to top-score with 43 in England's first innings total of 185 and could then afford to sit back and watch with admiration as Lohmann weaved an irresistible spell on the South African batsmen. His first-innings figures of 7 for 38 were impressive enough, but second time around he produced total panic in the ranks, taking 8 for 7 as the home side were dismissed for just 30, the second lowest total in the history of Test cricket.

Lord Hawke was not pleased to see an Englishman, Lieutenant R.M. Poore, playing for the South African team. He was in the 7th Hussars and, as a temporary resident, had 'earned' his place with centuries against the tourists for both Pietermaritzburg and Natal. He went on to play some brilliant innings for Hampshire when other commitments permitted, but fortunately on this occasion he did not tip the balance decisively against his fellow-countrymen.

The Second Test at Johannesburg was equally one-sided, although this time the English batsmen had more of a say in the outcome. They made a shocking start, but a partnership of 119 between Tom Hayward and C.B. deprived the South Africans of their early advantage. Fry was eventually dismissed for 64, but Hayward went on to make 122 and half-centuries from A.J.L. Hill, C.W. Wright and H.R. Bromley-Davenport enabled the tourists to make 482. The South African batsmen avoided the total humiliation of the First Test, but they were again exposed by Lohmann's guile as he recorded figures of 9 for 28 in the first innings, and Lord Hawke's side went on to win by an innings and 197 runs.

Although there was still one Test to play, C.B.'s tour ended prematurely at the beginning of March. He had already tried his hand at hunting while on tour – he was a very capable horseman – and was on the trail again when the team made a return trip to Douglas Logan's headquarters at Matjesfontein. Fry had previously ridden a reliable chestnut, but gave this up to Lord Hawke's 18-stone brother. The replacement, borrowed from a friend of Logan's, was a mercurial performer. C.B. had to go back to the Logan house to get a rifle and it was now, inexplicably, that his horse went berserk, coming within inches of colliding with a wall before heading out into the open country.

This is how Fry remembered the terrifying incident in *Life Worth Living*:

> When we had gone a mile or so at a rate of knots, I saw ahead an arch under the railway, and remembered with the instantaneous perception one has at such times that a very deep spruit ran under the railway at right angles. I had noticed it coming down in the train. I saw ahead a precipitous plunge in the chasm, which was much too wide to jump. So, disengaging my feet from the stirrups, I hunched forward and, picking a clear piece of ground, executed a jump forward out of the saddle and landed on my left foot and right hand. I rolled over once and then stood up and watched the disappearing beast, which stopped with all four toes jammed into the ground on the brink of the chasm . . . This was the nearest shave I ever had for my life, and I still admire my acrobatic feat – at a distance.

The irony was that it was Fry's right fibula which was broken, earlier in the escapade, he thought, and it was duly put in plaster. The only consolation for C.B., apart from his survival, was the ideal opportunity for recuperation on the boat home, giving him the chance to be fit for the new season in England.

The final Test Match in Cape Town was as one-sided as the previous two. Lohmann pushed up his tally to 35 wickets for the three international matches, while Hill dominated the England innings of 265 with a century. Fry still finished as the leading batsman on the tour, making 750 runs and averaging just over 34, but Lohmann was the dominant personality. In all, he took 157 wickets at the absurdly low average of 6.78, with Bromley-Davenport (48 wickets at ten apiece) and C.B. (37 at an average of 12.72) leading the support cast.

Notwithstanding his accident Fry relished the tour, which made it even more of a tragedy that it turned out to be his only overseas trip as a player. For he was subsequently forced to reject four separate invitations to tour Australia when his batting powers were at their height.

5

SUSSEX — THE EARLY YEARS

When Charles Fry joined up with Sussex in the middle of July 1895 for his first extended spell with the county side he had an equal band of devotees and detractors. The critics labelled him as a boring batsman, so obsessed with survival that he placed unreasonable restrictions on his attacking repertoire. There were beguiling glimpses, however, of the later, liberated player who eventually discovered that belligerence could be practised in safety.

In the second innings of Sussex's match against Somerset at Taunton at the start of August he came to the mature conclusion that cautious defence would be pointless on a tricky wicket. Sussex were heading for inevitable defeat, but in scoring 91 out of an all-out score of 143 C.B. demonstrated his ability to alter his tactics according to the state of the game and the prevailing conditions. He scored at almost a run a minute, prompting *The Guardian* to say: 'In the second venture Mr C.B. Fry became conscious that nature has granted to him exceptional physical advantages. Usually this famous athlete is as slow and deliberate when batting as a certain Marquis (Salisbury) when making a political speech. The tendency to yawn seemed almost irresistible; but on Friday Mr Fry roused himself.' However, it was an isolated success for C.B. He averaged less than 30 for the whole summer, but had more reason to be pleased with his bowling, taking 57 wickets at a cost of just over 25 apiece.

Fry announced his full recovery from the South African escapade when he played in two first-class matches before starting as a master at Charterhouse in May 1896. He was then unavailable until the start of August and had no opportunity to figure in the

Test series, but an innings of 92 for Sussex against the Australians suggested that he might have been in contention if he had been able to play throughout the summer. In the game before this C.B. had taken severe punishment as a bowler at the hands of his cultured former Oxford colleague, Lionel Palairet, who had joined Somerset. Fry was struck for 21 in an over, and this, it should be remembered, at a time when all boundaries were measured in fours.

It was at the end of August that Fry achieved his most notable feat as an all-rounder. He took 5 for 81 in Nottinghamshire's first innings at Trent Bridge, due reward for 44 overs of persistence, then made 89 in Sussex's modest total of 184. A return of 5 for 66 enabled Sussex to dismiss Notts for 280, but a target of 350 proved well beyond Sussex, whose major resistance came from the inevitable Charles Fry with a well-made 65.

There had been a brief rumour that C.B. would be lost to English cricket and the nation in general on the strength of a post which had been offered to him by the South African Chartered Company. There was general relief when it became clear that he would still be able to play for Sussex in 1897.

However, he still struggled to find any sort of consistency, playing one innings less than in 1896 and finishing with an almost identical average. The highlight of his season was a sparkling century against Kent at the end of August at Hove. Having scored his debut hundred for the county against Gloucestershire in 1894 he had waited for three years to reach the three-figure mark again. There was also a lesser premium on his bowling and a haul of just 12 wickets was disappointing for both him and Sussex, who were also faced with the prospect of losing Ranji on a permanent basis. It was rumoured that he would remain in India after touring Australia with Andrew Stoddart's team.

Sussex were deprived of Ranji's services in 1898, but it was only a temporary absence from the English game and, by way of compensation that season, Fry demonstrated that he had come to terms with the first-class game. No doubt he was improving technically, but the reason for his sudden emergence as a top-class batsman was more fundamental. In some ways he had been faced with the familiar problems of an amateur cricketer, trying to afford to play a game which placed severe demands on the pocket and offered minimal expenses by way of compensation.

In broad terms these amateurs fell into two categories: there were the out-and-out gentlemen of leisure who could rely on family wealth to ease their path, and others, like Fry, who lacked the necessary backing but still fell into a social category where they were obliged to play the game for love rather than money. It was often a mystery how these middle-class amateurs balanced their personal books and it was logical that there should be widespread allegations of shamateurism. Invisible income was somehow coming the way of the amateurs and the feeling was that they were either receiving under-the-counter payments or benefiting from the generosity of patrons.

In his first few years with Sussex, C.B. was able to rely on neither and the only way he could afford to play cricket was by teaching and writing, neither of which offered the prospect of an independent solution. Fry was confident of his ability as a journalist yet uncertain about journalism as a regular breadwinner. This insecurity clearly affected his batting—he averaged only 26 for his first six seasons in first-class cricket—and it is not beyond the bounds of possibility that he might have been lost to the game if a definite solution had not been found.

The answer, to both his personal and cricketing anxieties, lay in unlikely surroundings. Soon after he left Oxford, Fry visited the training ship *Mercury* for the first time. It had been set up by Charles Hoare, a member of the famous banking family, ten years earlier, and on the Hamble River in Hampshire teenagers learnt the basics of seacraft before joining the Royal Navy or the merchant service.

Assisting Hoare was Beatrice Holme Sumner, whose parents lived in Surrey. There were strong naval connections in the family and as well as becoming romantically involved with Charles Hoare she soon proved that she could make a great contribution to the work of the training ship. Hoare was already married, but he and Beatrice successfully complicated the situation by having two children together, Robin and Sybil. In other circumstances it might have been possible for the Hoares to divorce and the scandal would have been minimised by a marriage between Charles Hoare and Beatrice Holme Sumner. However, the Hoares were devout Catholics so a divorce was out of the question.

C.B.

Charles Fry began to make regular visits to Hamble and built up firm friendships with both Hoare and Beatrice Holme Sumner. Fry also played cricket on the grounds of the training establishment and soon discovered that Miss Sumner had an unusual interest in and understanding of the game. She was eight years older than C.B., but he greatly admired her intelligence and strength of character. There was no conventional romance between the two, but equally there was no future in the relationship between Hoare and Miss Sumner. The scandal of this extra-marital relationship had been successfully contained, but it could only cause increased embarrassment and there was a possible solution which could make life less complicated for all parties.

C.B. and Beatrice Holme Sumner decided, with Charles Hoare's approval, to get married, and since the arrangement suited Hoare well enough he also offered to help subsidise Fry's cricketing career, ensuring that he could turn out for Sussex for the entire duration of each cricket season without worrying if his income from writing articles would be enough to pay for his travels.

At the same time Fry was able to cut short his time as a master at Charterhouse and he had few regrets in leaving the school during the summer term in 1898. Teaching, at Charterhouse at least, had not matched up to C.B.'s expectations. He had hoped that he would be given his head and left to his own devices, but instead his duties were carefully prescribed and limited. It had been thought that his commitments at the school in 1898 would keep him out of county cricket until the end of July, but his acquaintance with Sussex was actually renewed a few days after his marriage on 4 June.

C.B. was also happy to swap the more claustrophobic surroundings of London's Tavistock Place for Glenbourne Manor, a lovely property in West End, only a few miles from Southampton and Hamble. It was not a house which Fry could have contemplated buying independently, but with Charles Hoare's assistance it was possible. The gardens soon housed something of a menagerie: both C.B. and Mrs Fry were very fond of animals and apart from a lively pair of Scotch terriers they also kept ponies and hens. They also wasted no time in raising a family. Charis, the eldest child, was born in 1899, and she was quickly followed by Stephen and Faith.

Fry began to discover a security that he had not known since early childhood. The new Mrs Fry not only shared his love of cricket, helping him to practise in the garden at Glenbourne Manor, but also shared his enthusiasm for the hunt—she held the unusual distinction of having been an honorary whip for the Duke of Beaufort's Hounds as a young woman. She was an interesting character. In her younger days she allowed her emotions to surface much more than anyone who knew her at the *Mercury* would have thought possible, and was quite happy to present herself as an attractive woman. Her affair with Charles Hoare confirmed that her phenomenal self-discipline sometimes conceded to logic of the heart. Like C.B., she had a shy side to her personality which she covered up with her gruff, abrupt manner, but people who knew her well would vouch for her fundamental kindness.

Fry got his share of the cricketing headlines in June 1898, but this was because he had become one of the prime scapegoats in the tough campaign against throwing. Fortunately the critical attention on his bowling did nothing to affect C.B.'s resolve as a batsman and it was in the third game where his action was called into question that his batting began to click. This was against Middlesex at Lord's in the middle of July. Fry carried his bat for 104 in the first innings and although he was dismissed for a duck in the second innings he had more suffering in store for the Middlesex bowlers a week later when he scored 108 and 123 not out in the return match. This was the first time he had scored two centuries in a game.

He then went on to make 93 against Gloucestershire and 110 against Somerset. *Cricket* said: 'On his present form Mr Fry is about the best batsman in England.' There was more to come: at the start of August he hit 99 and 133 against Hampshire and *Cricket* underlined its earlier plaudits: 'Certainly at the present time no one in England can hold a candle to him.' His purple patch from the middle of July to mid-August had brought him close on 1,000 runs, including five centuries and two other scores in the nineties. It was a mouthwatering taste of the run orgies in which Fry specialised for the remainder of his career.

In 1898 the best was saved for Yorkshire, whose formidable array of bowlers could hardly have known the trouble they would experience in trying to dismiss C.B. over the next ten years. He batted throughout the Sussex first innings of 311, making a brilliant undefeated 179. In the second innings he was bowled without scoring by Wilfred Rhodes, an illustration of cricket's genius as a humbling game.

Despite the occasional low score C.B. managed to finish second in the national batting averages behind Willie Quaife, having made 1,788 runs in his abbreviated season at an average of just over 54.

Sussex could only manage ninth place in the County Championship in 1898, but they were four places higher the following season when Ranji returned to the fray, rejuvenated and in quite remarkable form. Fry began on a highly promising note with a fluent innings of 98 against the MCC, then made 81 for the South of England against the Australians to announce himself immediately as a Test Match probable. However, big scores eluded him until the beginning of July when the vaunted Yorkshire attack were hit for an undefeated 162, and his very next innings produced another century, Fry's 104 helping the Gentlemen to an exceedingly rare innings victory against the Players.

His next burst of form came at the end of the month when a run-a-minute 94 against Middlesex was followed by a glorious 181 against the Australians. His dominant strokeplay was underlined by 25 boundaries in a four-hour stay, but even C.B. had to give second best as the inimitable Victor Trumper made an undefeated 300, then the highest score by an Australian in England.

VINTAGE FRY

Any doubts about the long-term credibility of the Fry/Ranji combination were swept away by their merciless trail of destruction in 1900. Ranji played 18 fewer innings than in 1899, but once again topped the 3,000-run mark, averaging almost 90; and the princely glitter was rubbing off on Charles Fry, who scored 2,325 runs at an average of 61.18. Cricket fans had never seen anything to match this—batsmanship of a sublime quality, which not only rewrote the record books, but also created a fresh set of standards for future players to follow. The two men faced bowlers of devastating speed, accuracy and guile. They showed techniques for run-making on rain-affected and damaged tracks which only magicians could contemplate.

Three half-centuries for W.G. Grace's London Counties team against Surrey at the start of the season gave C.B. immediate confidence, and Surrey were again forced to toil in his majestic wake as he cut and drove his way to an impressive 145 against them at the end of May. Then he switched his attentions to the Essex attack, scoring 69 and 101 not out at Leyton.

This was not a match which left him with feelings of total contentment, however. In the first innings he was astonished to be given out lbw to Walter Mead when well set for another century. Characteristically, he found it difficult to hide his feelings at the decision and knocked the bails off as he walked grumpily away from the wicket. In the second innings he was hit in the face by a ball which rose viciously off a length, but bravely resumed, his sights set firmly on the hundred which he had been denied in the first innings.

Sussex's game with Gloucestershire at the start of June is

discussed elsewhere in the book—it was here that Fry was called for throwing for the fourth and final time—but this match also signalled the start of a phenomenal run of scores by Ranji. He opened modestly with 97 and 127 against Gloucestershire, but then made 222 against Somerset and an undefeated 215 against Cambridge University. C.B. replied with a century against Kent and the two heroes played their part to the full in one of the most bat-dominated games in the history of the County Championship. Leicester was the venue in the middle of July, the home side giving Sussex a miserable day and a half in the field by making 609 for 8 declared. However, they were overtaken as Ranji made a career-best 275, capitalising on Fry's foundation of 135, and Sussex finished with a mammoth total of 686 for 8. Fry's innings was especially praiseworthy as he was clearly not well, repeatedly having to rest between deliveries.

The summer may have belonged to Ranji, but the next three weeks were dominated by Fry, who gave a broad hint of the end-of-season carnage which he would wreak the following year. Including his innings against Leicestershire he made 940 in eight visits to the crease at an average of 117.50, passing 50 on each occasion.

The long-suffering Surrey bowlers were on the chopping block again as he hit 125 in 170 minutes at Hove, then doubled the dose in the second innings with a breathtaking 229, made in just 260 minutes and laced with 28 sizzling boundaries. It was Fry's highest score and also the first time anyone had hit a century and a double hundred in the same match. A partnership of 196 in 100 minutes between Fry and Ranji, who made 103, assured the cricket world that these were geniuses in tandem.

Fry made it three centuries in a row when he made 110 against Middlesex, but the record-breaking in this match was provided by his Indian colleague, who hit 202 to become the first player to score four double centuries in the same season. C.B. took up where he had left off in Sussex's next match, against Worcestershire, and as he eased his way into the nineties seemed set to become the first batsman to score a hundred in four successive innings. When he had made 96, however, he was struck on the elbow, and although he carried on batting he was obviously shaken and was caught without adding to his score.

There was no longer-term damage to his confidence, as an

immaculate innings of 105 against Gloucestershire amply proved. Fry failed to reach double figures in his next three innings, but Leicestershire's bowlers felt the sting at Hove as he made 145 out of 217 in just 175 minutes. It was his ninth and final century in a wonderfully productive season, but Ranji still had one more gem to reveal, making 220 against Kent at the end of August.

Sussex's euphoria was the unrelieved depression of the other counties, by now fully aware that the law of averages was against them. On the rare occasions that Charles Fry failed there was an uneasy feeling among the opposition that Ranji would compensate. The most successful batting duet in the history of the game gave the Brighton faithful a pride which they had never known before. The county finished third in the championship in 1900, Ranji's first full season as captain. The taunts of 'Silly Sussex' were rapidly disappearing: but for an unreliable bowling attack they could have been challenging for the Championship itself.

The following year, 1901, was one in which C.B. leapt out of his colleague's shadow to steal the limelight in glorious fashion. His mastery on all sorts of wickets and against all types of bowlers set him apart from his indigenous contemporaries. Curiously, it was not overwhelming consistency which took C.B. past the 3,000-run mark for the one and only time in a season, with an average touching 80, but three all-devouring bursts of scoring. It is interesting to note that Fry went into June having played just five innings and amassed the grand total of 137 runs. A strained back had threatened to sideline him for some time and, with Ranji also unwell, Sussex hardly had the perfect introduction to a new season.

Fry's first half-century came against Nottinghamshire at Trent Bridge on 6 June, but the significant pointer to his record-breaking season came in the form of an extraordinary second innings. The remainder of the Sussex side, Ranji included, were all at sea on an awkward pitch, but C.B.'s technical mastery enabled him to carry his bat for 170 out of a total of 254. He had batted through an innings twice in 1899, but on neither occasion was his domination quite so complete. The runs came in just 225 minutes, including 22 fours, and an inspired Joe Vine, returning match figures of 15 for 161, ensured a comfortable Sussex victory.

Fry retained the golden touch for Sussex's next game at

Leicester. He batted throughout the first day and powered his way
to 244, easily the highest score of his career, in a total of 557. His
first 50 took over two hours, Leicestershire having good cause to
rue dropping him on 23, but he accelerated so effectively that his
remaining runs came at almost a run a minute. He was dropped
again, but by that stage he had made 190 and Sussex went on to
win the match by an innings, their fourth success in their opening
five games. The Brighton faithful began to flatter their heroes with
thoughts of a genuine tilt at the County Championship.

C.B.'s almost unfailing sense of humour was revealed in one of
his less successful knocks of the summer. Playing for London
Counties against the MCC at Lord's in the middle of June he wore a
sun hat when he went out to bat, in blatant defiance of the bitter
wind which was sweeping across the ground. It was almost as
though he could exert the same mystical influence over the
elements as he could over bowling sides.

Two mammoth knocks against the Universities took C.B. past
the 1,000 run mark for June. Cambridge suffered first: they might
have been happy with a total of 360, but a first-wicket stand of 203
between Fry and Vine soon put it in context and C.B. continued to
brutalise the student attack, finishing with 241 out of the county's
total of 571 for 5 declared.

A duck was the last thing pundits expected from Fry in Sussex's
match against Oxford at Eastbourne, the county trailing by 226
runs on the first innings, but somehow that failure lent a certain
inevitability to the rest of the game. Sussex avoided the spectre of
an embarrassing defeat by scoring 414 for 6 and Charles Fry was
still there at the end having made 219. Things could have been
worse for the young men, but for a rare failure in telepathy
between C.B. and Ranji. The pair had added 167 in 85 minutes
when Fry was called by his partner for a quick leg-bye. Unhappily,
as Ranji strode down the wicket from the non-striker's end Fry was
still rubbing his knee where he had been struck a painful blow.
Ranji was caught in no-man's-land and his glorious cameo of an
innings ended in ignominy, on 84.

Sussex's pretentions as true contenders were then put in rude
perspective as the reigning champions, Yorkshire, shot them out
for just 52 in 85 agonising minutes at Bradford and galloped
through to a ten-wicket win. The irresistible combination of

George Hirst and Wilfred Rhodes, with five wickets apiece in the first innings, swept through the Sussex batting with frightening alacrity. Fry would make Yorkshire pay for this humiliation in years to come.

In the context of the summer as a whole Fry's July was anonymous, a run of moderate scores relieved only by two excellent hundreds at the headquarters of cricket. The first came for the Gentlemen against the Players, Fry's 126 being notable for the strength of his on-side play, while his 116 against Middlesex was an altogether more cautious affair.

Fry and Ranji were both among the runs in Sussex's match down at Taunton against Somerset, who took a huge first-innings lead of 324, in spite of C.B.'s first bowling stint for almost a year. Sussex were faced with a daunting task to save the match on the final day, but a magnificent unbeaten 285 by Ranji, the highest score of his career, turned the match upside down and Sussex finished on 466 for 1. Fry's invaluable contribution of 119 not out went all but unnoticed and he admitted that he was 'rather ashamed' by the innings. Nevertheless, the two maestros shared an unbroken stand of 292 for the second wicket in only 170 minutes: it was the highest-ever partnership between Fry and Ranji. C.B. revealed in the *Daily Express* that it had been decided by committee that Ranji would make 300, and he certainly would have reached this landmark but for forty minutes being lost to rain. The innings was all the more remarkable because Ranji had been up all night fishing, although sleepless nights were not an unknown phenomenon for this asthma sufferer.

The beginning of an astonishing sequence of runs, which gave Fry an indelible place in the record books, came on a rain-affected wicket at Portsmouth. He had made 88 in more favourable conditions in the first innings, but his 106 second time round was an object lesson in how to play on difficult wickets. Supreme judgment, technical assurance and unfailing determination made Fry without peer on a damaged wicket.

Sussex cricket was in a state of euphoria on 19 and 20 August as Yorkshire were set up for the hiding of their lives. It started with a Sussex total of 560 for 5 declared, founded on a partnership of 349 for the second wicket between Fry, who made a chanceless 209 in just over six hours, and Ernest Killick, with an admirable 200. The seeds were sown and when Yorkshire were reduced, almost unbelievably, to 49 for 8 at the close of the second day's play there were visions of a famous Sussex victory. The weather came to the champions' aid, however, and they were able to save the match without any difficulty. Fry predicted a backlash after Yorkshire's near debacle: 'But there is a skeleton in the pavilion. My word: someone will suffer for this. Providence forbid that that someone be Sussex.'

There was the same infallibility about C.B.'s batting as he clocked up his third successive hundred, this time a smooth innings of 149 against Middlesex. Sussex totalled 501, so within the space of four days they had topped the 500 mark for the first time against two of their most powerful opponents. When Middlesex were dismissed for 189 it looked as though Sussex would pull off a notable win, but their inability to produce the same penetration in Middlesex's second innings cost them victory.

Meanwhile Fry was reluctantly being drawn into a showdown with the Surrey professional Bobby Abel as both men homed in on their 3,000 runs for the season. The race had its sideshow attractions for the national newspapers. It was amateur against professional and also they were two Surrey-born players, although Fry's connection was brief. Better still, Surrey met Sussex at the Oval on 26–28 August and it seemed as though Abel would keep his nose in front as Sussex were obliged to bat on a drying wicket. Once again, however, Fry dug deep into his rich vein of form to produce a purist's delight of an innings—105 on a difficult track against some of the finest bowlers in the country.

Cricket noted that the space devoted to this sprint finish to a marathon was exceeding that given to bulletins on the health of Mr Gladstone during his last illness. The magazine illustrated the contest with one of its customary excuses for poetry:

> Said Abel to Fry
> When Three Thousand was nigh,
> "Don't you find statisticians bore you?"
> Said Fry unto Abel,
> "Blow the average table!
> Don't mention such things, I implore you."

Fry even advised *Express* readers to put their money on Abel. At this stage Abel had an aggregate of 2,943 runs, Fry was on 2,901, and John Tyldesley, on 2,781, still had a slight chance of pipping both at the post. The two main contenders were both at the crease on 30 August, and it was C.B. who got a head start: by lunchtime he had already made 90 and was only nine runs short of the magical figure. Abel was 47 not out when lunch was taken at the Oval, but the afternoon session started earlier at Hove and Fry got home by a short head. *Evening News* readers were treated to a minute-by-minute breakdown of how the two heroes had moved towards their target. Fry was so delighted and relieved to have settled the argument that he launched into a burst of almost skittish hitting. His last 50 runs against Kent came in just half-an-hour and although it was not one of his most convincing innings he had the added satisfaction of completing his 1,000 runs for August as well as making his fifth century on the trot.

C.B. was persuaded to tell the nation how he had won the race, but he insisted on explaining his terms of reference: 'My remarks must in practice be prefaced by the statement that as a serious cricketer there is nothing more abhorrent to me than the individual averages and aggregate competitions into which one is liable to be bustled nowadays.' As a caveat he added: 'It is not given to every batsman to celebrate his own exploits in the columns of the Press . . . It seems to me that between my bat and my pen I shall get into difficulties some fine day.' And indeed he did—though seldom at one and the same time.

Team game or not, the spice of individual competition which Fry and Abel had inadvertently brought to the cricket field had great significance for the sport. The *Daily Express* wrote: 'No season has ever lain a-dying under similar circumstances of interest as those under which the season of 1901 is passing into history. But this season the old order is gone and a new interest, unknown in the history of the game, has risen.' The Golden Age, with Fry and Ranji its key figures, had truly emerged.

Indeed, Charles Fry's personal exploits carried that interest right through to the middle of September when he turned out for the Rest of England against the re-crowned champions, Yorkshire, at Lord's. The crowd were enthralled by some ferocious hitting by Gilbert Jessop, but their attention was diverted as Fry, although understandably nervy, came to the crease in search of his sixth successive century. Thanks to some brilliant running between the wickets C.B.'s score mounted steadily and when he finally made it to three figures it seemed as though the crowd's tumultuous applause was echoed by a standing ovation throughout the country. He was dismissed after making 105, but for two reasons it was a most praiseworthy effort: he had not played a first-class innings for a fortnight and he had been up until two o'clock in the morning the previous night plying his journalistic trade.

A measure of Fry's overall achievement was the fact that no one had previously scored more than three successive centuries, and no one indeed had come close to matching his thirteen hundreds in a season. (Inevitably it was Don Bradman who equalled the first record, just before the Second World War, Mike Procter repeating the feat in 1970–1, while it was twenty-five years before Jack Hobbs compiled a total of sixteen centuries in a season.)

It was entirely appropriate that great names should be needed to match Charles Fry's momentous feats; and it is not outrageous flattery to nominate his six successive hundreds as the outstanding spell of run-making in the history of the game. The opposition were tough throughout, the pitches and conditions were variable and for once in his career C.B. could milk the praise without his attitude or motivation being queried.

For the best part of eight months Fry's devoted fans were left to wonder whether he could extend the wondrous sequence at the start of the 1902 season. The odds were very much against him: on 19 April he had played in the FA Cup Final and a week later in the replay which Southampton lost 2–1, still suffering from the after-effects of 'flu. Two days after that disappointment he was turning out for London Counties against Surrey. For a couple of hours he offered genuine hope that he would make his seventh century on the trot, but when he had made 82 he was caught.

There is a familiarity about the 1902 season which for once had little to do with Fry and Ranji. Two of the most remarkable finishes in Test cricket were fought out to give the year an eventual aura of glamour which it had done nothing to deserve up to then. Appalling weather early in the season and differences between the two Sussex stars and the county committee about fielding standards were hardly the prerequisites for a vintage summer.

Ironically, Sussex managed to finish as runners-up to Yorkshire in the County Championship. Previously unrecognised players like Fred Tate responded magnificently to the extra pressure placed on them by the disenchantment of C.B. and Ranji. Fry, although physically and mentally out of sorts for most of the year, was at least faithful to the cause and played in the majority of Sussex's games, but Ranji was only 'available' for 12 out of 27 games.

Fry began the season on a fairly promising note, but he experienced a long barren spell before making his first century of the summer on 19 June. He was unusually productive on the off-side in his innings of 122 against Middlesex at Lord's and was then able to sit back and watch in contented admiration as Fred Tate, father of the more famous Maurice, charged through the Middlesex batting. He bowled unchanged in both innings to finish with match figures of 15 for 68.

Fry attributed his poor season to being 'knocked up' by playing in the latter stages of the FA Cup while suffering from 'flu. Archie MacLaren had been out of health and runs a year earlier and Fry's subtle observations then could equally have been applied to himself in 1902: 'None but a rather bad player makes runs if he is out of health. Cricket is a stalwart, hard-hewn game to look at, but in point of fact it is in some ways a delicate game made up of a minute differences. There is the whole world between timing a ball exactly right and being a fraction of a second too soon or too late. When a man is out of health his batting mechanism falls out of gear. There is a misty something between his eye and the ball; he seems to catch sight of the ball not at the first, but at the second intention.'

In the light of a plethora of miserable totals on rain-affected wickets Sussex's game with Surrey at Hastings in the middle of July seemed absurdly out of context. A stand of 238 for the first wicket between C.B. and Joe Vine set the pattern for a match of extravagant scoring. Vine made 92, while Fry, averaging just over 30 going into the game, relieved his protracted depression with a chanceless innings of 159. The scene was set for the tiring bowlers to be pummelled into submission and Ranji presided over the demolition of the Surrey attack. He made 234 in just 200 minutes to lift Sussex to a total of 705 for 8 declared, which remains their highest-ever score in the County Championship.

Bobby Abel (179) and Tom Hayward (144) then added 246 for Surrey's first wicket as the match headed for run-drenched deadlock. The end result was the highest aggregate yet in an English game – 1427 runs for the loss of 21 wickets. Interestingly, the previous record had been set up in Sussex's match with Oxford University in 1895, with Charles Fry playing for the students.

Any hopes of the Sussex giants running into rampant form were undermined by internal politics. C.B. and Ranji opted out of the county's game with Worcestershire and although Fry made a brilliant undefeated 159 against Middlesex there was a highly public show of dissent against the Australians. Ranji bowled himself and Fry in harness to the amazement of the Hove crowd. It was the Indian's second bowling stint of the season, while Fry had not turned his arm over at all for Sussex that season. He started off bowling overarm, then switched to lobs, giving Monty Noble a few untroubled runs on his way to 284. The *Sussex Daily News* was not impressed with Ranji's tactics, calling the unusual bowling partnership an 'unwonted sight'.

Neither he nor Fry played in Sussex's next two games. Rumours were rife about a serious rift between the two amateurs and the county committee concerning the poor standard of fielding among Sussex players. In an attempt to clear the air the *Sussex Daily News* offered this explanation in the middle of August, failing to conceal the fact that Fry and Ranji were discontent:

> The Sussex cricket world have been full of talk lately about differences in the Sussex team and prospective changes. It would be singular if a cricket team went through an entire season without some little disputes. The keenness with which the game is conducted, the responsibilities for losing or 'drawing', the disappointment of dropped catches, are calculated to test the most amiable tempers. The most satisfactory answer to recent reports, however, is that Mr C.B. Fry took part in the Leicester match—a part again disappointing to himself as a batsman, though he is too good a sportsman to get down-hearted at runs of ill-luck—and that K.S. Ranjitsinhji will be in the team against Hampshire this week. The latest rumour about the Indian Prince was that he had accepted a post with the London County Club at the Crystal

Palace. The Prince's answer to this, in a telegram to the *Sussex Daily News*, is emphatic. It is sufficient to state that it is quite untrue.

It may have been untrue, but a holiday in Yorkshire deprived Sussex of Ranji's services for the Hampshire game, which both illustrated Fred Tate's golden touch with the ball and Charles Fry's disconcerting lack of confidence with the bat. Tate took 8 for 28 in Hampshire's first innings, finishing off with an amazing spell of 7 for 5 in six overs. Sussex went on to win the match without any difficulty, but C.B. had little influence on the occasion. He was caught off a no-ball before he had scored in the second innings, dropped on seven, then legitimately caught when he had made nine.

It was a mark of Fry's reputation that he finished in the top twelve in the first-class averages, but was still regarded as an unmitigated failure. His unhappy footballing experiences with Southampton at the end of 1902 did nothing to lift the gloom, but it was only a temporary hiccup–the best was yet to come.

The transformation in Charles Fry between 1902 and 1903 was astonishing. The weather, for the most part, was equally hostile to cricket, but C.B.'s boundless energy was restored and the runs flowed energetically from his bat.

His first innings for Sussex that summer produced a worrying duck, but the world was set to rights in the second innings of the match against Worcestershire. He made 174 in four hours of masterful strokeplay, including 20 boundaries. Sussex's next game, against Nottinghamshire, was abandoned in unfortunate circumstances, after the sudden death of the famous Notts opener Arthur Shrewsbury, who was top of the first-class batting averages in 1902.

It was Lancashire who next suffered at Fry's hands as he made 181 in five hours. It was not one of his more fluent innings–he went 45 minutes without scoring at one stage–but he offered only one chance, well after he had completed his century, and with Ranji also making a hundred there was clear indication that the deadly duo were back in business.

Neither could match the explosive hitting of Gilbert Jessop at Hove on 1 June when Gloucestershire came down to play Sussex. He made the fastest double hundred in the history of the game and went on·to make a thunderous 286 in 175 minutes. An unbeaten 162 by Ranji enabled Sussex to draw a game they never had any chance of winning, while C.B. had a lucky escape during an innings of 83. When he had made 78 he started for a run when it was noticed that the leg bail had come off. The fielding side appealed, but the umpires were uncertain whether Fry or the wicket-keeper had dislodged the bail. He was given not out, but explained afterwards that he had nudged the leg stump with his heel while starting to run.

A definitive illustration of Fry's capacity for subjugating the best attacks in the land came in Sussex's game with Yorkshire at Bradford in the middle of June. Yorkshire had won the County Championship in the previous three seasons, but they were totally outplayed in this fixture. The prime reason for this was an innings of monumental application by Charles Fry, 234 runs of scientific genius mingled with subtle improvisation. His seven-hour knock was the longest of his career and after Sussex had declared on 558 for 6 Yorkshire were bowled out for 120 and 258.

The internal rumblings in Sussex were less distinct than they had been in 1902. Pressure from Ranji and Fry had resulted in a trainer being engaged by the county. His background was in football and C.B. had already seen him at work at Southampton. It was redolent of a 'professional' attitude to the game and the two Sussex stars approved of any measure which might help to turn the team into a more efficient unit. 'The Sussex trainer', the *Sussex Daily News* explained, 'travels provided with the best known remedies for a variety of accidents in the cricket field, and is also in attendance to give the players a rub down after a long spell in the field or before they go in to bat.'

Fry became the first player in the country to complete his 1,000 runs for the season when he made 89 against Middlesex, but his batting moved onto a higher plane in the first two weeks of July. He made exactly 200 against Surrey at Hove, hitting 28 fours in his 280-minute stay at the wicket.

C.B.'s next date was at Lord's for a Gentlemen v Players encounter. When the professionals made 478, then dismissed the amateurs for 185, it seemed inevitable that the Players would maintain their record of domination in the series. At the close of the second day the Gentlemen, following on, were 74 for 1, with Fry undefeated on 41. He had been joined by Ranji and it looked as though a large partnership would have to materialise between the two for the Gentlemen to save face. The rest is the story of what many people considered the finest innings of Charles Fry's magnificent career.

A century stand between Fry and Ranji eased the amateurs' demise, but the fireworks started when Archie MacLaren joined C.B. In the space of three hours these two great players demolished an attack, which, although shorn of the services of an injured Sydney Barnes, was still formidable. When the declaration came at 500 for 2 they had added 309, a record for these games which remained intact until the end of the Gentlemen v Players matches. Fry batted for five-and-a-half hours in making an unbeaten 232, the fourth highest score in these matches, pummelling 32 fours with some on-drives of awesome power. MacLaren's contribution was 168, made at almost a run a minute.

A modest score of 160 in his next innings, against Hampshire, was not only Fry's sixth century of the season, but also took his aggregate past the figure which he achieved in the whole of the troubled summer of 1902. At the end of July he was within a single run of scoring two centuries in the match against Leicestershire, following up 99 with an undefeated 127. This game also demonstrated the dependable opening partnership which had grown up between C.B. and the professional Joe Vine. They put on 170 in the first innings and 179 in the second.

Fry sauntered past his 2,000 runs for the season in the middle of August, and although his average fell back a little from close on 90 there was no noticeable loss of form. Reputation preceded C.B. and Ranji to cricket grounds throughout England, but they could not guarantee thrilling entertainment and crowds were not slow to pass on the message when they saw gods posing as mere mortals. When Sussex took on Middlesex at Lord's towards the end of August the first two days were completely lost to rain, and bar dramatic happenings a result was out of the question. Middlesex declared at 162 for 5 and when Ranji joined Fry, Sussex had lost their first two wickets for eight.

They were determined to avert an embarrassing collapse and went along with such caution that the crowd got restless. The *Sussex Daily News* said: 'Mr Fry was the first recipient of ironical applause, on venturing to pat the tricky pitch, where it had been cut up by the bowlers' deliveries; and, ultimately, both batsmen shared the barracking.' Wallis Myers offered a more precise account in *The Man and his Methods*: 'To smooth out a slight eruption on the pitch, Mr Fry walked a few yards up the wicket and prodded the ground slowly with his bat. In the middle of this incident came the shout, "Mind the worms, Fry!"–an allusion to an article on worm-killing from the pen of the famous batsman that sent a ripple of laughter over the ground. Mr Fry himself was highly amused. But a minute later came the unworthy jeer from the same quarter, "Mind your average, Fry!" There was no smile this time, but a tight compression of the lips, and the next ball that came down was sent with one terrific drive to the boundary.' Fry and Ranji had the last laugh, both completing half-centuries. They broke free from their self-imposed shackles by making 35 runs in the last 15 minutes, but this only convinced the spectators that they should have batted with greater freedom earlier in the proceedings.

C.B. lifted his tally to nine hundreds for the season when he scored two in the same match against Kent at Hove. Neither innings was particularly speedy, but his 138 in the first innings was a technical masterpiece on a tricky pitch and a slow outfield. This was the third time he had made two hundreds in the same game, equalling the record then held jointly by W.G. Grace and R.E. Foster.

As it was, the *Westminster Gazette* were sufficiently in awe of his prodigious run-making in inauspicious conditions to propose him as the '*fons et origo*' of the dismal weather. In a dry summer, they suggested, his average would probably have exceeded 100, and went on: 'We fear we have no real chance of a really hot dry summer so long as Mr Fry can get an average of over 80 in a year of rains and floods. It seems more than ever a pity he is not going to Australia–they actually want rain there!'

There had been two months of agonising between the offer of an Australian tour and C.B.'s reluctant refusal. He said he would be unable to go more than six months without the steady income from journalism which subsidised his cricket during the summer. He also had a wife and young children to consider, but he might well have made the trip if he had been able to write about the tour for an Australian paper. England could ill afford to be without the batsman who had been in a class of his own during 1903. Ranji was second in the national averages, having scored 25 runs an innings less than Fry, while the next in line, George Hirst, averaged only 47.

Sussex again finished second in the County Championship, which was dominated by Middlesex, and Charles Fry's crucial part in that success was rewarded by the initiation of a presentation fund. It was not just in recognition of his prodigious exploits in 1903, but also loyalty to his adopted county during the previous nine years.

Therefore, it was a source of no great joy to Fry when the *Daily Mail* got hold of a rumour that he was transferring his allegiances back to Surrey, for whom he had appeared briefly in 1891. C.B. took the opportunity to scotch the story with a letter to the *Daily Express* which said: 'I have never had the remotest intention of playing for Surrey, nor have I expressed my wish to do so. I have not, nor ever have had, the remotest intention of applying for the secretaryship of Surrey. The post, so far as I ever knew, is not vacant. And, in any case, it is not a post that has, or is likely to have, the very least attraction for me.

'The only interest I have in the Surrey secretaryship is the hope that my old friend, Mr C.W. Alcock, will be quickly restored to health.'

It was a denial which brooked no argument and when, two months later, another rumour was confirmed by C.B. moving up from vice-captain to take over the Sussex captaincy from Ranji, the future seemed secure.

The status quo was largely preserved in 1904, but there were subtle changes and variations from previous seasons. Fry and Ranji were still destined to be the dominant figures in terms of both quality and quantity, but spectators were privileged to witness a revision in C.B.'s approach to batting. Whereas before he had made his runs at a fairly predictable rate—around 40 an hour—he reacted to the selfless demands of captaincy by putting a greater premium on fast scoring. The best attacks were still treated with immense respect, but less accurate bowlers found themselves cruelly punished in a way which they would not have previously expected.

Fry had to wait until the end of May for his first century of the summer, but it was well worth the wait. Somerset bowlers were on the receiving end as he made 120 in just 110 minutes, a spectacular innings with the unusually high proportion of 19 boundaries. The pattern was similar in his very next innings, against Leicestershire. He went for his shots from the start and was missed early on, but rode his luck against erratic bowling and sketchy fielding to finish with 191 not out in a total of 279 for 7 before rain wiped out the final two days. This was another run-a-minute affair, replete with 28 cracking fours.

These back-to-back hundreds heralded the start of a splendid spell, even by Fry's exalted standards. In the space of fourteen innings he topped the three-figure mark seven times, and the majority of these were big hundreds. He slammed 226 against Derbyshire, who were playing Sussex for the first time in twenty years, gave the Yorkshire bowlers their usual heartache with 177, and ended the purple patch with 191 against Leicestershire, an identical score to his unbeaten innings in the first game between the two sides that season.

He had good reason to be delighted with the success of his new liberated method, but there was one aspect of captaincy which regularly defeated him. Fry's tactical instincts were sound, if uninspired, but he had appalling luck with the toss and lamented that inferior teams were getting first use of placid wickets then ploughing through the Sussex batting on ill-tempered tracks. In the first eleven Sussex games that season they were able to bat first only twice and Fry eventually became so disillusioned with his poor fortune that he entrusted the toss of the coin to George Brann for the match with Essex on 7 July. Sussex won the toss, but they were still unable to force a win.

The death of an aunt at Tunbridge Wells kept C.B. out of action for a week, but on his return he slammed 181 against Surrey. He was notably inconsistent during the final month of the season, and his average, which was over 85 at one stage, dropped to 70, but two magnificent double hundreds reminded the cricket world that he was still very much in business. He made 211 against Hampshire at Hove and added 287 for the first wicket with Vine. This was the highest of the 33 century-stands between the two players and the third time during the 1904 season that they had made more than 200 together. They were the most reliable opening partnership in the country at this stage and the only consolation for counties playing Sussex was that Ranji couldn't appear to wreak further havoc until one or other were dismissed.

C.B.'s other double hundred came, almost inevitably, against Yorkshire, whose bowlers had grown to view matches with Sussex as cricketing purgatory. Their desperation was captured in an evening paper cartoon, which depicted Lord Hawke, the Yorkshire skipper, trying to restrain his star bowlers, George Hirst and Wilfred Rhodes, from throwing themselves into the sea at Brighton. The caption read: 'Children, don't be foolish! Don't do anything rash. Remember, there is tomorrow.' The duo replied: 'That's just it, Pa: 307 for one wicket; Fry not out and Ranji not in. Here goes!'

Fry's one dismal failure of the summer came in Sussex's return match with Lancashire in the middle of August. During the first game between the counties that year, at Manchester, C.B. had been presented with a travelling writing case by the Sussex professionals and scorer, in recognition of his remarkable batting in 1903. He thanked them in style, with an unbeaten century in the second innings, but made miserable scores of two and nought against the same opposition at Hove. On both occasions he was lbw to the left-arm bowler James Hallows, and he was clearly displeased by the umpire's decision in the first innings. J.A.H. Catton, who had handled Fry's copy as editor of *Athletic News*, offered his commiserations and said 'hard luck', to which C.B. replied, with customary contrariness: 'Not at all – rank bad play.'

This match was seen as a head-to-head between Fry and the Lancashire professional, John Tyldesley, who had taken over at the top of the batting averages. It was almost like a repeat of the race between Fry and Abel for 3,000 runs in 1901, but Tyldesley failed against Sussex and finished the season with some poor scores, leaving the way clear for Ranji to steal ahead of the field.

Charles Fry was accorded élite status among England's cricketers on the grounds of run-making alone, but there was another feature of his *modus vivendi* which gave him the march on his fellow-amateurs. A journey between London and Portsmouth in an old Daimler at the turn of the century had given him a taste for this novel form of transport. Driving, at this juvenile stage in the development of the motor car, was at worst a captivating hobby and at its most sublime a thrilling adventure.

The fund started for Fry at the end of the 1903 season was so generously supported that the Sussex members were able to present him with an immaculate Clement-Talbot the following spring. It immediately became a familiar sight on the county circuit, with C.B. and Madame, as he referred to his wife, a perceptive supporter and critic, relishing their new-found independence. They were so enamoured of this new toy that the chauffeur was often relegated to the back seat. C.B. was captured in the 'Out of Harness' section of his own magazine, singing the praises of the motor car: 'Motoring is the finest nerve-bracing pastime I know, and during the cricket season I found it an infinitely more genial mode of transit from town to town than the railway train. You have no adequate idea of the varied beauties this England of ours can offer until you have toured its roads and explored its highways and byways in a smooth-running car which has an immunity from punctures.'

The Talbot may have had immunity from punctures, but it did not have immunity from accidents, as Fry discovered during Sussex's game with Hampshire in the middle of August 1904. After the second day's play he was driving back to his home at West End when he collided with no less a celebrity than Admiral Moresby, who was riding his bicycle near his home at Fareham. The *Sussex Daily News* reported: 'The car and the bicycle upon which the Admiral was seated touched each other, Mr Fry being engaged at the time in endeavouring to avoid a dog in the roadway. The gallant officer was thrown violently, but was enabled to regain his legs and walk home within a few minutes. The gentlemen exchanged cards. The wheel of the Admiral's bicycle was badly twisted, and the machine was otherwise undamaged.'

Fry failed to turn up at Portsmouth for the final day's play, which was wiped out by rain anyway, evoking this response in the *Daily Express*: 'The Sussex skipper's absence from the ground at Portsmouth yesterday evoked the facetious comment that an old-fashioned duel of the "pistols for two dinner for one" nature was in progress, which necessitated this absence.'

The anti-car lobby interpreted the incident as further evidence for their campaign against this new monster of the highways and Admiral Moresby, a gentleman of advanced years, received great sympathy. One paper felt Fry's choice of 'victim' rather ill-considered: 'C.B. Fry, ahoy! Shiver my timbers, messmates, you mustn't go about this country upsetting real, live Admirals. We like to see you play cricket, and we like to see you play football, and it gives us great pleasure to read your contributions to the "Express", and we think your magazine well worth the money; but when it comes to careering about in motor-cars and cutting up naval officers we really must draw the line. If it's actually essential to your happiness that you should run over somebody you will find plenty of Italian organ-grinders, fish hawkers, and such impedimenta knocking about.'

Fry was not the least deterred and he was the proud owner of a succession of cars in the period up to the First World War, two of which deserve special mention. After he had sold the Talbot, Fry bought a splendid French car, a de Dietrich, from the ex-racing driver, Charles Jarrott. It was unusually reliable and gave honest service right up to the war. The other car of note was a Humber, which was originally offered as a prize in a competition run by *Fry's Magazine*. The winner was a contributor to the magazine, which caused a certain amount of comment, but Sir Perry Robinson did not want the vehicle and after a year the Humber found its way via a friend of Fry's to C.B. himself.

Fry not only became the keenest of motorists, but also turned himself into one of the earliest skilled mechanics. It is not generally appreciated that quite apart from excelling as a student of the arts he had a ready understanding of science-based topics. It recalls a story C.B. told of when he was invited on the maiden voyage of a ship round the Isle of Wight. He happened to go into the wireless room and saw a man who seemed puzzled by the various instruments. C.B. explained coils and capacity to him and when, at lunch, Fry's wireless friend was called upon to make a speech, it turned out to be none other than Marconi!

Just before he severed his connection with *The Captain* in 1905 Fry wrote a piece, 'Sparks from a Christmas Fire', in which he reminisced vividly: 'Old England, how much more familiar you have become since we took our first trip, my car and I . . . A dog or two, one or two walls, one admiral, several sharp corners, two cows, one sheep, which went in by the radiator and came out by the "tail-lamp".'

Fry's contretemps with Admiral Moresby was followed by more misfortune when Sussex entertained Yorkshire at Hove on 18 August. He was stung on the arm by a wasp while fielding in Yorkshire's first innings, but any suggestion that his resolve had been undermined was dispelled the following day as he resumed his battle of wits with the Yorkshire bowlers. In some ways the story was a familiar one: Fry dominated the Sussex innings, making 229 out of a total of 377. He hit 27 fours, batted for 370 minutes and added 181 for the first wicket with Vine, but C.B.'s tenth century of the season did not attract universal praise and the Yorkshire bowlers Rhodes and Haigh were so frustrated by his refusal to attack balls which could safely be left alone that they deliberately bowled wide outside the off stump.

The *Yorkshire Post* pointed out that after Fry had completed his double hundred it took him another 70 minutes to compile 29 runs, hardly the correct tactics, they felt, when quick runs were needed prior to a declaration. They accused Vine of being a less talented version of C.B., using his pads more than his bat, and said the whole Sussex side tended to respond to Fry's negative promptings as captain.

There was a snide, bitchy overtone about the *Post*'s verdict on the match:

> The plain fact is that Mr Fry will only hit balls that, in his opinion, he can hit safely in front of the wicket or on the leg side. A great factor in his large scores is his avoidance of risks, and herein he shows more self-restraint probably than any other batsman of modern times. But a sporting risk is, after all, one of the attractive features of batting, and if a batsman, however eminent, either excludes, or is unable to include, the hits behind the wicket in his repertoire, bowlers cannot be blamed for refusing as far as possible to supply him with the opportunities for making the strokes in which he is so great a master.
>
> Mr Fry must be absolved from any assumption that the

position of his name in the averages is at all likely to influence his play, for it is a cardinal principle with all amateurs, we are told, to look upon averages as more or less an excrescence upon the game. Yet if any professional cricketer had adopted the same tactics that the Sussex captain did on Saturday, when it was essential his team should get runs and get them quickly, amateurs would have promptly accused him of forgetting the interests of his side in his desire to advance his own average.

The accusation was implicit, but the reasoning was faulty; there is no doubt that Charles Fry did not always serve the best interests of his side, but his quest was very much that of the perfectionist rather than the statistician. The contentment he gained from a minor score against testing bowling in trying conditions confirmed that his ultimate purpose was honourable. His constantly high standing in the batting averages was simply a by-product of that attitude, and in 1904 Ranji and C.B. again stood proudly at the head of the pack, both averaging more than 70.

There was no Ranji in 1905. A combination of asthma and malarial fever kept him in India and the responsibility for Sussex's success as a batting side came to rest squarely on Fry's shoulders. He responded magnificently to the challenge and after a sticky patch in the early Test matches against Australia finally translated his County Championship form into international achievement.

He began promisingly for the Gentlemen against the Australians, then played himself into a spectacular run of form with two centuries in Sussex's match against the MCC. He made 156 and 106, giving not a single chance, and became the first player to make two hundreds in a match on four separate occasions, beating the record which he shared at that time with W.G. Grace and R.E. Foster. He was within three runs of repeating the feat against Nottinghamshire, following up 97 with an undefeated 201. As he homed in on his double century he gave notice of the ferocious hitting powers which were so often concealed beneath the surface. One hit bounced off the stand roof at Hove and out of the ground.

In the space of six days C.B. had made 560 runs and with the First Test starting at Trent Bridge at the end of May his prospects seemed bright. But misfortune was always waiting to pounce and on 24 May Fry split a finger in his right hand while batting in the nets at Hove. Predictably, he had been included in the England 13 for the Test, and would have been an automatic selection, but he telegraphed Lord Hawke to say he would probably be unable to play.

His fears were justified, but he bounced back at the start of June with 233 against Nottinghamshire, who had therefore suffered two double centuries from the great man in the space of three weeks. His average for Sussex at this stage of the season was a phenomenal 134.43. A few years later the *Daily Express* related an amusing tale of this match:

> Some years ago C.B. Fry was due to play against Notts. at Trent Bridge. On his way to the ground he went into an athletic outfitters and bought two new bats. He was so eager to test his new purchases that on his way to the Notts. cricket ground he stood up in the Landau and practised imaginary strokes.
>
> As the Landau passed over Trent Bridge C.B. was observed by many hundreds of passers-by. Among them was a Notts. professional, who dashed off to the ground and shouted to a brother professional: 'Look out, here he comes!'
>
> 'Who?' was the query.
>
> 'Why, Fry, of course,' was the answer, 'and he's already made 200–on the bridge!'

The Nottinghamshire bowler Tom Wass had his own highly individual assessment of C.B: 'He were a woon, were Mr Fry,' he said.

C.B. kept the momentum going with successive hundreds against Kent and Yorkshire. His 175 against Kent was a particularly fluent innings, compiled in just 210 minutes, but there were more worries for Fry in County Championship games during the remainder of the season.

His sense of protocol was rudely offended when Sussex played Warwickshire for the first time at the beginning of July. A century by Fry enabled him to set Warwickshire a target of more than 350 on the last day, but it soon became clear that their ambitions, not unreasonably against a side as formidable as Sussex then were,

were restricted to playing for a draw. A section of the Hove crowd became frustrated by the dogged resistance of Warwickshire's captain, J.F. Byrne, and started barracking, but Fry was so angered that he ran over to make his feelings known, shouting to the crowd: 'If you don't stop this nonsense I'll take my team off the field and we'll chuck the match up at once. I'm not going to have it on this ground.' Needless to say this sharp rebuke had the desired effect.

C.B. came out of this incident with great credit, but the same could not be said of Sussex's game with Lancashire a week later, when two of the most respected amateurs in the game, Fry and Archie MacLaren, sought to prove that they could be as petty and childish as the next man when their patience was tested. The game began on a gloomy note for C.B., as rheumatism kept him off the field for much of the first day, but it was on the second day that the match took a bizarre turn. At this stage in cricket history teams were not allowed to declare until lunch on the second day and with Lancashire standing on 587 for 6 at this point it was fair to presume that Sussex would be batting immediately after lunch.

However, MacLaren did not close the innings and Fry was so peeved that he instructed his bowlers, Smith and Chapman, to bowl daisy-cutters by way of protest. The declaration came soon afterwards and C.B.'s chosen response would have been a long and particularly obdurate innings, but he was caught off his first ball. Sussex finished more than 200 behind Lancashire on the first innings, but MacLaren refused to impose the follow-on and was not even prepared to set Sussex a target in the hope of winning the match. The Hove crowd became so disgusted with his curious tactics that most left the ground at tea-time.

No one was very impressed. The Lancashire batsmen had played the grubbers with horizontal bats – 'as little girls play in a nursery', said the correspondent in *Play the Game*, continuing, 'I protest against such a contemptible travesty of the game: Is not such a proceeding calculated to bring a noble sport into disrepute and unpopularity? Will people pay to see this?'

There was also a curious occurrence in Sussex's game with Hampshire in the middle of August, although this resulted from pure absent-mindedness on Fry's part. He scored 127 in Sussex's total of 498 and when Hampshire were dismissed for 297 early on the final day it seemed inevitable that they would be asked to follow on, but there was confusion when the Sussex openers were seen with their pads on. It transpired that Fry thought it was the second day of the match, not the third, and he immediately changed his mind. Just before Sussex took the field C.B. ran out to the umpires, who were waiting near the pitch for the resumption of the game, to consult them upon the alteration of his decision.

He followed up his century in that game with 155 against Kent, and a half-century in the first innings of Sussex's return match with Yorkshire meant that, in aggregate, he had scored more than 2,000 runs against the most feared bowling side in England.

Sussex finished the season in third place in the County Championship and it was not just Ranji's absence which made this a remarkable achievement. England calls, representative games, illness and other commitments had conspired to deny Sussex of C.B.'s presence in 14 of their 31 games, but there was a tremendous opportunity for other members of the side to disprove the taunts of one-man team and they were not found wanting. Cox beat Tate's record by taking 164 wickets in the season and Killick did the double.

Even more pressure was placed on Sussex's resources in 1906. Already deprived of Ranji's services they soon had to adapt to the loss of their other resident hero. Charles Fry's first game of the season did not come until 20 May when Sussex played Somerset at Bath. Scores of five and nought hardly set the world alight, but a well-made 67 against Middlesex at Lord's promised another run of high scores.

He was going well again in the second innings and had made 36 out of 54 when disaster struck. He set off for a sharp single, but after he had completed a couple of strides he collapsed in pain and after being run out he was carried off to the pavilion by his now sympathetic opponents. He was seen in the Long Room by Dr Warton Hood, who had been watching the game. As Fry lay on his back in the pavilion, still unaware of the extent of the damage, he was asked to give a message to the nation: 'I had been doing my best to brighten cricket,' he said, which in the circumstances was a remarkably humorous reference to the current obsession with cricket providing greater entertainment for spectators. Fry was then driven away to see a specialist, Dr Frank Romer, and that evening he was able to reveal chapter and verse on the injury. He had not actually torn the Achilles tendon of his left leg, but he had badly ruptured it, and it was doubtful whether he would be able to play again that season.

On 29 May he was seen at home by two more doctors, including Dr Russell Bencraft, the president of the Southern League and ex-captain of the Hampshire cricket team. The result of these consultations was that Fry's leg was put in plaster and a reluctant C.B. was forced to come to terms with a long period of recuperation. Wallis Myers wrote: 'He bore the enforced rest with surprising cheerfulness, giving the mind its complement of exercise, and adding, I do not doubt, to his large store of practical philosophy. For some weeks he was not permitted to stand up; then came an interval of crutches (a cruel irony of fate this seemed), and finally in August almost complete recovery. Ever optimistic, he joined in a village match near his home, only to suffer a relapse. There was nothing for it but a long rest.'

C.B. had a boot specially made with an iron stanchion to support his injured leg and a strap round the knee and was able to go out hunting in the autumn, but there was still considerable doubt about his future sporting career. 'The next spring', he wrote in *Life Worth Living*, 'I went to consult a specialist in London as to my prospects. He told me that I had had a great career, but must never again go in for anything athletic. I paid him three guineas. I consulted another specialist. He said the same thing. I paid him three guineas. I consulted a third. He said that if he were I he would forget about the accident and go on as if nothing had ever happened. I paid him three guineas.'

The prescribed inactivity took him through to the start of the 1907 season and there was exceptional interest in his first appearance of the season, against Kent at Hove: it was the first opportunity Sussex supporters had had to see their hero in action since the end of the 1905 season. However, there was very little to cheer them. Still wearing his iron support, Fry showed none of his customary agility and verve at point; and the lack of confidence in his all-round fitness also infected his batting, with scores of five and one offering little evidence of a quick return to form.

79

He was so dissatisfied with his physical condition that he dropped out of the Sussex side for a fortnight and when he returned for the Surrey match he was dismissed for a duck as Sussex were skittled out for 43. He did contrive to make 26 in the second innings, but Fry's depression had communicated itself to the whole Sussex team, who frequently found themselves struggling on drying pitches and lost six of their first eight games in the County Championship, drawing the other two.

There was added pressure on C.B. because the South Africans were touring and had been offered their first official Test matches in this country. If Fry had been able to show a semblance of fitness and form he would almost certainly have been given first refusal of the captaincy as the senior amateur in contention for a place, but with the First Test only a fortnight away he had done nothing to satisfy the selectors on either score.

Nevertheless, he had not been forgotten and was already being offered the chance to tour Australia the following winter. At the same time F.S. Jackson was turning down the dual opportunity to captain England against South Africa and skipper the touring party.

There was a hint of the old Fry, appropriately against Yorkshire, on a fiery wicket at Sheffield, when he made 85 in the first innings, but there was another scare as he was hit on the foot just before being dismissed, and he failed to trouble the scorers in the second innings. This was also the first game in which umpires had provided towels for bowlers to dry the wet ball.

C.B. was back on the record-breaking trail in his next match, against Lancashire, but for once in his career it was failure which made the game noteworthy. He made the first and only pair of his career, which meant that he had been out for nought in no less than four of his last six innings. This was hardly Test form, but modest scores of 35, 45 and 27 somehow convinced the selectors that he was worth including in the England side. It appeared to be a gamble, but C.B. had lost the slight limp with which he started the season, the stanchion had been shed, and it was a fair bet that his batting form would return as he became completely confident about his physical fitness. We shall see shortly how he fared in the Tests themselves.

The real Fry began to shine through (if such could be a valid description in a miserably wet summer) when Sussex played Lancashire at Eastbourne in the middle of July. He was naturally intent on burying the memories of his double disaster at Old Trafford and made a faultless unbeaten 102 in the second innings to begin his rise from the unknown depths of 55th in the first-class batting averages.

He then came within one run of scoring two hundreds in a game for the fifth time. The Worcestershire bowlers were slammed for 125 in the first innings, but Fry paid the penalty for not going in first on the second evening, being stranded on 99 when the second Sussex innings drew to a close. It was both a comment on Fry's sudden discovery of form and the failures of other batsmen throughout the country that he had now leapt to second in the averages.

Apart from C.B.'s brilliant efforts for England in the Test matches his most praiseworthy and courageous innings came against Derbyshire at the beginning of August. The Hove pitch contained more gremlins than usual and Fry was hit several times on the hand as he struggled to make 17 in his first hour at the crease. He then decided that attack was the best form of defence and the remainder of his 187 runs came at the rate of one a minute. The innings not only took Fry past his 1,000 runs for the season, but also lifted him to the top of the batting averages, a remarkable achievement in view of his early doubts about his fitness and the run of appalling scores.

The summer of 1908 represented a crossroads for Charles Fry. Charles Hoare, the founder and director of the training ship *Mercury*, died at the end of May, and for some time afterwards Fry's major energies were directed towards taking over the ship— and releasing it from debt. At the same time the rumours about his transferring his allegiances from Sussex to Hampshire gathered momentum.

In the early part of the season he had been turning out for Trojans, the club in Southampton, and it was widely expected that this would be the forerunner to the announcement that he would start playing for Hampshire. This is what the *Southern Daily Echo* said on 28 May: 'Disappointment will be felt locally at the absence of C.B. Fry's name (for the game with Leicestershire), for the rumour that the brilliant Oxonian intends to play for Hampshire is still being persistently circulated, and generally accepted.'

His name was optimistically pencilled in at Hove for many of Sussex's games during the first month of the season, but it was not until the middle of June that it actually became clear where his loyalties would lie. The red carpet was brought out at Horsham when Sussex played Essex and it was so confidently assumed that C.B. would be turning out that when he had not arrived at midday the start was delayed in anticipation of his imminent arrival. A quarter of an hour later a telephone call was made and it was established that his return would be delayed once more.

He finally did play on 22 June, against Cambridge University at Hove. The match had added significance, signalling the long-awaited reunion of Fry and Ranji (who had now inherited the title of Jam Sahib of Nawanagar) on the first-class cricket field. It was the first time since the end of the 1904 season that Fry and Ranji had played together for Sussex, but it did not take long for C.B. to find his feet. He made impressive centuries against both Lanca-shire and Somerset in the first half of July.

It was inevitable, in view of Fry's indecision about his future, that the game between Sussex and Hampshire would attract even more interest than usual. The match at Portsmouth between the two sides had been uneventful, but the return game at Chichester was notable for a complete breakdown in communications. The first day's play was lost to rain, and it seemed that the second day would be similarly blank when the Sussex players woke to the depressing sound of a downpour at Shillinglee Park, which Ranji had rented from Lord Winterton. However, the weather was a good deal more promising twenty-two miles away at the Priory Park Ground in Chichester and the umpires decided that play could start at 11.30 if no rain fell. A telegram was sent to Shillinglee Park, but before it arrived C.B. and Joe Vine had set out for Chichester on a reconnaissance mission. The communication eventually got through to Ranji, but he was so certain that the weather must also have deteriorated at Chichester that he and the rest of the Sussex team stayed put. Fry and Vine got to the ground shortly after midday, two more telegrams were despatched to Shillinglee Park and the remainder of the Sussex players arrived in Chichester at 3.30. The umpires made a hasty inspection and decided that they could start at 4.15 if no more rain fell. Sure enough the heavens opened and play had to be called off for the day much to the frustration of the Hampshire players and the embarrassment of the Sussex contingent.

There were some meaningless exchanges on the final day of the game, but the confusion was swiftly forgotten in Sussex's next two matches as Fry and Ranji conjured up glorious memories of their halcyon days of 1901 and 1903. C.B. was at his most imposing in the game against Worcestershire at Hove, making 214, while Ranji scored exactly 200 against Surrey at the Oval. Sussex supporters were not to know it, but these were the last double hundreds that these two great players would make for the county.

A hand injury put Fry out of action for almost a month, but he and Ranji were back for the first-ever cricket week at Hove at the end of August. However, the scheduled games with Yorkshire and Gloucestershire fell foul of some highly eccentric weather. During the second game violent gales tore down marquees and left a trail of havoc – 'damage exceeding anything of the kind in the annals of the county club'. It was a sad way for the Sussex public and C.B. to bid their fond farewells. The supporters hoped that Fry would be back for another term, but he himself knew that the rumours would finally be given substance.

GIANTS OF THE GOLDEN AGE

7

The immortal W.G. Grace had signalled the emergence of the brilliant band of amateurs who gave the game of cricket a self-confidence, arrogance even, which glowed right up until the start of the First World War. But if there were any two cricketers who exemplified the Golden Age they were Charles Fry and Kumar Shri Ranjitsinhji—an irresistible combination of the Englishman who distinguished almost every field of endeavour and the urbane Indian with a gift for extravagant hospitality and exotic strokeplay. Apart from Fry and Ranji the other notable figures in this surge of amateur pride were Archie MacLaren, Stanley Jackson, Gilbert Jessop and Plum Warner.

But it was the charismatic Sussex pair who established new vistas for the art and science of batting. An average of 50 for a season was no longer a fantasy figure. C.B. and Ranji brought a self-belief to Sussex cricket which marked them out as the stuff of which legends are made. It can be said with some confidence that outside Test cricket the game has never seen two such outstanding players in one team at the same time.

Their fitful careers in Test matches can be discounted. In those days Australia and South Africa were the only international opposition for England—and it was not until 1907 that South Africa were considered worthy of Tests in England. The greatness of players had to be judged largely on their performances in the County Championship, which was bulging with excellence during the Golden Age. Between 1898 and 1905, however, in this arena, there was no one to touch Fry and Ranji.

In his prologue to *Cricket on the Green* by R.S. Young, Fry recalled his first meeting with Ranji. C.B. was playing at Beverley in Yorkshire during the long vacation from Oxford and the opponents were Cambridge Cassandra. 'A slim young Indian was bowling. I hit him over the wall into a shunting-yard. An engine was slowly puffing around. The ball hit the barrel of the engine, cannoned forward off the brass beehive, and went into the funnel. The engine puffed away with the ball in its belly.' The bowler was none other than Ranji.

There are a couple of popular misapprehensions about C.B. and Ranji which require explication. The first, quite understandably, is that they were highly consistent. In fact, they were both prone to inconsistency, and it was only the magnitude of their big innings which gave the impression that they were reliable scorers from May right through to September. The second illusion concerns the partnerships between the two players. In view of the immense number of runs they made it was surprising how few they compiled together. The reason was simple enough: for the most part Fry opened the Sussex innings, whereas Ranji would often go in as low as six or seven. The familiar scenario for bowling sides was of Fry dominating the first part of the Sussex innings, then Ranji taking over the mantle of responsibility by farming the strike away from the lower half of the Sussex order. Lengthy stands between C.B. and Ranji were disappointingly rare, but when they did occur crowds were rarely denied sublime entertainment–Fry's ferocious power dovetailing superbly with Ranji's delicate wristwork and subtle placement.

There was little doubt who was teacher and who the pupil, but that is not to suggest that Fry made any attempt to model himself on Ranji, who was beyond imitation. C.B. learned from Ranji that genius was not simply God-given talent, but a pursuit of perfection by observation, consideration and an immense amount of practice. Neither found it easy to place anyone above the other in the batting roll of honour. Between 1900 and 1904 they scored no less than 23 double hundreds between them and the allocation of genius, which had been solely Ranji's until 1899, extended without jealousy to Charles Fry.

They were box-office darlings and if it was Ranji whose improvisation proved the bigger draw, Fry was still an essential part of the double act. Neville Cardus described them like this: 'Ranji cast his magic all over his team; we saw them in the glow of his Eastern splendour. And C.B. Fry was his Grand Vizier, the subtle adviser to the Prince, the Machiavellian logician, who evolved a comprehensive statecraft of batsmanship from Ranji's first and governing principle: "Play back or drive".'

It was often an uneven struggle between Fry and Ranji and the honest toilers who plugged away on plumb batting wickets at Hove. Jack Fingleton wrote of the bowlers' dilemma in *Cricket Crisis*:

> One day a fellow English player said to Ranjitsinhji: 'Ranji, I could stop you and Fry making those big scores at Hove.'
> The Indian prince was amused.
> 'How?' he asked.
> 'By packing the leg field and making the fast bowler aim at your leg stump,' was the reply.
> Ranjitsinhji thought for a while, and this was his response, significant in its conception of what then constituted a proper outlook on the game.
> 'Yes,' said Ranjitsinhji, 'that would stop Fry and me to a great extent, but surely you would never do that.'

The imposing shadows of Fry and Ranji denied the limelight to Sussex players whose honest efforts would have been better applauded in counties without such idols. Indeed, less successful Sussex sides right up to the present day have been harangued by veteran supporters who remember those balmy days at Hove when the sun always shone and Fry and Ranji always scored magnificent centuries.

But it could not have been due simply to the run-making of two great batsmen that Sussex shed their Aunt Sally image at the turn of the century. In the seven seasons from 1899 to 1905 they finished in the top six each time and were runners-up in both 1902 and 1903. The professional, Joe Vine, nicknamed The Creeper, started and ended his long career with Sussex as a hitter, but his approach to batting was radically altered by Charles Fry, especially when Vine became his regular opening partner just after the turn of the century. It was hardly unique for a professional to be warned of the perils of upstaging his amateur colleagues, but in this case Vine was under precise instructions to hit no more than one boundary an over. On occasions he took the advice rather too literally and for a long time held the dubious honour of the record for the longest time before making the first run of an innings. This was against Nottinghamshire in 1901, when he took 75 minutes to get off the mark. The following year he went 65 minutes without scoring against Gloucestershire at Hove.

However, to a great extent, the tactics paid off. Fry and Vine put together century stands on no less than 33 occasions and a feature of their partnership was some tremendous, if occasionally hair-raising, running between the wickets. Vine was almost as fleet-footed as C.B. and he was also a very useful bowler, performing the double in 1901. In 1911 he was capped twice for England against Australia, at the ripe old age of thirty-six, by which time he had reverted to the freer style of batting which graced the early part of his career. The straitjacket which Fry had imposed clearly rankled with him and he was pleased to be able to play his natural game when C.B. switched his allegiances to Hampshire. In *Sussex Cricket*, Arthur Gilligan remembered praising Joe Vine for some bright hitting in a match in the post-Fry era. 'I wouldn't have dared do that when Mr C.B. Fry was playing,' he answered. 'I once hit three fours in the same over, and Mr Fry came up to me and told me plainly that it was my job to stay there, and leave that sort of cricket to him.'

Another reliable and ever-present member of the Sussex team was Ernest Killick, the bespectacled left-hander, whose high point was an innings of 200 against Yorkshire in 1901, when he and C.B. added 349 for the second wicket. Between 1898 and 1912 Killick made 344 successive appearances in the County Championship for Sussex, but this figure was exceeded by Vine, who played in 399 consecutive championship games from 1899 to 1914.

Then there was George Brann, a Corinthian like Fry, who had played football for England against Scotland as far back as 1886. He proved to be a late developer as a batsman, but went in first with C.B., before Vine stole the position, and made useful runs before moving out of first-class cricket in 1905. Although not quite in Fry's class as an all-round sportsman, Brann was also a fine golfer.

Fred Tate earned unwanted fame as the man who lost England the memorable Fourth Test against Australia in 1902 – this was his lone appearance for England–but he had recommended himself for selection by a vast haul of wickets for Sussex. He finished with 180 victims that season, and set a new county record.

The leading bowler for Sussex in 1903 was Albert Relf. On the nod from C.B. he was chosen for the touring party to Australia that winter and developed into one of the most successful all-rounders in the history of the game. He completed the double eight times, making over 22,000 runs and taking 1,897 wickets between 1900 and 1921. He also played thirteen times for England.

Two other Relf brothers played for Sussex, notably Bob, who managed to put one over Charles Fry in 1907 when Sussex played Kent at Canterbury. Having bowled Kent out Sussex were faced with an awkward spell before the close of play. A wicket fell with 20 minutes to go and C.B. had no intention of risking his own hide so he sought out a nightwatchman. The story is related by Alan Hill in *The Family Fortune–A Saga of Sussex Cricket*:

> He looked out of the window of the Canterbury pavilion and called out: 'Where's young Relf?' Bob, who did not then bat high in the Sussex order, was already in his street clothes, waiting to dash away for a night on the town. 'Tell him to get his pads on; he's in now,' urged Fry.
>
> Relf was back in flannels and padded up in record time. As he hurried to the wicket the Kent fieldsmen ragged him about the two-minute rule. Wicket-keeper Fred Huish told Relf he was really out and added: 'You ought not to be here.' Bob panted with fury and replied: 'I'll be here all day tomorrow.'
>
> At the wicket he remarked to his Sussex parnter Joe Vine: 'Do you know what I'd like? I'd like to keep that old devil (Fry) with his pads on and sitting in his chair all day tomorrow.'

Vine was happy enough with the arrangement and the two professionals stuck to their pact, batting for most of the next day. Vine was eventually out for 108, but Relf went on to make 210, rubbing the salt into C.B.'s wounds by dominating a third-wicket partnership with the great man. It was an incident fairly typical of Fry's prickly relations with the Sussex professionals–amateur skippers were either liable to have a paternal attitude towards their paid charges or treat them with scarcely concealed contempt.

Percy Fender, who was just moving into first-class cricket when Charles Fry's days at Hove reached an end, confirmed that Fry had little to do with the young professionals, whose pranks he found rather tiresome. He was more likely to be found joining his wife in the stands to take a detached view of the cricket, on the rare occasions when he was not either batting or leading his men in the field.

Nevertheless, Sussex had good reason to be grateful for the dependable qualities of their professionals, since Fry and Ranji made themselves less available as year succeeded year. *Wisden* was moved to an unusually fertile image: 'Playing in some matches and standing out of others Ranjitsinhji and Fry might be compared to the stars of an opera company. They did brilliant things themselves but they did not help the ensemble.'

Charles Fry was the embodiment of that less-than-romantic definition of genius—an infinite capacity for taking pains. His natural talent as an athlete was exceptional, but his application and self-discipline were even more exceptional. When he quit Charterhouse in 1898 he devoted himself to perfecting the art of batting. It was a quest which he never abandoned. Right to the end he explored the dynamics of strokeplay, and in later years the bat would be replaced by an umbrella or a stick.

Neville Cardus remembered a conversation with C.B. in a hotel lounge during the 1934 Test Match at Leeds. Fry was replaying an innings against Middlesex over thirty years earlier. At the close of play he had been just short of his century, but instead of cruising to three figures he was bowled at 89 by an off-break from Albert Trott. 'I can't think what I was doing!' he said to Cardus, still baffled by that dismissal in 1903. He might just as easily have admitted that he had instructed Trott where to bowl in order to get him out.

C.B.'s remarkable consistency between the turn of the century and the First World War earned him the misleading tag of run-machine, but he was no Boycott. Batting was never a purely mechanical process for him and if he found it a more interesting challenge by giving broad hints to the bowler who was sweating blood to try to dismiss him, so much the better.

The player on the verge of greatness was described in the *Book of Cricket*, which Fry edited in 1899. He had hoped to receive the assessment from someone else, but in the absence of acceptances being matched by words on paper he had to conduct his own medical. This is what he wrote about himself:

In his earlier schooldays Mr Fry was a stiff, ungainly bat. Thanks to the kind coaching of the Rev Arthur Forman to whom he owes much of any athletic prowess that has fallen to him—he improved into a fairly free driver with a soundish defence. He was fortunate enough to gain his Blue at Oxford as a freshman. It was some time before he found himself able to play first-class bowling with any freedom. A good length bowler gave him a feeling of being very shoulder-tied . . .

Mr Fry is aware that from the moment he had the privilege of playing with Kumar Shri Ranjitsinhji he began to improve his game—a fact which, when the absolute diversity of their styles is remembered, emphasises the value of observing the methods of a great player. Mr Fry learnt such cricket as he knows from K.S. Ranjitsinhji and Mr F.S. Jackson. He is by nature an on-side player. He can drive fairly hard straight and to the on, and has some useful leg strokes. He is no cutter, and a very intermittent off-driver. He plays chiefly with shoulders and fore-arms; not enough wrist. He has a confidence in his back play which is not always justified. He would do better with more patience, and with a little more judgment in hitting.

Despite his caveat about the influence of Ranji there were still foolish presumptions that he was trying to model his batting on the style of the Indian. Fry wrote an article for *The Cricketer* in 1945, entitled 'Now and Then', in which he said: 'Ranjitsinhji was the first effective innovator in batsmanship. He, curiously enough, was notably correct but his peculiar quickness enabled him to walk about and turn straight balls into balls to leg and he made a cult of scoring boundaries by back play, i.e. with his weight (light enough then) on his back foot. He was an original and his physical qualities enabled him to be apparently "incorrect", when really he was only making "correctness" much more elastic and adaptable.'

Fry went on to explain that imitation was futile: the lesson was not in impersonation but inspiration. C.B.'s personal quest was to develop a technique which would enable him to maximise his natural ability. Ranji was capable of playing a variety of shots to the same ball, whereas Fry, even at the height of his powers, was accused of having just one shot, which he somehow managed to play in a great variety of directions.

C.B. was the master of the secondary position of batsmanship. That is, he would greet the bowler with the bat held high, so that by the time the ball arrived the downward stroke had been completed without undue haste. W.G. Grace, Lord Harris and Archie MacLaren were other notable exponents of this stance, which subsequently went out of favour and has only been revived during the last ten years as a desperate measure to combat the extreme pace of modern bowlers. The Golden Age produced a comparable troop of pace bowlers—Kortright, Mold, Richardson, Lockwood, Jones—but the exaggerated backlift served Charles Fry equally well against bowlers of more modest pace. He also found that his footwork and balance at the crease were enhanced by adopting a two-eyed stance.

Few men saw more of Fry as a batsman, outside his county colleagues, than Pelham Warner, whose first sight of C.B. was when he was playing in the Repton team in 1888. He refuted the suggestion that Fry was a production-line player, writing in *My Cricketing Life*: 'Even at this stage he showed great natural aptitude for the game.' He saw no reason to alter his verdict at the end of Fry's first-class career and said this in one of the earliest editions of *The Cricketer* in 1921: 'No one has studied cricket more thoroughly than Mr Fry, who brought a great brain to bear on the game. His powers of observation are immense, and in his prime it may be said that he reduced run-getting almost to a certainty . . . A batsman must be judged on his ability to play on every kind of wicket, and Mr Fry comes out of this test as well as any other player. On all sorts of wickets he was an absolute master; on a hard true wicket he was as good as any one else; and on a fiery wicket he was only inferior to W.G. or the Jam Sahib.'

The Leicestershire professional, Albert Knight, said in 1906 that Fry's 'infinite painstaking capacity is unexcelled in the whole history of the game'. He added that there was 'no batsman who is more likely to rival the long, long records of Dr Grace; the same untiring tenacity, the same great studied effort and regulated experimentation are his, and if his limitations are more apparent than those of the "Champion", Mr Fry is so conscious of them as to render them an additional strength and stay.'

His judgment was so precise that he was able to reduce risk to a bare minimum; but this quality did not endear him to bowlers who bemoaned his lack of adventure. There is no doubt that he struggled to get going against accurate bowling and did not have Ranji's powers of improvisation, but most batsmen through the ages have experienced identical problems. The fact remains that C.B. made his runs at an average of 40 an hour and was so proficient at despatching wayward deliveries to the boundary that his caution was rarely an embarrassment to either him or his side.

He was capable of playing all shots, of both attacking and defensive breed: the ones he rejected or used sparingly were those that had failed to prove their worth. If Fry were caught unexpectedly he would immediately analyse the mechanics of the shot and store away the answers for future reference, if not further use. Plum Warner gave a telling, if eccentric, illustration of the ferocious power Fry could unleash. In 1905 Middlesex blooded an Afridi, Ahsan ul Hak, who was included in the team to play Sussex at Eastbourne. Warner recalled: 'Fry hit a ball tremendously hard by mid-off, where Ahsan was fielding, and in the dressing-room afterwards Ahsan said to me: "I hope, Skipper, you noticed that I did not put my hand near that fearful drive of Fry's. It would have been foolhardy to have done so!" '

C.B. was a true disciple of Ranji's guiding principle: play back or drive, and his judgment of length was so precise that he rarely picked the wrong option. It would do modern batsmen no harm to note that front foot play should be intrinsically aggressive, while back foot shots can be both defensive and attacking, according to the length and line of a particular delivery.

At Oxford and in his early games with Sussex Fry was repressed in his shot-making, but through exceptional powers of observation and that much-maligned activity, practice, he made the grade. This is how Wallis Myers described C.B.'s devotion to the cause: 'He pursued his private practice with unabated zeal. In the early spring months, no matter what the character of the weather, he would improvise a wicket in the garden, don an old sweater, and rub up those weapons in his armoury which he considered needed polish. After he was married Mrs Fry would "bowl" to him, throwing balls to him with sufficient accuracy to tease his defence; while the fielding could be done, and done with almost human intelligence, by a couple of Scotch terriers whom their master had trained to anticipate every stroke, and recover the ball wheresoever it wandered.' When practising in the nets at Hamble, Fry got into the habit of using a bat which had been reduced to three inches in width. Life would then seem so much easier out in the middle!

Even when C.B. had become a master in the art of batting he needed constant reassurance, especially from those like Ranji, whose own relaxed brilliance made him the perfect comforter. By the start of the century Ranji's former qualms about Fry's calibre had disappeared. He wrote in the *Daily Express*: 'We find in him a batsman of the highest class, free and easy in his methods, pleasing to the eye in his play, and executing all the strokes that are possible in batting with perfect confidence . . . The working of the legs is beyond reproach; the attitude and poise of the body and the swing of the bat are quite majestic. His driving is terrific, being low and beautifully timed.'

Frank Woolley, the great all-rounder for Kent and England, began his career in 1906 and although Fry was into his mid-thirties by this time, Woolley confirmed that none of the ability or application had been lost. 'He was a great batsman', wrote Woolley, 'one of the very few right up at the top who really knew how to bat for the particular wicket against the bowlers then engaged. He would not use the same methods against every bowler, and on soft or difficult wickets nobody in my experience moved his right foot farther back than Mr Fry did as a habit. I question whether he was ever out "hit wicket" in spite of the full use he made of his ground.'

Another interesting observation made by Woolley referred to C.B.'s uncanny ability for leaving dangerous balls which were going to miss the stumps, however narrowly, a talent which would not go amiss among some of the so-called world-class players of today, their judgment impaired by a surfeit of one-day cricket.

Woolley remembered bowling to Fry in a match at Canterbury and said, 'I think I learned more that day than on, perhaps, any other one day of my whole career.' The Canterbury wicket offered some help to the spinners, who were able to turn the ball quite quickly, but it was not an impossible track to bat on. Woolley explained: 'Over and over again I would bowl a ball pitching about on the leg or leg and middle, expecting a catch in the slips. As regularly as I pitched on more or less the unplayable length Mr Fry would draw away slightly to the leg-side, leaving his wicket open, and the ball would go over the top, or outside the off stump.' As ever, Fry was ready to explain his thinking to the baffled bowler, even in the heat of the action. By considerable observation he had reasoned that the slow left-armer's most dangerous ball, pitching around middle stump on a good length, was always likely to miss the stumps. However, if the right-hand batsman was tempted into playing a shot at such a delivery he would almost certainly end up being caught in the slips. Fry's theory was that the ball which bit and turned was also liable to lift more than the straight delivery and he reckoned that batsmen ought to be able to 'draw back quickly after having watched what the ball is doing after pitching, and let the wicketkeeper return the ball to the disappointed bowler!'

C.B.'s dedication waned little with advancing years. Wally Hammond, who, by contrast, played almost exclusively through the off side, recalled the Fry of 1921. This was the veteran, semi-retired from first-class cricket and closing in on his fiftieth birthday, who was persuaded back into the big time in the hope that his experience might lead England to victory over the formidable touring Australians. Hammond wrote in *Cricket My World*: 'In 1921 it was almost painful to watch the intensity with which this player of model book-shots dug himself in, cautiously ground down the strength of young attacking bowlers striving with every heartbeat to win places in the first post-war Tests in England, and then almost mechanically sent the ball cracking away to the boundaries.' Hammond believed that the inclusion of Fry as captain might well have resulted in the 1921 series bringing a healthier return for England.

8

PASTURES NEW

The procrastinations about Charles Fry's county allegiances were finally ended in the spring of 1909 with some swift dealings–the stuff multinational agreements are made of. A letter from C.B. was read out to a Sussex committee meeting on 4 March, saying that because of the 'honorary though exacting and responsible work' which he had undertaken in connection with the management of the training ship *Mercury* he would not be able to play for Sussex any more. It was unanimously resolved that the Sussex secretary, Colonel Bruce, would write to Fry, imploring him to change his mind, but on 5 March the Hampshire committee were hearing the news they had waited for: C.B. was finally ready and able to play for them. The euphoria in Hampshire was only matched by the despondency in Sussex. He had been living in his new county for ten years, but there were still some supporters of Sussex cricket who questioned his right to guillotine a relationship spanning fifteen years. Those with long memories even recalled Fry's previous assurances about his loyalty to Sussex. As long ago as April 1902 he had expressed great annoyance at the slightest suggestion that he might take up a career with Hampshire. 'I shall play for Sussex as long as I play first-class cricket,' he had said.

It would be pleasing to record that C.B. immediately bestrode his new kingdom like a Colossus–and his first game for the county did find its way into the stores of statistical squirrels–but it was the magnitude of Hampshire's defeat at the hands of Surrey at the Oval which stuck in the memory. Jack Hobbs slammed 205 on the first day and, with E.G. Hayes going on to make 276, Surrey amassed the mammoth total of 742. This in itself was, and remains, the highest score ever made against Hampshire, but the pain would not have been so acute if they had gone on to save the match. Unfortunately, even that minor compensation proved beyond them, and they were bowled out for 129 and 145 to give Surrey victory by an innings and 467 runs. It ranks as the second most one-sided match ever between two counties. The record margin, of an innings and 485 runs, was also achieved by Surrey, and their victims twenty-one years earlier had been . . . Sussex! It should be noted that the only player who stood between Surrey and an even more convincing margin in 1909 was C.B. Fry, whose scores of 42 and 60 looked quite impressive in the context of Hampshire's dismal totals.

He made his first duck for the county in his second game, but when C.B. replaced the unwell Archie MacLaren as captain of the MCC side to take on the touring Australians at the end of May it was openly suggested that he might at last achieve his ambition of captaining England in a Test match. However, MacLaren recovered in time to take his place as skipper, but Fry, when available and uninjured, was still an automatic choice for the national team.

He wisely opted out of both Hampshire's games with Sussex that summer, but a measure of the interest in his possible appearance against his former colleagues was that 10,000 people turned out at Southampton at the end of May in the vain hope of seeing Fry make runs against Sussex.

C.B. was unable to play a great deal for Hampshire in 1909, but there were some fleeting glimpses of the genuine article and even the sort of exuberant strokeplay which had rarely been given true expression. He made an unbeaten 72 in 50 minutes against Gloucestershire at Portsmouth and almost transformed an obvious draw into an improbable victory for Hampshire. Nevertheless, his only century of the season, and his first for the county, came against Warwickshire at the end of August when he made 132 on a wicket which no one else on either side could master.

It was an abiding image for Hampshire supporters to conjure with during the winter, confident that the hero they had coveted for so long would play throughout the summer of 1910, undistracted by Test calls, and inspire the county to unknown triumphs. He had played just fifteen innings for the county in 1909: there had to be a greater return to come on Hampshire's investment.

These hopes had no chance of fulfilment in 1910. The start of a new season usually found C.B. practising with boyish enthusiasm, whether or not other commitments would restrict his first-class involvement. However, Mrs Fry had been seriously ill and in May 1910 she was recuperating in Brighton. C.B. not only found himself cast in the unaccustomed role of nursemaid, but also had to cope with the day-to-day administration of the *Mercury*, something his wife had so far handled with total confidence.

At the same time C.B. was receiving a torrent of criticism as the result of a bitter article entitled 'The Humbug of County Cricket'. Amateur he may have been, but it was generally felt that he still owed a degree of loyalty to cricket and should not vent his spleen at the expense of the great game. He had argued that county teams were not representative of the talents within their borders and had labelled county members as glorified season-ticket holders. He also said this of the County Championship: 'We know that the best team generally comes out top, that the general order means little or nothing, that a team can be champion without ever having played, say, the second and third on the list, and, in a word, that the championship is a considerable farce.' He felt that the notion of a league competition should be abandoned, believing that sides would play more attractive cricket and draw larger crowds if they were released from the shackles of competing for points. His idea of a knockout competition for the counties, first broached in the autumn of 1903, came to mind once more.

In the middle of June there were whispers that he might begin serious practice and have a few games with the Trojans before easing himself back into the hotter climate of county cricket, but in the end his sole contribution to Hampshire's summer was two games during cricket week at Bournemouth at the end of August and beginning of September. There were incidents in both to warm the hearts of Fry followers.

C.B. made a negligible mark with the bat against Kent, but an amusing anecdote was related in *The Field*:

He was fielding close to the crowd when Knott was batting, and an amateur photographer, anxious to improve the occasion, stepped into the field of play, and, placing himself in the approved manner, proceeded to peer anxiously into the 'finder' of his camera. At this moment Fry had to rush in to field a hard drive, and the photographer fled, to return with boldness directly afterwards. A humorous request to Fry to pose himself in an elegant manner was met by the laughing reply that a catch might come to him, and the words were hardly out of his lips when the catch came – a hard drive by Knott – Fry taking the ball on the left side after running for some yards. Apparently the photographer gave up after this.

In the second match, against Worcestershire, C.B. made a superb hundred, but could easily have been dismissed right at the start of his innings of 115. Before he had scored he played forward to Lyttleton and the wicket-keeper Bale appealed for a catch, but the umpire at the bowler's end judged that the ball had touched his pad rather than his bat. While the appeal was being turned down, however, Bale had noticed that Fry was still leaning out of his ground and the toe of his back foot was elevated, so he made a motion to break the stumps with the ball. The square leg umpire instinctively responded to this secondary appeal for a stumping in the affirmative, until it was pointed out to him by C.B. that the wicketkeeper had neglected to disturb the bails when he struck the wicket!

There was a good deal more to savour in 1911 and from Fry's bat came the articulate assurance that his days as a masterful player were far from over. He was forced to restrict himself for the most part to games at Southampton and Portsmouth, but he announced his intentions by plundering centuries in successive matches against Derbyshire and Kent at the beginning of June. He then hit 121 against Worcestershire and his place at the head of the national averages was secured by a phenomenal burst of run-making between 7 and 12 August. Hampshire's match at Canterbury, in which C.B. made two centuries against the reigning county champions, is mentioned elsewhere in connection with Fry's allegations of unfair play against Colin Blythe. The critical flak which flew around after that incident obviously galvanised rather than depressed him because he went straight down to Southampton and hammered the Gloucestershire attack for the highest score of his career, 258 not out, overtaking the 244 which he had made against Leicestershire ten years earlier.

C.B. then scored three successive hundreds at parochial level, one for the *Mercury* officers and the other two for the *Mercury*. In an unofficial sense he beat his own world record by scoring an unbeaten 102 for the Rest of England in the traditional end-of-season game against the county champions, Warwickshire. *Wisden* was sufficiently impressed at the time to mention the feat, but as far as first-class cricket was concerned he had made only four successive centuries.

In the middle of the season Charles Fry had been invited to lead the MCC touring party to Australia the following winter. By now, of course, the equation, never an easy one for him to balance, had been further complicated by his responsibilities to the *Mercury*. On these grounds he might have been expected to turn the invitation down immediately, but, as usual, Fry's protracted soul-searching reached the hearts of the nation. He was naturally flattered by the MCC's earnest desire to see him lead the touring party and at the age of thirty-nine he probably knew, although his powers as a batsman were undiminished, that it would be his last chance to tour Australia as a player.

His unenviable dilemma was recognised by *The Field*, who took it upon themselves to organise a fund which would not only clear the *Mercury*'s debts of £1,600 (see p. 174), but also provide sufficient additional finance to release C.B. for his cricketing crusade. By giving their time and labour *gratis* the Frys had already managed to reduce the annual requirement for running the training ship from £3,500 to £2,200. *The Field* then put an arbitrary estimate on the cost of Fry's absence for six months and came up with an appeal target of £5,000.

The Field's initiative came at the start of August and Fry was quick both to express his gratitude and accept the kind offer. Furthermore, he used their gesture as a springboard for appeals to newspapers in the hope that their readers would also get behind the *Mercury*. The hope was that cricket-lovers would rally to the cause and the national hero would be able to lead the assault on the old enemy, but the plan went disastrously awry for a number of reasons.

There were parts of C.B.'s letter to *The Field*, supposedly one of pure endorsement, which could hardly have struck a chord with cricketers, for instance: 'Fond as I am of cricket, and keen as I am on doing anything I can to help maintain its prestige, cricket is after all, at best, a game. The *Mercury* is a serious national work ... The most enthusiastic idolater of cricket, if he knew the value of the *Mercury* and its work, and all the difficulties we have had in preserving it and carrying it on, would never ask me to put cricket before it. Nor should I for one moment even think of so doing.'

It was hardly surprising that there was confusion among potential subscribers. If Fry had such a mature perspective on the relative merits of cricket and shaping young cadets, was there any decision to be made? A week after the appeal had been launched *The Field* announced without obvious embarrassment that the fund had reached the grand total of £66 14s and that included a contribution of £21 from the magazine's proprietors.

On August 15 C.B. wrote again to *The Field*, asking them to call the appeal off. He thanked them for setting the ball rolling, but added: 'As, however, the response to your kind appeal has been so small, and it is clear that in the time available no adequate sum can be raised to relieve the *Mercury*, I have definitely decided to inform MCC that I cannot go to Australia. When I consented to your appeal on behalf of the *Mercury* I had in mind that the membership of MCC runs into some 5,000, and that the committee of MCC had not once but repeatedly pressed me not to refuse the invitation if there was any fair chance of my being able to go.'

The magazine *M.A.P.* (*Mostly About People*) reacted rather cynically to *The Field*'s gesture, but possibly grasped some of the unanswered questions which had led to the dismal failure of the appeal. They suggested that C.B. should have squared up with the public when he was first offered the captaincy six weeks earlier; and then there would have been ample opportunity for any appeal to gather momentum. On 19 August a correspondent wrote in *M.A.P.*: 'What I don't understand, however, is whether the whole of the sum asked for by *The Field* is to be devoted to the needs of the *Mercury*, or whether only part of it is intended to recoup Mr Fry for any loss his magazine may sustain during his absence from England. This is a point which *The Field* last week did not make quite clear. Nothing could be more damaging to the reputation of English cricket than that an impression should arise that the hat has to be sent round before a distinguished amateur could afford to take a holiday in Australia from his business in England.'

The same writer went on to speculate in future issues about the danger of amateur status being infringed and wondered how *The Field* had arrived at the stated figure of £5,000, the magnitude of which might lead people to suspect that C.B.'s own nest was being feathered. It was also suggested in *M.A.P.* that the appeal might have had a better chance of success if it had been organised by the MCC themselves, but these observations met with an angry response from *The Field*, who went so far as to demand a retraction from *M.A.P.* following their 'ignorant remarks' about the nature and justification of the appeal.

It obviously had not worked in Fry's favour that he was involved in the controversy with Colin Blythe at Canterbury just a week after *The Field* had launched the appeal. The unfavourable reports which greeted C.B.'s action in this match preceded the inevitable finger-wagging and question-marks about his suitability as England skipper. Inevitably, *M.A.P.* got in on the act, saying: 'Mr Fry showed himself quite devoid of that tact and self-control which are so necessary in a captain of a touring team.'

As a batsman C.B. earned almost universal admiration, but more doubts were expressed about his qualities of leadership. The Rev. R.S. Holmes offered a nicely balanced appraisal in *Cricket Notches*: 'He has been called "an ideal captain"; but is he? To me he has always seemed an isolated figure on the cricket field, answering to Wordsworth's famous description of Milton–"like a star that dwells apart"; self-contained, never in closest touch with his fellows, a man to be more admired than beloved. A man after my own heart, reserved, and not "hail fellow" with all comers. But on that account scarcely an ideal captain of a cricketing team which is composed of all sorts and all conditions of men.'

The bonhomie may have been missing, but there were definite compensating factors. Over a period of fifteen years C.B. had established himself as the most prolific and reliable English batsman. He was astonishingly fit and agile for his age and his understanding of the mechanical aspects of the game could not be bettered. He could lead by example, if not by inspiration, and the example was normally sufficient; but the spontaneous gifts of captaincy eluded him. As leader of a successful side he could follow the blueprint unerringly, making the appropriate bowling changes and placing fielders with subtlety according to the strengths and weaknesses which he had observed closely in opposing batsmen. But it was the gift for improvisation in adversity that was outside his repertoire—he did not have much to say on the subject and knew that this aspect of captaincy was beyond the zealous research of a student.

Fry was, however, finally rewarded with the England captaincy in 1912 and, with six Tests to be played against Australia and South Africa, his Hampshire outings were restricted to a minimum. Nevertheless, C.B.'s success in the few county games he was able to play confirmed the underlying tension which affected him so severely in the international matches.

Early in the season Fry made an undefeated 152 against Somerset and he followed up with 143 against Kent at the end of May. At the beginning of July he scored what proved to be the last of his sixteen double centuries in first-class cricket, 203 not out against Oxford University. He made an excellent century for the Gentlemen at the Oval and subjugated another generation of Yorkshire bowlers at Southampton at the end of July, but he still could not carry this form into the Tests and it was only the eventual success against Australia which got him off the hook as far as the public and newspapers were concerned. When the clouds were lifted the scenario changed with dramatic speed. The crowds cheered endlessly and everyone wanted to pat C.B. on the back, as if they had always been on his side. The papers changed tack with admirable swiftness. This tactical buffoon, allegedly past his prime, was born again as a rejuvenated hero.

C.B. was not easily fooled by fickle adulation and when the 1913 season came around he was in no hurry to bounce back on to the cricket fields to milk the remnants of the praise from the previous summer. The *Athletic News* wrote at the end of May: 'The Sphinx-like silence of C.B. Fry, both with pen and bat, is shortly to be broken, with the mightier of the two implements, at all events. As to when Fry will don armour we must look to the sun whence cometh our help in this as in many other matters.' And sure enough, in the June issue of *Fry's Magazine*, there appeared 'The Truth about County Cricket', an examination of the problems facing the first-class game in this country. However, the other part of the bargain was destined not to be fulfilled. There were the usual rumours about C.B. renewing his part-time acquaintance with

Hampshire cricket, but he eventually decided to ignore the county game altogether that season.

His first appearance in 1914 came at the beginning of June after he had recovered from a heel injury. In the light of an absence of almost two years from first-class cricket it was nothing short of miraculous that Fry should manage to score 41 and 112 in the game against Gloucestershire at Portsmouth. Miraculous maybe, but typical: the usual painstaking net practice at Hamble ensured that he was as well tuned as anyone could hope to be after twenty-one months of self-imposed exile. The *Southern Daily Echo* marvelled: 'There is only one C.B. Fry. What other batsman could have played as he did yesterday after having been out of first-class cricket for over 12 months?'

Fry's season almost began and ended with that game. He played just six more innings for Hampshire in 1914: the war intervened and cricket's already tenuous hold on C.B. was severed, perhaps for good. However, 1914 did provide one more cherished memory in the shape of a match between the MCC South African XI and the Rest of England, which was part of the centenary celebrations of the opening of Lord's. Fry was captain of the England side and he and his opposite number, Johnny Douglas, were introduced to the King on 23 June when he visited Lord's with the Prince of Wales. George V spent some time talking to the two captains in front of the pavilion, with Fry, the true patriot, standing rigidly to attention in His Majesty's presence.

TESTING TIMES

In modern times Charles Fry's promising form on the tour of South Africa would have been rewarded with crass newspaper assurances that he had a guaranteed place in the England side for the next fifteen years. However, he wasn't in contention when the Australians toured in 1896–Charterhouse duties kept him out of first-class cricket until the three-match Test series was all but over.

He forced his way into the reckoning when the Australians were in England again in 1899, following up 98 against the MCC with an even more significant 81 for the South of England against the tourists. His subsequent efforts were less impressive, but he was fortunate in having a confirmed fan in W.G. Grace, who not only pressed for his inclusion in the side for the First Test at Trent Bridge, but also succeeded in getting C.B. co-opted onto the newly formed selection committee. The 'Champion's' confidence seemed well-founded as he and Fry added 78 for England's first wicket. According to C.B. the stand would have been worth 100 or more if, Grace (improbably at the age of fifty) had been able to match Joe Vine's speed between the wickets. Fry was 'bowled' early on by a no-ball from Ernest Jones, whose lightning deliveries suggested that he would be a key man in the series. A legitimate ball from Jones eventually shattered C.B.'s stumps–but not before he had made an encouraging 50 in 95 minutes, the top score in England's total of 193.

That gave Australia a first innings lead of 59, but although they posed a feasible fourth-innings target England set the pattern for a rather dreary series by concentrating obsessively on survival. The leading batsmen were not even successful in that limited ambition, collapsing to 19 for 4. No one struggled more than C.B., who was in for an hour making just nine. It was only thanks to Ranji's unbeaten 93 that England contrived to save the game.

It was not immediately apparent, but there was deep significance in the selection committee's meeting at the Sports Club to decide the make-up of the England team for the Second Test at Lord's. Fry arrived late and almost before he had a chance to sit down he was asked by W.G. whether Archie MacLaren should be drafted into the side. He replied in the affirmative, little knowing that he had effectively signed Grace's death warrant as a Test player. It would be misleading to regard the change as a simple swop, for only six of the England team who took the field at Trent Bridge were retained for the Lord's game. But Grace had understandably lost his youthful agility and did not want to be a liability in the field.

Archie MacLaren not only got back into the England side, but also assumed the captaincy, despite rival claims from F.S. Jackson, and eventually confirmed the solid impression he had made against the Australian bowlers on the 1897–8 tour. It was a gloomy match for C.B. at Lord's. He made just 13 and 4, being dismissed both times by Jones, who took his tally for the first two Tests to 17 wickets. The tourists owed their first innings lead of 215 to brilliant centuries from their young stars, Victor Trumper and Clem Hill, aged twenty-one and twenty-two respectively. MacLaren hung on gamely to make 88 not out in England's second innings, but Australia still sauntered to a ten-wicket win.

In the Third Test at Leeds Jack Hearne performed the hat-trick in Australia's innings, on an illustrious trio at that – Monty Noble, Syd Gregory and Clem Hill. Nevertheless, the weather put paid to England's chances of victory. C.B. made 38 in his only innings of the match but, as in the final Test, he was out at the start of the second day's play, having failed to add to his overnight score.

England's bowling resources let them down in the Fourth Test at Old Trafford after 130 from Tom Hayward had put them in complete control. C.B. might have been expected to prosper when Jones put down a sharp caught-and-bowled chance when he had made nine, but instead he played on next ball. The Australian batsmen fought back well in their second innings and England were left with a futile one-hour spell for batting at the end of the match. Their frustration was reflected in some cavalier shots, but C.B. had the minor consolation of being dismissed by a brilliant catch from Frank Iredale when he had made only four.

Bill Lockwood came in for the final match in the series, but his return of 7 for 71 in Australia's first innings at the Oval only served to underline the patternless selections earlier in the series. C.B. was left with the impression that when selection committees were given the powers to co-opt additional personnel there would always be fatal differences of opinion. He favoured dictatorial judgment—preferably his own! At least there was a convincing display from the English batsmen. The openers, Jackson and Hayward, both made centuries, but the most exciting batting came from C.B. and MacLaren, who added 110 in just 70 minutes. Fry slowed down towards the end of his knock of 60, but his half-century came at almost a run a minute. England totalled 576, but the Australian batsmen were able to save the match without too many problems and clinched the series 1–0.

The summer of 1902 offended the Trade Descriptions Act by bringing rain, rain and more rain. By his own immaculate standards Charles Fry's batting matched the weather. He made an encouraging start, but there was none of the sparkle of the previous year and it was really on the strength of earlier glories that Fry was chosen for the First Test at Birmingham. He succeeded in making his first duck in Test cricket, but 138 from John Tyldesley saw England through to a declaration on 376 for 9. Australia were then bundled out for 36, their lowest-ever score against England, and doubtless would have lost by an innings if the rain had not predictably intervened. C.B. had the slight consolation of dazzling the critics with some brilliant fielding. His catch to dismiss Howell in the first innings was described as 'a marvel of athletic springiness' and he produced another superb effort to get rid of Duff in the second innings.

The elements permitted less than two hours' cricket in the Second Test at Lord's, but there was still something to make the world sit up and take notice. Both C.B. and Ranji were dismissed for nought: it was unheard of. Had these gods really been reduced to the status of mere mortals? In the circumstances it was quite an achievement for Fry to provide *Daily Express* readers with a humorous account of his dismissal by the previously unvaunted

Bert Hopkins, who also grabbed Ranji's wicket, but was so unnerved by his brief dalliance with stardom that he took no more wickets in the series. This was Fry's description of his own demise: 'His second ball, which pitched on my legs about 4 ins clear of the wicket, I was able, with a stroke I do not reckon in my repertoire, to cock up into the hands of short-leg near the umpire. That comes of playing the new-fangled leg-glance instead of the old-fashioned leg-hit. I hope to forget how to play the shot I invented for that ball: it is not a good one if there is a man where the ball happens to go.'

C.B. was given the opportunity by total inactivity on the second and third days to indulge in a little prophetic speculation about pitch covering. This classic piece of bad weather journalism recalls R.C. Robertson-Glasgow's first meeting with Fry, more than thirty years later at Lord's: 'Rain had prevented the start of the match; but he was hard at work, standing. I ventured to ask him what attracted his pencil, and he said, "My dear fellow, I am writing about what ought to be happening if anything were happening at all. In short, the perfect critic." '

Fry wrote in 1902: 'It sounds artificial, but, by Hercules! the idea of covering up the wicket with a big tarpaulin is not so very unreasonable. Here are fourteen men who have come thousands of miles to play us at cricket. It rains, and they might just as well have stayed at home. The tarpaulin would mean that play could go on nearly all the time rain is not actually falling. The outfield would be wet and slippery, but that would not matter so very much. The ball would be greasy, but a square foot of flannel would be used to dry it: and with resin and sawdust we might manage. Of course, all this sounds odd; but a cycle of summers of the kind in vogue at the present will accustom us to greater oddities.' He also threw in the suggestion that Test matches should be played to a conclusion, irrespective of how they interfered with the county programme.

C.B. could have no cause for complaint when he was left out of the England 12 for the Third Test at Sheffield, but Ranji injured a leg and his county colleague was called up as a replacement. Sussex were completing the last rites of their high-scoring game with Essex at Leyton when the telegram came through on 2 July. A buzz went round the ground as Fry rushed from the field and five minutes later he could be seen in front of the pavilion, hurriedly buttoning up his overcoat before being whisked away to start his journey up to Yorkshire. This late reprieve was celebrated by 'Spedex' in the *Daily Express*, who clearly held great store by the charisma of the amateurs, saying: 'Fry, MacLaren and Jackson are the figureheads of the younger champions, and are the mainspring of present-day cricket impetus. From the boy who plays with a bat of "father's fashioning" to the colt on the eve of his promotion to first-class cricket, "C.B.", "A.C", and "F.S", are the models—nay, idols—and the deeds and personality of this triumvirate are the fostering incubators of their emulation.'

These noble sentiments failed to break Fry's run of misfortune, but he deserved particular sympathy in the first innings. It was the sort of summer where rain was succeeded by bad light and the first day at Sheffield came into the funereal category. Sydney Barnes took 6 for 49 as Australia were bowled out for 194 and England looked well set at 86 for 1, but they collapsed in the gathering gloom. The background was especially poor from the pavilion end and when C.B. had made just a single he failed to pick up the flight of a ball from Saunders outside the off stump. He aimed a futile drive, over-balanced and was duly stumped. The message immediately got through to the incoming batsman, Leonard Braund, who successfully appealed against the light as soon as he reached the wicket.

Fry could only manage 4 in the second innings and a tally of 5 runs in four innings hardly recommended him for further inclusion. It was a shame: the England side in 1902—and, of course, the Australian team—ranked with the best sides put out by the two countries in the history of the Ashes. England's batting strength, on paper at least, was so formidable that Wilfred Rhodes, a scorer of Test match centuries, went in at number eleven.

Charles Fry was reduced to a reporting role for the remaining Tests at Old Trafford and the Oval, which just happened to go down as the most exciting pair of games in the history of Test cricket. The first produced a memorable hundred for Stanley Jackson, a personal nightmare for Fry's Sussex colleague Fred Tate, and a three-run win for Australia to assure them of victory in the series. England gained a measure of revenge at the Oval in a match which was rightly remembered for a magnificently belligerent century from Gilbert Jessop and for the apocryphal exchange between Rhodes and George Hirst as they gathered the 15 runs needed for a one-wicket win–'We'll get 'em in singles.'

C.B. was in such majestic form at the start of the 1905 season that the Australian tourists appeared to be condemned to toil in the Tests. He made two hundreds in Sussex's match against the MCC and in the space of nine days amassed 628 runs. He was an automatic choice for the First Test at the end of May, but while batting in the nets at Hove on May 24 he was hit on the right hand, split a finger, and had to have three stitches put in. He immediately telegraphed the chairman of the selectors, Lord Hawke, to say he would be unlikely to make Trent Bridge. George Hirst was also out of action because of an injured knee, which meant that the top two in the national batting averages, both running at more than 100 an innings, were unable to turn out.

In the event their absence did not matter as England won the First Test by 213 runs. Nevertheless, Fry was back for the Second Test at Lord's and top-scored with 73 in England's first innings, but the first day's play hardly ranked as a scintillating spectacle. The whole England side had struggled to make headway against some mean, negative bowling from the Australians. The chief culprit was Warwick Armstrong, whose leg breaks were fired in outside the leg stump and with a packed on-side field the batsmen were at a loss. The large crowd were unsympathetic to their problems and jeered loudly as C.B. and the England skipper, Stanley Jackson, put together a tedious fourth-wicket stand. Fry, who had come close to being bowled by Frank Laver early on, was missed off the same bowler when he had made 46. He was just beginning to come to terms with his difficulties and jealously eyeing his first Test century against the old enemy when his innings was ended by a dubious piece of umpiring from his old adversary, the Australian umpire Jim Phillips. He gave Fry out caught at the wicket although C.B. maintained that the ball had come off his boot rather than his bat. C.B. pulled no punches in his report for the *Daily Express* the following morning: 'There is no doubt that the cricket at Lord's yesterday was the dullest ever seen in a Test match.'

Fry once again won his spurs in the field with a brilliant running catch to dismiss Noble and was unbeaten on 36 at the close of the second day, his runs again having come at a depressing trickle. A declaration loomed, but rain wiped out the whole of the third day.

In the Third Test at Leeds Fry was played in his accustomed role as opener and responded with a more agreeable 32 in the first innings, but his basic failure to dominate the Australian bowlers was again revealed second time round as he crept to an unconvincing 30 in 100 minutes. There were the same unmistakable signs of over-anxiety, curious from a man who constantly asserted that no player should be nervous in a Test match if he was physically fit. A few years earlier *Tit-Bits* had said in a profile of C.B.: 'If Mr Fry were only a compiler of moderate totals he would be valuable to an international side on account of his entire freedom from anything like nervousness.' C.B. himself would have liked to treat a Test match like a casual game on the village green, but his temperament proved suspect on the international stage and he was never able to justify the confidence of that writer.

England clinched the series against Australia with an overwhelming innings victory at Old Trafford at the end of July, but there was still no personal glory for Charles Fry. England had built a sound base when he came in at the fall of the second wicket, but he took twenty-five minutes to get off the mark and was bowled by Armstrong when he had made 17.

The Australian bowlers had developed a highly tenable theory that if C.B. was restricted in his shot-making on the on-side he would be effectively neutralised and frustration would eventually lead to his dismissal. These tactics might have worked in the last Test at the Oval, but for a golden opportunity for Fry to work out his antidote in a more relaxed environment. Sussex played the Australians at Hove soon after the Old Trafford match, and although they lost the match by an innings C.B. found a solution to his personal dilemma. He was almost decapitated by Cotter early on, but put his trust in positive thinking: eighty minutes and 70 runs later, by playing a highly attacking game, he had released himself from the mental stranglehold which the Australian bowlers had exerted.

Two weeks later he had the chance to test the quality of his rehabilitation. England batted first at the Oval and made a poor start, losing their first two wickets for 32, but from the moment C.B. arrived at the wicket it was clear that his nervous prodding had given way to assertive strokeplay. The Australians stuck to their game plan – a plethora of short-pitched deliveries outside the off stump, but this time C.B. had the answers. He unleashed a series of rasping cuts and on the odd occasions when the ball was pitched up he drove with great authority through an arc between cover and the bowler. This dramatic escape from the shackles of submission was very much to the liking of the 22,000 crowd, who roared their approval at each of C.B.'s 23 fours. He was in for 215 minutes for his 144, adding 100 for the third wicket with Tom Hayward (59) and 151 in 125 minutes with Jackson (76) for the fourth wicket. It was to remain as Fry's highest score in Test cricket. England's total of 430 ensured that they would not lose the game, which turned into a tame draw. C.B. scored only 16 in England's second innings, but his reputation was intact . . . for the moment. He averaged 57 for the series, only Jackson having better figures, and the battle of wits and nerve had finally gone his way.

The serious Achilles tendon injury which Fry suffered at the start of the 1906 season threw his Test career into jeopardy. A fully-fit C.B. would have been the natural choice for captain against the South Africans in 1907, but even though he defied expert advice by trying to make a comeback at the start of the summer his form was sketchy and his troubled movement in the field suggested that he was still a long way from complete recovery. In the circumstances R.E. Foster was offered and accepted the captaincy.

Meanwhile, Fry showed no signs of a return to confident batsmanship until the middle of June when he made 85 against Yorkshire. 'Linesman' in the *Daily Mail* wrote: 'All the world rejoices at the recrudescence of Mr C.B. Fry.' However, he followed that brief ray of light with three successive noughts and it was a shock when he was included in the England 13 for the First Test at Lord's on 1 July. 'Linesman' described his selection as a 'sentimental compliment' and 'quite astonishing', suggesting that Lord Hawke had been unduly influenced by that one innings of merit against Yorkshire. It seemed to underline Fry's view that it was hard to force one's way into the England side, but once picked it was just as hard to be dropped.

When the iron stanchion which had been supporting his injured leg was removed Fry looked more like the magnificent athlete he was, but the runs stubbornly refused to flow and this item appeared in the *Daily Mail* on the morning of the First Test: 'It was rumoured on Saturday that Mr C.B. Fry had withdrawn his name from the list of selected players, and so chivalrously, if quixotically, rectified an apparent injustice to other players who on the season's form are much more worthy of a place.'

It was a rumour without foundation, however, and Fry took his place in the side, scoring 33 out of 54 before playing on to Vogler. England went on to make 428 and with the fragile South African batting collapsing dramatically on the second day a big defeat was only averted by the intervention of rain on the last day.

There was almost a month between the First and Second Tests, and considerable relief was felt by Fry, his supporters and the England selectors as he played himself into tremendous form. The question remained: could C.B. switch his attentions to Tests without mysteriously losing his touch?

The opening overs of the Second Test suggested that the answer was a definite no. Fry misjudged a full toss from Vogler and was bowled, but no one else found life any easier on a challenging Headingley wicket and England were starting their second innings before the end of the first day's play. Fry (12 not out) and Tom Hayward (13 not out) were still together at the close, but only by virtue of an extraordinary piece of luck for C.B. His middle stump was clearly hit by a ball from Faulkner, but although the leg bail was disturbed it did not come off.

Fry responded to this extravagant good fortune by adopting an admirably positive approach at the start of the second day. In Vogler, Faulkner and Schwarz, South Africa had a tremendous trio of leg break and googly bowlers, but Fry's judgment on the still unreliable wicket was impeccable and he raced to 50 in seventy minutes. He was not impressed by the lbw decision which ended his innings at 54, but nothing could detract from his splendid performance. It was even suggested in some quarters that this was of equal merit to his 144 against Australia two years earlier. The other hero for England was Colin Blythe, who bowled with phenomenal accuracy to take 15 for 99 in the match.

C.B. kept the momentum going in the Third Test at the Oval, which was rapidly turning into his favourite Test match ground. He was the dominant figure in a stop-start first day which was restricted to four hours by a succession of showers. It was hardly the perfect setting to build a long innings, but Fry's determination was total. He was bowled by a no-ball when he made 13, then almost caught and bowled by Schwarz on 27, but he settled into a defiant role as his partners came and went at the other end. The crowd of 12,000 were overjoyed when C.B. completed the worthiest of hundreds. He might have been stumped when he had made 81, but he accelerated quite effectively towards the end and was still unbeaten when stumps were drawn with England on 226 for 7.

He went on to make 129 before being caught and bowled by Faulkner, having batted a total of 285 minutes. The fact that he had hit just seven fours was indicative of the struggle on a far from easy wicket. 'I look back on the match', Fry later recalled, 'with fine self-appreciation, because I scored 129 without a chance against very difficult bowling on a foul wicket. Tell it not in Gath, but this was the best innings I ever played in my life.'

C.B. failed in the second innings, making just 3, but his original selection for the England team had been more than vindicated and the advantages of persevering with the players of greatest ability and dedication were again underlined.

In 1909 Fry joined Lord Hawke, Archie MacLaren and 'Shrimp' Leveson-Gower on the selection committee for the Tests against Australia, but if any of these had known the lambasting they would receive from the Press they would probably have quit in advance. The First Test at Edgbaston gave no hint of the imminent moans as England moved confidently to a ten-wicket victory. Both sides were bowled out cheaply in their first innings on a wet wicket and C.B. was dismissed first ball by Macartney. Jack Hobbs was also dismissed without scoring, which made it all the more extraordinary that he and C.B. should be the heroes for England as they chased the 105 runs needed for victory in the last innings.

Fry had gone in at number four in the first innings, but despite his failure he persuaded skipper Archie MacLaren to let him open the second innings with Hobbs. The wicket was still difficult when they started out thirty-five minutes before lunch on the third day, but some glorious shots by Hobbs changed the course of the match. When lunch was taken he had made 33 out of 43, with C.B. hanging on grimly with 5 to his name. After the interval the two batsmen scored at a more even rate and it was C.B. who had the satisfaction of making the winning hit, an all-run four, as England sped to 105 without loss. Fry's contribution was 35, while the magnificent Hobbs was undefeated on 62. C.B.'s appreciation of his partner's innings could scarcely have been couched in more flattering terms: 'I have to say that this was as great an innings as I ever saw played by any batsman in any Test Match, or any other match. It is the only innings I have seen when batting the other end that I rank with some of the innings I saw Ranjitsinhji play when I was in with him.'

The crowd were ecstatic at the end of the match and ninety minutes after the game had ended they were still shouting for their heroes, Hobbs, Fry, MacLaren, Blythe, Hirst and the Australian skipper Monty Noble. The enigmatic Blythe, who had taken 11 wickets in the match, could be seen watching the celebrations from the far side of the field. He was in his day clothes and hardly looked like the demon bowler who had destroyed the cream of Australia's batting.

Blythe's nerves got the better of him and he was advised by a specialist to drop out of the Second Test at Lord's. C.B. himself was in the original 13, but scratched from the side because he was tied up with legal matters, giving evidence on behalf of his brother-in-law, Frank Holme Sumner, who was facing fraud charges at the Old Bailey. While he was being acquitted the England selectors were watching anxiously to see if their unbalanced selection could beat the Australians. They had tempted retribution by leaving out Gilbert Jessop and neglecting to include a fast bowler, although Lancastrian Walter Brearley could easily have been drafted into the team. Nowhere was the criticism of the selectors in general, and Fry in particular, more pronounced than in the *Daily Express* where Sir Home Gordon frequently spoke his mind.

He suggested that C.B. should have been left out of the England side anyway: 'He has failed in Test matches with greater frequency than any one else played solely for his batting, while his fielding at Birmingham fell far below the magnificent standard of his ten colleagues.' It was no help to the selectors that Australia's nine-wicket victory at Lord's was followed by two centuries for Jessop against Hampshire and a return of 6 for 49 by Brearley against Kent.

The persistent Sir Home Gordon wrote on 19 June: 'Calm consideration only intensifies the universal and profound disgust at the way in which the national prestige has been lowered by the team chosen to represent England in the second Test match against the Australians on Monday, Tuesday and Wednesday last. Granted that the Selection Committee did their best, that best was so flagrantly bad that they ought to be debarred from repeating the offence which is now a matter of unfortunate history.'

The advice on selection was well followed for the Third Test at Leeds, where Fry, Jessop, Brearley, Rhodes and Barnes all came in, but the end result was the same as at Lord's. Jessop ricked his back early on and was unable to bat, while C.B. failed twice, endorsing the opinions of critics who felt he should have been excluded from the side. There was a particularly humiliating end to his second innings, in which he made 7. He succeeded in dragging a ball from Cotter onto his stumps from a foot outside the off stump.

C.B. did not appear in the Fourth Test, an absence which was initially explained by a hip injury he had picked up in the Gentlemen v Players game in the middle of July. However, it is worth underlining that he did turn out for Hampshire on the same three days as the Old Trafford Test and, ironically, played an exhilarating innings of 72 not out in fifty minutes at the end of the game.

Fry was back in tow for the Fifth Test at the Oval. Australia needed just a draw to win the series and centuries in both innings by Warren Bardsley ensured that their wishes would be granted. C.B. made 62 in England's first innings and was looking good for a few more when Wilfred Rhodes, with whom he had added 104, hit a ball from Noble straight to Syd Gregory at cover-point. Fry charged down the wicket, was sent back by Rhodes and run out by the bowler despite a valiant attempt to regain his ground with a full-length dive. At the end of the match C.B. was undefeated on 35 in England's second innings, so a series which had been rather trying for him as both a player and selector ended on an encouraging note.

The 1912 season has gone down in history as the one which played host to the one and only Triangular series, but it was also a year of massive peaks and troughs for Charles Fry, who finally claimed the England captaincy and was still undefeated at the end of six Tests which brought four wins and two draws. The series was pronounced a failure, but the weather refused to give the experiment a fair crack of the whip and this, more than any other factor, was responsible for the low-key events of 1912.

It was a plain insult that C.B. should originally be offered the England captaincy for just one match. No other captain since the formation of the independent selection committee had been chosen on approval, and Fry wrote to Lord Harris, the chairman of the Board of Control, to say that he would not accept the captaincy on that basis. He also sought permission to head a selection committee consisting of just two other members. Happily, his arguments were persuasive to Lord Harris, who told the Board of Control: 'I think this fellow Fry is right.'

The other selectors were Harry Foster and Jack Shuter, and according to C.B. they met once in May to choose their best side, nominated substitutes who could come in to replace injured players and agreed to stick by their original selections, irrespective of the vagaries of form. It was an approach which C.B. was still preaching forty years later. The continuity of selection, he always felt, was of prime importance, and gave confidence to the players who were recognised as the best in the land. With a few exceptions, he argued, it was generally possible to nominate the outstanding batsmen and bowlers, and there was no justification for chopping and changing in fickle fashion.

The Fry philosophy may have bred confidence among the chosen players in 1912, but his own security of tenure was not reflected in individual success. Even at the ripe old age of forty he still exhibited over-anxiety, and if anything the added pressures of captaincy made him even more prone to nervousness. Nevertheless, his enthusiasm was decidedly infectious. In the Test trial at the start of May he posted himself suicidally close at short leg, like an army commander leading a charge, and the same desire to be obtrusively involved was evident in the match between the MCC team that had played in Australia the previous winter and the Rest of England. The *Daily Telegraph* reported: 'Mr Fry worked untiringly, in a sense almost unnecessarily, for it made needlessly long distances in the field for him to cover between the overs, and he fielded in any number of positions during the innings.'

England's first game in the Triangular series was against South Africa at Lord's. They won by an innings, but C.B. would have had more cause for contentment if his own form had been good. He began very nervously and was frequently beaten by Aubrey Faulkner, eventually being bowled for 29 by Pegler at a stage where he looked as though he might be assuming control.

The South African batsmen were at a complete loss to deal with the wiles of Sydney Barnes, who took 34 wickets in the three Tests against them, but they again had a strong bowling side and C.B. was only able to make 55 runs against them in the four innings he played. This is how the *Daily Express* reported his dismissal in the first innings of the Second Test at Leeds, lbw to Pegler for 10: 'Fry's return to the pavilion was a melancholy one. Surely there is not a player in England who takes his marching orders so much to heart as Fry. His face was a picture of misery.' The story was equally gloomy in the second innings and the paper again spoke of his 'doleful tread back to the pavilion'.

Fry was no more convincing in his final innings of the summer against South Africa. He gave no indication of permanence and it was no surprise when he was caught off Faulkner after he had made just 9.

England's first game with Australia was ruined by rain. A Jack Hobbs century gave the home side the smoothest of starts, but Fry, 24 not out at the close of the first day, was still batting on the third day after rain had ripped out most of the middle day's play and ran himself out on 42 as a declaration loomed. C.B. knew that a result was out of the question and confounded the *cognoscenti* by holding back Frank Woolley, potentially an ace card on wet wickets. Frank Foster and Barnes had been ineffective, but Fry also kept Wilfred Rhodes out of the attack until late in the proceedings. The critics were baffled, but Fry's logic was revealed in the hour of genuine need, for the element of mystery about Woolley's bowling helped him to matchwinning spells in the last Test at the Oval.

The Second Test at Old Trafford was even more of a washout and C.B.'s timing completely deserted him in an innings of 19 which lasted for an hour and confirmed that the responsibilities of captaincy could not inspire him as a batsman.

The events of the whole summer were then effectively distilled into four days at the Oval at the end of August. South Africa had been beaten by both England and Australia, so this last Test was like a knockout final and it was agreed that it would be played to a definite result. The intense interest in the match was reflected in

England's caution on the first day, despite a century opening stand between Hobbs and Rhodes. Fry was even more introspective than usual and all he had to show for forty-five minutes' batting was five singles. F.B. Wilson wrote in the *Daily Mirror*: 'His innings was as unworthy of Fry as a lie of George Washington. He seemed paralysed, fascinated like a rabbit given to a snake. There was some barracking when he was in, and when he was out, caught at mid-on off a wretched mis-hit, it was a decided relief.'

The 30,000 crowd had booed him as he strode out to the wicket, unhappy about his refusal to start play on time. Fry's opposite number, Syd Gregory, saw the value of catching England on a drying wicket. C.B., however, was well aware that the match would run its full course and unwilling to concede unnecessary advantage on the opening day.

The Australians got to 90 for 2 at one stage in reply to England's total of 245, but then Fry took the wraps off Frank Woolley and the Kent bowler operated to devastating effect on the drying wicket, taking 5 for 29. Barnes also bagged five victims as Australia were bowled out for 111. A measure of C.B.'s total commitment to the job in hand was his reaction when Charlie Macartney came close to giving Rhodes a catch off Barnes's bowling. Fry did a handstand in uncontrollable excitement!

At the close of the third day England were teetering precariously on 64 for 4, but at least their skipper was still there, undefeated on 17. The purpose of his dour struggle was revealed on the following day when he went on to complete an invaluable 79 in 225 minutes. England's dependence on C.B. was reflected in their swift collapse after he was dismissed with the total on 170. Hazlitt took five wickets for one run as 170 for 5 became 175 all out.

A target of more than 300 was always going to be too much for the Australians, who were shot out for just 65, Woolley again taking five wickets. The England side were heroes all in the eyes of the spectators, but, as Fry subsequently explained, they could not expect to have it both ways: 'When the crowd gathered round the pavilion and shouted for me I would not go on to the balcony, because I felt that the time for them to cheer was when I was walking out to bat as the captain of my side to try to win the match on a foul wicket. Ranji was in our dressing-room and he said to me, "Now, Charles, be your noble self." But I said, "This is not one of my noble days." '

The papers spoke of how Fry had vindicated himself and praised his 'batting masterpiece' to the heights, but they had been just as fickle as the fans. Before the game Fry's own form and his grasp of the art of captaincy had been roundly criticised—now he was genius incarnate.

CONTROVERSIES

It was hard to ignore Charles Fry at any stage in his life. Physically dominating and mentally arresting, he had to be the focal point in any gathering. Cricket supporters grew accustomed to his perpetual motion. In the early part of his career he was liable to wander away from his allotted base as a fielder: it was not intentional disobedience, simply the expression of a restless spirit. In time his perambulations were curbed and he contented himself with prescribing concentric circles and absent-mindedly plucking blades of grass, as if wrestling with deep philosophical questions.

As a batsman he was equally self-possessed, waltzing round the crease between balls and overs. It looked for all the world like posing, but he was so self-aware and such a keen student of movement that it became utterly natural for him to strut around masterfully, his head held contemptuously high and shoulders militarily tensed.

To some people it betokened arrogance–and it was not an altogether deceptive impression. C.B. was not only highly self-opinionated, but also low on tact, so it was inevitable that there would be flashpoints, both on and off the field. Three such examples are recounted here in some detail and the very fact that they happened at the beginning, in the middle, and towards the end of his career in first-class cricket demonstrates that experience taught him very little about hiding his feelings.

The first incident came when C.B. was barely out of nappies in terms of cricketing know-how, in a game for Sussex against Gloucestershire over the 1894 August Bank Holiday. It was his first sight of the legendary W.G. Grace, either as a spectator or an opponent, but this landmark was superseded by the bizarre events of the first day.

A crowd of around 3,000, many of whom had travelled a considerable distance to attend the match at Bristol, obviously hoped for some engaging cricket, but a prompt start was ruled out by overnight rain. The sun was shining brightly, however, and the multitude grew restless. The players on both side sensed the tension and several of them, including Fry, decided to stage an impromptu football match, emerging from the pavilion with their trouser legs rolled up.

This magnanimous gesture did not have the intended result, as the feeling among the crowd was that if football was possible so was cricket; and it was cricket they had paid to watch. According to Gilbert Jessop, 'They were orderly until Charles Fry "cocked a snook" at them.' This may or may not have been the prime catalyst, but the crowd were sufficiently moved to augment their clamouring with a show of strength, cries of 'play the game' having met with no response from umpires or players.

A section of the crowd showed their disgust by turning their attentions on the square. Gilbert Jessop said they 'raided a portion of the playing area, devoting considerable attention to one portion which Spry, the astute groundsman, had hastily roped in. The sight of that twenty yards of turf was not good to look upon when the game was resumed next morning, but as Spry had "laid the crowd a brick" by roping in an unused portion of the square, the real wicket remained unscathed.'

The unfortunate players who were out on the ground when the tumult arose were mobbed and harangued. They beat a hasty retreat to the pavilion, which was then surrounded by around 2,000 spectators who had no intention of letting the cricketers leave without making their feelings well and truly known. The two captains, W.G. Grace and Billy Murdoch, appealed for calm from the comparative safety of the pavilion, but even the local demi-god could not alter the mood of the crowd. Wallis Myers reflected a side of Fry's character which was more sensitive to the grievances of the paying public, writing in *The Man and his Methods*: 'For several hours the teams were kept prisoners. Eventually, on Fry and Brann essaying to steal away unawares, the crowd surrounded them and held them up. Blows were threatened, and only the good sense of the two amateurs prevented further disorder.' Grace and Murdoch even needed police protection to enable them to reach the waiting cab.

In the cold light of day newspapers reflected gravely on the anarchic scenes at Bristol – it was certainly no help that spectators were still being let into the ground after it had become fairly clear that there would be little if any play. *The Times* said: 'The public had before been informed that they would receive passes for admission to the ground today. It was something of a pity, however, that the gates were not sooner closed. Yet this was no excuse for the disgraceful behaviour of the people and the wilful damage done to the turf.'

C.B. could have been none too shaken by the experiences of that curious day for he made his maiden century for Sussex when play resumed. His innings of 109 took three hours and enabled Sussex to make 302. The other notable feature of the day's play was the bowling of C.L. Townsend, still at Clifton College and making his debut for Gloucestershire. He took 6 for 125, announcing an illustrious career with both his county and England.

The remainder of this match was the domain of F.H. Parris, who enjoyed himself immensely on a beast of a drying wicket, taking 15 for 98 on the third day as Gloucestershire were dismissed for 121 and 77.

Charles Fry enjoyed something approaching all-round status as a cricketer at the start of his career, although he was not taken seriously as a bowler until his final couple of years at Repton. However, he fell foul of an energetic campaign to rid the game of 'chuckers' at the end of the 1890s and the start of the twentieth century. He pleaded his innocence with typical vigour and in-genuity, but there was a powerful lobby prepared to dispute his right to bowl. 'That his action was curious,' said Wallis Myers, 'not to say unorthodox, may be at once admitted; no man bending his arm and ducking his head as he did, and nearly sitting down on his left knee at the time of delivery, could fail to excite comment.'

This eccentric style, fair or not, succeeded in baffling some experienced and capable batsmen, who found it difficult to pick up the ball in flight and judge its pace off the wicket. He was never a prolific wicket-taker, but dangerous enough on one occasion to grab eight wickets for the Gentlemen against the Players at the Oval in 1895 and to perform the hat-trick for Oxford against the MCC the previous year.

The man most closely identified with the no-balling of Fry and the whole crusade against unfair bowling was the Australian umpire, Jim Phillips. His determination first became apparent in the 1897–8 season in Australia, when he twice called the speedy Ernest Jones, the second occasion being the Second Test between Australia and England.

His reputation was quickly forged and when Phillips came over for the 1898 season in England there were strong rumours that he had his sights set squarely on C.B. Ironically, it was not Jim Phillips, but one of his disciples, W.A.J. West, who first no-balled Fry for throwing. West, the man who had dismissed Fry during his one and only game for Surrey back in 1891, took his stand for Sussex's game with Nottinghamshire at Trent Bridge during the middle of June.

There was an element of surprise about West's pronouncement, but there was nothing unexpected about Phillips's verdict a week later when Oxford University went down to Hove to take on Sussex. The county side were fully aware of the significance of Phillips standing in this match and Billy Murdoch did nothing to avoid the imminent confrontation. Sussex totalled 301 on the opening day, Charles Fry making 62, and when Oxford batted Murdoch brought him on to bowl at Phillips's end (bowlers could then be no-balled by either umpire). The outcome was predictable: Fry was immediately no-balled twice and had to complete his single over with a mixture of slow round-arm and overarm deliveries.

C.B. was convinced that Phillips had prejudged the issue – and incorrectly at that. In *Life Worth Living* he revealed an ingenious plot which he hatched to expose the Australian's decision. He claimed that he encased his right elbow in splints and bandages, then buttoned his sleeve to the wrist, before going out to field in Oxford's second innings. Fry's recollection was that Murdoch refused to co-operate with the devious plot and wouldn't put him on to bowl. 'Too good a game to spoil, old boy,' he was supposed to have told C.B. However, the record books show that Fry delivered four overs in the University's second innings and was not no-balled.

Judging by this choice piece of verse in *Cricket*, C.B. escaped further punishment by bowling lobs in the second innings:

> Charles B Fry
> Was no-balled at Brigh-
> ton by Phillips, the umpire for throwing:
> When Oxford went in,
> With two hundred to win,
> Charles tried lobs, his true penitence showing.

There was enduring mutual distrust between Fry and Phillips. They were obviously very different as people, but they shared a common determination and an unshakeable belief in right being on their respective sides.

They clashed again during the Second Test between England and Australia at Lord's in 1905. Fry had played with great application to make 73 and seemed well set for his first century against the old enemy when Phillips gave him out caught at the wicket. Fry maintained that his bat had struck the toe of his boot— a foot away from the ball. He claimed that he succeeded in concealing his annoyance at the time, but sought an explanation from Phillips after the match. Phillips said he definitely heard a click, but Fry wondered, with customary mischief, whether he had heard the slamming of a door in the pavilion.

C.B.'s final infringement in 1898 was at Lord's in the middle of July. The match against Middlesex began memorably for Fry as he carried his bat for 104 in Sussex's first innings total of 197, but a third umpire, Sherwin, confirmed the opinions of Phillips and West by no-balling Fry in Middlesex's second innings. The misery was prolonged as C.B. was bowled for nought by Albert Trott.

Sydney Pardon, the editor of *Wisden*, was not slow to endorse the umpires' stand. In the 1899 edition he referred to the no-balling of Fry as 'long-delayed justice' and went on: 'As a matter of a fact he ought never, after his caricature of bowling in the MCC and Oxford match at Lord's in 1892, to have been allowed to bowl at all.' *Wisden* had carried a similar message in 1895: 'A very well-known cricketer, who does not wish his name to appear, writes:- "It is rather a difficult matter and I personally got such a real sickener from the performance of the committee of the MCC in allowing Fry to bowl in the 'Varsity match of 1892 that I there and then made up my mind that throwing must not be allowed." '

It was generally recognised that C.B. made efforts to adopt a more acceptable action after his first year at Oxford, but there was still a host of critics. He did little bowling after he had been pulled up short in 1898, but his name still loomed large in the mounting controversy about throwing. However, it was not until he had been no-balled for the last time, in 1900, that county captains began to put their heads together in the search for a united stand against throwing. W.A.J. West was again the dissenting umpire as Sussex were put to the sword by Gloucestershire's human typhoon, Gilbert Jessop. Interestingly, C.B. was no-balled in his first spell, but returned for a second helping without again incurring West's displeasure. The bowler who dismissed Fry for nought in Sussex's first innings, the slow left-armer, A. Paish, was himself no-balled for throwing three years later.

Sydney Pardon took the mature view that it was unnecessary to feel excessive sympathy for Fry. His batting had always been the more significant part of his cricketing make-up and his astonishing success in 1901 seemed to suggest that he benefited as a batsman from being spared the additional responsibility. On the other hand it was galling for someone who prided himself on all-round ability to be virtually barred from bowling.

At the end of 1900 the county captains met and decided on united action to stamp out unfair bowling. Lancashire asked for an opinion on their fast bowler, Arthur Mold, and said he would not be bowled again if his action was considered to be unfair. The captains unanimously condemned Mold as a chucker, but felt obliged to draw up a list of bowlers whom they regarded as throwers. Fry was quoted as one of the prime offenders and he and another suspect, Captain Hedley, were known as Captain Chuckley and Mr Shy!

Ranji, Fry's Sussex captain, was unhappy with the 'blacklist', as *The Times* reported at the start of 1901: 'Last season he (Ranji) had asked several of his brother captains if Mr Fry threw. They had replied "No." Mr Fry had asked several of them himself, and had got a favourable reply. It seemed strange, if the account was true, that they should have unanimously voted against him. As he himself certainly did not consider that Mr Fry threw, he should certainly bowl him if he thought it was to the interest of his side to put him on. He was not a party to that agreement, and his club never empowered him to be a party to it.' Ranji found it difficult to decide on C.B.'s action. On occasions he gave him a public vote of confidence, but he was also quoted as saying that he thought his colleague was a chucker.

The controversy about throwing reached fever pitch in the 1901 season when Mold was no-balled sixteen times by Jim Phillips at Old Trafford. His action was not challenged in the second innings, but the damage had been done and he never played in a first-class match again. Phillips was moved to issue a manifesto, published in the *Daily Telegraph*, which said he was 'determined to apply Law 48 with a severity that may occasionally do injustice to a bowler'. Phillips may have been regarded in some circles as over-zealous and self-righteous, but there was undeniable courage in his convictions and his determined stand was followed by a lengthy period in which there was very little suspicion about illegal bowling.

Fry's opportunistic critics found high-powered ammunition when Hampshire played Kent during Canterbury week in 1911. Kent had won the County Championship in the previous two seasons and were poised to repeat their success that year. C.B. scored two centuries in the match, the fifth and final time in his career that he achieved the feat, but it was not for this notable milestone that the game was remembered.

Hampshire batted first, and with Fry in sparkling form they moved serenely through the opening session, scoring at the highly respectable rate of 80 an hour. This was not enough to appease the Kent supporters, however, who were now so unaccustomed to obstacles being put in the way of their heroes that they booed Fry, more in frustration than in comment on the quality of his batting. It was not long after lunch when Fry completed his century and he was eventually stumped on 123. Hampshire were dismissed for 332 and Kent replied with 324, inspired by a hundred from Frank Woolley.

The flashpoint came at the end of the second day's play, by which time Fry, although not playing as fluently as in the first innings, was firmly entrenched and approaching another half-century. The final over of the day was bowled by the slow left-armer, Colin Blythe, whose prodigious feats had been a crucial factor in Kent's run of success. The *Kentish Gazette and Canterbury Press* reported those fateful final balls of the day like this:

Blythe tried Fry with two full pitches, which the batsman despatched for a two and a four. Some diversion was caused by Fry appealing to the umpire on the ground that he could not see the ball because the sun was in his eyes. The umpire requested Blythe to bowl on the off for the remainder of the over, but the Kent skipper (E.W. Dillon), so it was stated, told Blythe to bowl as he liked. The Old Oxonian declined to continue, but after some demur he decided to do so. Blythe simply truckled up the remaining balls on the off, so that the batsman might be in no danger of losing his wicket. On his return to the Pavilion Fry was the recipient of a somewhat hostile demonstration, a section of the crowd indulging in derisive cheers and groans.

The Times seemed to be referring to a bereavement in speaking of 'one of those unfortunate incidents which occasionally happen at cricket'. The severe tone was maintained as the report concluded: 'Whatever may be thought of the tactics of Blythe in bowling the full pitches, they are within the rules of the game. No doubt it was unfortunate that Mr Fry should have showed his displeasure so obviously, but for those who jeered there was no excuse whatsoever. They surely had no right to show their feelings in the matter. It is greatly to be deplored that anything should have occurred, especially at Canterbury, to detract one whit from the dignity of the game.'

On returning to the pavilion Fry was heard to respond to his detractors with a defiant, 'Very well. I shall now bat all day tomorrow.' He didn't quite achieve that, but his scrappy innings of 112, prolonged significantly by three dropped catches, both ensured that Kent were unable to force a victory and ultimately denied them a hat-trick of championships.

Curiously, it was Fry who bore the brunt of the newspapers' invective. It seemed to be accepted that Blythe had bowled the full tosses intentionally, but it was C.B.'s want of sportsmanship which was called into question rather than the dubious motives of the bowler, an epileptic who was killed six years later in the First World War. It was even claimed in one particularly hysterical report that Fry had challenged one raucous spectator to an impromptu boxing match behind the pavilion. It was also pointed out, with rather more justification, that similar tactics had been used before by bowlers without adverse comment.

The Old Stagers translated the confrontation between Fry and Blythe into a sketch for Canterbury theatregoers. In this a batsman was bowled by a ball delivered while the limelight was shining into the eyes of the striker. The batsman objected and was given a packet of Fry's chocolate to soothe him and keep him quiet.

But C.B. didn't share the audience's amusement. He was understandably peeved by the unbalanced reports which had appeared in newspapers and was grateful to J.A.H. Catton, his one-time editor on *Athletic News*, who saw the incident in a less myopic light. Fry wrote him a letter of thanks which was reproduced in Catton's *Wickets and Goals*. In it he said:

> The truth is a considerable number of the Kent players are so uplifted with the success of the Kent XI that they have arrived at a pitch of vicarious pride which admits of no merit or dessert outside the Kent players: and they don't like the Kent bowling collared.
>
> The crowd booed me on the first day of the match when Bowell and I were scoring eighty runs or so an hour . . . for slow play! Lord Harris endeavoured to stop it. Of course I don't care a snap whether they boo or cheer, but I do not like my friends, whose opinion I value, to read garbled accounts, reflecting on my sportsmanship. And I do think the spectators on all county grounds should be encouraged to regard the visiting teams as the guests of the home club; to be treated as such. And by the way, I did not invite anyone to fight behind the pavilion. Some one got hold of a cock-and-bull story.

Incidentally, *The Times* man who watched the match appeared to see a different contest from that in which C.B. took part. This was his impression of the first day's play: 'There was a splendid attendance and the crowd was ready and willing to cheer both sides impartially and often . . . The large crowd, whether judges of cricket or not, must have appreciated his (Fry's) innings, and expressed their approval at the end of it with no uncertain voice.'

C.B. wrote a guest chapter in *Cricket Typhoon* by Keith Miller and R.S. Whitington in 1955. It was entitled 'Appointment with Speed' and in it Fry maintained, improbably, that Blythe's bowling on that fateful day ranked with the quickest deliveries he had ever had to face. During the intervening forty-four years the incident had shed much of its original acrimony, but C.B. still took delight in remembering that he had answered the tactics in the most appropriate manner by scoring a century.

CRISIS CALL

In times of crisis England cricket selectors have been apt to glance over their shoulders for geriatric salvation. Such was Charles Fry's lot in 1921: he was a sprightly forty-nine, but a buoyant England side would not have beckoned him back from semi-retirement into the Test arena. However, Johnny Douglas had led England in Australia the previous winter and returned with the stigma of an embarrassing 5–0 defeat.

C.B. was amazed to get a letter on his forty-ninth birthday from Harry Foster, one of the selectors, asking him about his form and wondering whether he would be prepared to take on the England captaincy again. He was not too enamoured of the idea of facing the hostile bowling of Gregory and McDonald, but he was understandably flattered and thought it would be more sensible to turn to him if England's fortunes continued to plummet.

Fry had played no first-class cricket in the 1919 season and in the summer of 1920 he restricted himself to two matches: the first was in aid of Phil Mead's benefit and then C.B. scored 137 and 57 against Nottinghamshire to show that he had not lost his old ability. When he made himself available for Hampshire's early games in the 1921 season rumours were rife about a dramatic England recall. He made little impression in the first couple of county games, but despite scores of 14 and 4 against Middlesex *The Times* reported that his footwork was still good and he appeared confident, adding that 'The failure of Commander Fry in the second innings was a great disappointment. It cannot, however, be put down either to advancing years or loss of activity. In the field he was quite fast, one brilliant piece of fielding at cover-point nearly costing Middlesex a wicket from a run-out.'

Innings of 96 and 45 against Kent appeared to tip the balance in Fry's favour, but injury then kept him out of the MCC game against the Australians and when, on 22 May, the first eight names were announced for the opening Test at Trent Bridge, C.B.'s was not among them. In the event England's gloomy sequence continued, again under Douglas's captaincy, and when Fry was again pressed by the England selectors he agreed to play in the Second Test at Lord's—as long as he made some runs against fast bowling in the meantime.

He was chosen for the Test side, but scores of 0 and 5 against his old bogey team, Lancashire, were hardly the ideal preparation, and on the eve of the Lord's game Harry Foster was obliged to release the following statement: 'Mr C.B. Fry has stated frankly that he is not satisfied with his present form and has asked to be allowed to stand down tomorrow. His acceptance of the invitation originally was subject to his being satisfied with his form at the time of the Test match.'

Fry's withdrawal from the side—and he was clearly worried about his decreasing mobility in the field as well as his doubtful batting form—opened the door for his county captain, Lionel Tennyson, who said in his autobiography, *Sticky Wickets*, that Fry 'had on his own responsibility and counting on his tremendous prestige travelled up from Southampton to interview the selectors and to impress upon them the fact that, in his opinion, I was the most likely bat available at the moment to knock fast bowlers off their length.' The selectors took Fry's advice and Tennyson justified the confidence shown in him by scoring 74 not out in the second innings, but it could not prevent another defeat and Johnny Douglas's seventh successive loss against the Australians demanded that another captain would have to be found.

Fry had an ideal opportunity to claim the leadership for the Third Test at Leeds because Hampshire were playing the Australians at Southampton in the middle of June. The *Southern Daily Echo* said prior to the game: 'C.B. in form against the Australians would be one of the best things which could happen for the county—and England—at this time of cricketing slump.' His answer was fairly conclusive: in two innings of 59 and 37 the tried and trusted technique was an effective barrier to the Australian fast bowlers and it was the leg breaks of Arthur Mailey which brought about his dismissal in both innings. The selectors would have been prepared to take a chance, but Fry injured a finger when catching Warren Bardsley and was forced to pull out of the firing line. The selectors then decided to throw their support behind Tennyson as captain, who was certainly not found wanting in terms of bravery. His left hand was badly injured while fielding, but he somehow managed to score 63 against the formidable Australian attack, playing with just his right hand.

The comparative success of his 'protégé' convinced C.B. that he could now move off centre-stage, although naturally with mixed feelings. It was in 1921, then, that his first-class career ended. But the story of how he was recalled to the England captaincy at the age of forty-nine would be vigorously related in his old age. At the time, intense pride in his performance was the prime consideration in his decision. He knew it had to be more than reputation which gave him the right to lead England out against the Australians once again.

12

SOCCER STAR

In the 1980s the Corinthian spirit seems a remarkably remote concept. Yet less than 100 years ago the cream of English amateur footballers played the game with true regard for gentlemanly conduct. The Corinthians were born in 1882, the brainchild of N.A. 'Pa' Jackson, who was assistant secretary of the Football Association. In the light of England's dismal record against Scotland in the previous few seasons he wanted to get the top amateurs together for a few matches each season. Tours were an integral part of the Corinthians' existence and at Christmas and Easter they could be confident of summoning up their finest troops to take on the best professional sides both north and south of the English border.

Charles Fry was enlisted for the glittering circus when he went up to Oxford. He had turned out for the Casuals, later to be amalgamated with the Corinthians, since his days at Repton, but Jackson's band of all-stars were on a different plane. They eschewed all competitive football and their behaviour was expected to be exemplary. A code of conduct was imposed on their players which not only demanded great self-discipline but also left them vulnerable to jealous jibes.

It was not easy for someone as self-opinionated as C.B. to remain tight-lipped when his Corinthian principles were being offended. In October 1900 he confided to readers of *The Captain* that all was not wholesome in the world of professional football:

Formerly many of the northern and midland players indulged only too frequently in tripping and pushing and other illegalities. There were always some who were scrupulously fair, but I fear they were in the minority. I remember being extremely annoyed and exasperated by their tricks: they seemed to me to trip you and shove you as a matter of course, and to reckon on taking every possible advantage, however illegal. But I do not now think so badly of them as I did then. The truth is, they played the game in a totally different manner from we southerners; their standard was different. They all played, as it were, 'on the cross'; it was a recognised thing that it did not matter what they did as long as the referee did not see, and they expected everyone to play the same game. If you and I played a game of écarte on the understanding that we would try to cheat, cheating would be part of our game and not really cheating at all. Well, the northern 'pro,' as a rule, played football that way. I am bound to say that it was not right or good for the game. Many of the best teams played a very fair game; the worst offenders were the second and third raters, who were atrocious. Still, I remember once, in a match against Sunderland, the then centre forward made a bracket of his forearms and carried the ball through the goal from a scramble just in front. I told him in round terms that he was not an honourable man. He looked at me in contempt for a moment, then jerked his thumb towards the fat and distant referee, and remarked: 'Ya daftie, yon could na' see.' It was being found out that mattered—the Spartan code of honour, in fact. And the spectators encouraged this sort of thing; nothing pleased them so much as a successful trip—they shouted with laughter at us slow-witted loons who did not know the game as played up north.

Fry's nerve and his willingness to stand up and be counted in the face of discouraging odds were awe-inspiring. He resembled a moralist warning Al Capone about the evils of corruption when he wrote an article on the illegalities of football for the *Strand Magazine* in January 1903. Enlisting Southampton colleagues for pictorial explanations he worked his way through all the sordid tricks of the trade, including the calf-kick—'a relic of barbarism'—the hook-foot trip and the artistic snick-trip.

The Corinthians side of which C.B. became a regular member in his first year at Oxford was not quite as strong as that of a few seasons earlier, but formidable nonetheless. Fry's all-round qualities were at a premium when the Corinthians challenged the Barbarians to a tournament in 1892. Soccer, rugby, cricket and athletics made up the competition.

The Corinthians proved too strong for their opponents at the round ball game, winning by the comprehensive margin of 6–1, but the logic of that result was not matched by the rugby game, where the Corinthians raised a few eyebrows by winning 16–13, taking advantage of the hard ground to play the ball with the feet whenever possible. Fry said that 'the match created much more than a mild sensation', but judging by contemporary accounts the result owed considerably to the charitable attitude of the Barbarians.

The athletic events also went the Corinthians' way and it was no surprise that Charles Fry played a significant part in this victory. He won both the high jump and long jump, but his distance of 21 feet 9½ inches in the latter was rather disappointing considering he had set his English record of 23 feet 5 inches at the Queen's Club the previous day.

Success in the soccer, rugby and athletics gave the Corinthians an unassailable lead in this forerunner to the modern Superstars competition, but the cricket match was still to be played (without Fry in attendance) and resulted in a win for the Barbarians.

There were more important challenges for the Corinthians on the soccer field and they particularly relished their New Year tours of Scotland, with matches against Queen's Park, the top Scottish amateur side, topping the bill.

Fry wrote the story of the Corinthians for one of the early editions of his magazine and related an anecdote from a game with Bolton Wanderers (although in *Life Worth Living* he said that it happened at Hampden Park when the Corinthians were playing Queen's Park). Fry's full back partner was the heavyweight F.R. Pelly, who preceded C.B. on to the field. A spectator pointed to Pelly and said to his neighbour, 'That's the cove who jumped 23ft 6ins.' 'Is he then?' was the reply. 'What a 'ole he must ha' made in the floor!'

The Corinthians' games against the leading professional teams were intrinsically interesting, but they were given additional purpose by the inauguration of the Sheriff of London's Shield, initially known as the Dewar Shield after Sir Thomas Dewar. The intention was to pitch in the top professional side of the year against the top amateurs. The first of these matches was played in 1898, with the Corinthians meeting Sheffield United at Crystal Palace. The game ended in a 0–0 draw, with *The Field* commenting: 'Fry displayed a great deal of speed and activity.' The teams agreed to replay a week later, but they were again evenly matched, drawing 1–1, and the Shield was shared.

Queen's Park received the amateur vote in 1899, but the following year saw the Corinthians take on Aston Villa in what was not only an enervating contest but a personal triumph for Charles Fry. He defended brilliantly and his performance was an eye-opener for critics who had doubted his reliability. The Corinthians were lucky enough to have both G.O. Smith and R.E. 'Tip' Foster in the forward line, and won 2–1. Smith, who followed Fry into the soccer and cricket sides at Oxford, ranks among the very best centre-forwards in the history of the game, while the double international Foster was another splendid all-rounder.

The teams in opposition a year later were exactly the same, but although C.B. again defended stoutly Villa won 1–0. Then in 1902 Tottenham Hotspur overwhelmed the Corinthians in the second half to pull off a 5–2 victory.

Fry felt that there was an absurdly biased attitude to the true merits of the Corinthians. He wrote in *Athletic News* in November 1900: 'I wonder why it is that so many papers and periodicals which devote attention and space to football news and criticism are so deeply impressed with the *a priori* superiority of the professional players.' Reflecting on when the Corinthians took on professional teams at the Queen's Club he added, 'No matter how well the Corinthians may play, they are never the better side.'

This was obviously one of the reasons why Fry attached himself to the professional game at the end of 1900. Paradoxically, in the light of his views about competitive cricket, he was quite content to embrace the vulgar cut-and-thrust of league and cup football. The Dewar Shield matches for the Corinthians had given him a taste of this and when Southampton, the leading lights in the Southern League, offered him the chance to play for them he was keen to accept the challenge. His home was just four miles away from Southampton and there was the added incentive of pursuing full international caps for England: the game against Canada in 1891 did not merit that status.

On 17 November 1900 the Corinthians beat Southampton 3–1 in a friendly, with Fry giving his usual impression of perpetual motion at right back for the amateurs. It was not the first time that he had played in a game between the two sides, but this fixture proved more significant as the forerunner to him signing forms for Southampton in the middle of December. The *Football Echo and Sports Gazette* glowed with the knowledge that C.B. would turn out for the Saints whenever his services were required: 'A player of Fry's stamp would be a distinct gain for the best club in the kingdom. He is, without doubt, the finest amateur back playing, a player who shines conspicuously in a constellation of football stars.'

He was not yet the complete footballer, for when he joined Southampton he had not mastered the art of heading the ball. However, there was the traditional Fry solution of practice, more practice and even more practice. The training ground was his garden at home: he would get his wife to throw the ball up for him and thousands of headers and headaches later the perfectionist was finally satisfied that he could meet the ball properly, head it with suitable velocity and in the intended direction.

When C.B. was on song he was an inspirational sight and everything that the hero-worshippers expected, dispossessing the man he was marking, distributing with precision and then covering for more uncertain colleagues. At his most energetic he could give the uncanny impression of taking on the opposition single-handed. But occasionally there were bad days when he mistimed tackles, when he exceeded his responsibilities and attempted to convert a team game into an individual quest for glory. He had little appetite for the physical excesses of football and a harsh tackle or a piece of misjudgment was liable to sap his confidence for the remainder of a match.

There were no qualms about his debut for Southampton against Tottenham Hotspur on Boxing Day 1900. People talked about the finest display ever seen by a full back at The Dell, Southampton's ground. The *Football Echo* said: 'The famous amateur's screw-kicking under difficulties was simply astonishing. When he had an attack of cramp in the closing stages of the game the spectators accorded him a spontaneous compliment by singing "For he's a jolly good fellow." '

Despite Fry's brilliance Southampton lost that game 3–1, but, ironically, a 3–2 victory over West Ham was achieved without great heroics from C.B. The win established Southampton's position as leaders of the Southern League table. In previous years they had shown admirable consistency, winning the title three times and coming third on three occasions between 1894 and 1900.

Fry's thunderous start with the club immediately put him in line for international honours, but Southampton suffered a major disappointment when they were knocked out of the FA Cup by Everton. They led 1–0 at half-time, but the Lancashire side dominated the latter part of the match and when Fry, who had played well up to then, ricked his knee, Southampton sensed that it was not going to be their day.

Nevertheless, C.B. was chosen for the South team to take on the North in the trial match and was then selected to play for England against Ireland on March 9. There were a couple of interesting sidelines to the game: it was to be played at Southampton, the first international to take place at The Dell; and on the same day the Saints were due to meet the Corinthians. Fry experienced a brief crisis of loyalties, but sensibly decided that his first obligation was to his country. In the meantime, however, he played twice for the Corinthians. He was re-acquainted with his amateur friends in their match with Sheffield Wednesday, then a week later turned out in the Sheriff of London's Shield match with Aston Villa.

The international should have been a joyous celebration of the pre-eminence of English football, but it was the original damp squid. Local interest had been heightened by the inclusion of two other Southampton heroes in the England side, goalkeeper Jack Robinson and outside right Arthur Turner, while the inside right was R.E. Foster. In just three months Fry and Robinson had built up a telepathic understanding. It was said that C.B. struck his back-passes with such ferocity that opposing strikers would have been happy to have claimed them as shots, but the assured Robinson fielded them with aplomb.

News of a stormy crossing for the Irish players hardly augured well for the big match, which was already projected as an embarrassingly one-sided affair. England led 1–0 at half-time, then added two more in the second half, but there was little attacking verve to please the enthusiastic crowd. There was understandable melancholy in the England camp afterwards, Charles Fry summing up the depressed mood of the players by saying that 'It was a very bad match. It was one of those games which, without any obvious reason, are aimless and vague and watery; nothing in the atmosphere of play to buck one up or incite one to effort . . . It was one of the least enjoyable games from a player's point of view that have ever fallen to my lot.' The end result was that Fry, who according to one source exhibited 'more spirit than coolness', was not retained for the game against Wales nine days later. This was a little harsh as the English performance against Ireland had reflected collective lethargy rather than individual frailties.

This also proved to be C.B.'s only opportunity to play football for England in maturity, but judging by the way he bounced back for Southampton the week after the international his resolve had not been weakened. A crucial Southern League match at Bristol City was the setting for one of his inspired performances. City were the major threat to the Saints' hopes of carrying off the title, but exemplary, disciplined defending by Fry was the main reason that the Southampton castle was not reduced to rubble. The *Football Echo* man at the match was left with the abiding memory of C.B., teeth clenched, tracking the tricky Bristol left-winger, Hugh Wilson, as though his life depended on it. The home side did manage to take the lead, but a late goal for Southampton maintained their breathing space at the top of the Southern League table, and, in retrospect, resulted in a two-point lead over City at the end of the season.

Fry's re-introduction to Southampton followers in the 1901–2 season came in the shape of their match with the Corinthians on 5 October. He slightly marred a superb display for the amateur giants with a mistake late in the game which contributed to Southampton's winner, but was happy to announce that he would be available for Southampton's game at Portsmouth on 12 October. It is interesting to note that Fry recognised his dual footballing allegiance by turning out for Southampton in the striped socks worn by the Corinthians!

It is also worth stating the obvious here by pointing out that amateurs owed nothing more than basic human loyalty to professional clubs. Fry, contrary to suggestions in his autobiography that he was regularly available for Southampton, had reached a stage in 1902 when he restricted himself almost exclusively to cup football, although this was partly due to illness during the Saints' highly successful run in the FA Cup. There were only a handful of amateurs playing for professional sides at this time and Fry could never have been classed as one of the boys at The Dell. His reputation earned him tremendous respect, even popularity, but he insisted on making his own travel arrangements for Southampton's away games.

This assessment is challenged, if not conclusively refuted, by Wallis Myers, who quoted the Southampton secretary E. Arnfield's description of Fry as 'a wonderfully good chum of all our professional players', and added himself:

It is not every amateur, especially an amateur of Fry's distinctive personality, who could throw in his lot with ten wage-earning professionals, and gain not only their esteem but their love; not every amateur who could so conduct himself on and off the field that differences of class and education created no barrier of reserve, or in any measure arrested social intercourse. If the Southampton team were proud of C.B. Fry the player, they were prouder still of C.B. Fry the sportsman. With both the officials and the team he was immensely popular, and the Southampton crowd, by virtue of his residence among them, took a great personal interest in his performances. Many times he invited the members of the team to Glenbourne Manor, until recently his Hampshire home—visits entirely free from patronage or ceremony—and many times when on tour with 'the Saints' he joined in their diversions and shared their pleasures.

He certainly started the 1901–2 season in fine style. According to the *Football Echo* C.B. 'performed prodigies' at Portsmouth and the paper saw fit to comment on his steady improvement since he had started playing for Southampton: 'C.B. Fry, when he joined Southampton, could not head a ball; now he can almost rival

George Molyneux in this respect, and by becoming proficient in this art, he has strengthened his claims for international honours.'

However, there was nothing for Southampton, Charles Fry or the jingoistic local paper to celebrate three weeks later as the Saints went down 4–3 at home to Portsmouth, who were destined to depose Southampton as Southern League champions. There was a curious incident during the game which proved a good deal more amusing to the crowd than to the unfortunate player who took the brunt of it. Jack Robinson came out to punch the ball clear, but his follow-through made contact with C.B.'s head. Judging by the distance the ball went this must have been quite a blow and Fry was dazed for some time afterwards. His blunder led to one of Portsmouth's goals and he never quite managed to recover his confidence or equilibrium.

Southampton got back to winning ways with a 2–0 victory at Luton on 9 November, but the headlines attracted by this game were concentrated on the supposedly modern phenomenon of hooliganism. The man in the middle of the incident, almost inevitably, was Charles Fry: the reports which followed the game are a revealing indication of the contradictory opinions expressed about this complex man. The *Football Echo*'s version went like this:

The personal damage sustained by the Southampton players pales before the hostile demonstration against C.B. Fry at the conclusion of the combat. Missiles were hurled at the famous athlete, and one, going straight for its mark, accidentally struck one of the Luton directors on the shoulder as he ranged up alongside 'C.B'. For a few minutes matters had an ugly appearance, but, fortunately, the mob were prevented from committing any act of personal violence. The root of the mischief was a duel between Colvin, the diminutive outside left of the Luton team, and Fry. The former, who had been carefully nursed by his comrades, found it a difficult matter to either circumvent or out-manoeuvre the old Oxonian, and then resorted to tripping. Once 'C.B.' almost turned a somer-sault over Colvin. This was more than human nature could stand without retaliation, and Fry promptly accepted the challenge with unsavoury results to Colvin who was bowled over twice. This roused the ire of a section of the crowd, who booed and hissed vigorously. The officials of both clubs heaved a sigh of relief when the amateur was safe in the dressing quarters again. This was a nice reception for one whose presence had been specially desired by the Luton Club and their supporters.

No doubt a fair proportion of the 4,000 crowd had paid for the exclusive privilege of seeing the legendary C.B. Fry, but in a world yet to sample the delights of radio and television there was an understandable tendency for sporting heroes to be expected to resemble gods in bearing, deeds and attitude. People seeing Fry for the first time were instantly assured that he was the genuine, all-conquering article, but the magnificence of his exploits could be exaggerated and his apparent aloofness could be misconstrued. Fry the footballer never quite matched the infallibility of Fry the in-form batsman, but there were always crowds, and less forgivably reporters, who were more than happy to hoot with derision when the aura of angelic genius was ruffled.

The *Luton News*, concerned that the local club's ground might be closed in response to the juvenile threats to Fry, placed the initial blame firmly in his court, saying:

> Fry, the man whom most people wanted to see, had been for some time losing his head, and the spectators soon lost their tempers . . . Of course, I know that the primary cause of all the unpleasantness on Saturday was Fry. This distinguished amateur, who has a reputation second to no man's, displayed anything but a sportsmanlike spirit, his feelings apparently first being ruffled by Colvin's hampering movements. Colvin is a little man and he quite upset the dignity of a big one.

The *Football Evening News* was so sycophantic as to harm Fry's case rather than assist it. They seemed to work on the dubious premise that someone as brilliant and dignified as C.B. could not possibly be infected with the same base instincts which had overtaken a section of the Luton crowd. Their sole relevant observation was this: 'Mr Fry bore himself bravely through it all, and of those who witnessed the outburst of churlishness and

Above Skipper's Hill near Mayfield in Sussex was home for Charles Fry in the first part of his life. The house is now a preparatory school.

Below Fry photographed in Repton School's XI, 1888 (standing, second from left). (*Courtesy Repton School*)

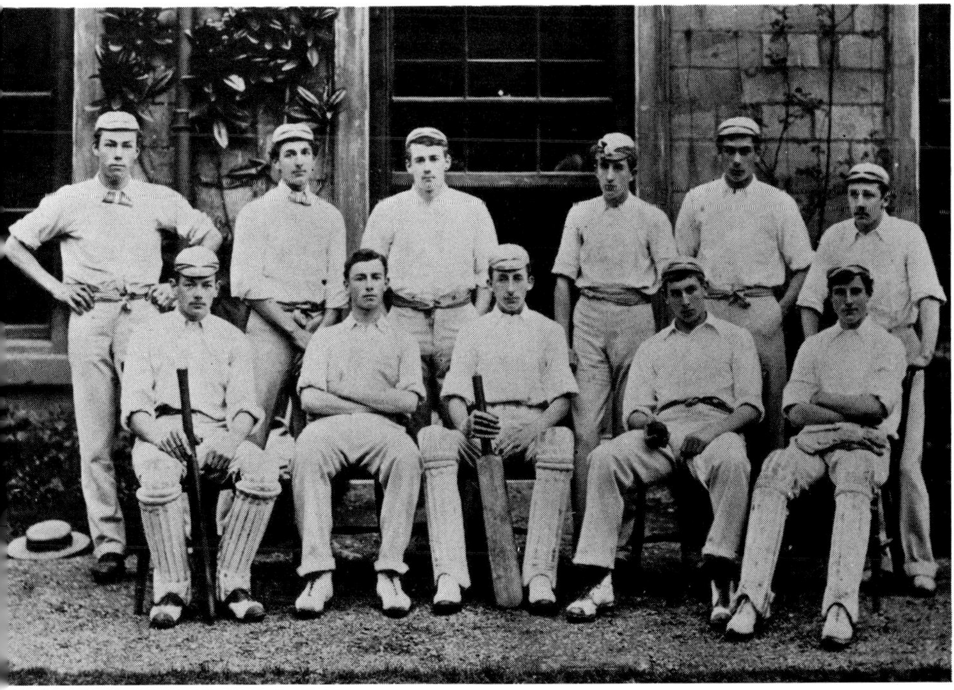

Above Fry the actor. He created great interest by appearing as the Prince of Morocco in Oxford University Dramatic Society's 1895 production of Shakespeare's Merchant of Venice.

Left Oxford Athletics—Fry captured by the cartoonist, Spy, in one of a series of athletic studies which appeared in the magazine *Vanity Fair*. (*BBC Hulton Picture Library*)

Below Fry's loyal service to Sussex was rewarded with the presentation of this magnificent Clement-Talbot car by county members in the spring of 1904.

Opposite Charles Fry was a magnificent on-side player and this photograph, taken when he was in his prime, shows his imperious manner at the crease. (*BBC Hulton Picture Library*)

Above The Prince of Wales, later Edward VIII, was the honoured guest at the *Mercury*'s speech day at the end of 1927. C.B. (in the naval uniform) follows behind as the Prince makes his inspection.

Below The magnificent collection of ship models gathered together by Charles Hoare and sold to the National Maritime Museum in 1929 for £30,000

Right Religion, and more particularly Catholicism, was the cornerstone of all teaching at the *Mercury*. This is the interior of the chapel.

Below Mrs Fry, complete in unflattering outfit, presides over another inspection at the *Mercury*. Her son Stephen (in plain clothes) is pictured behind.

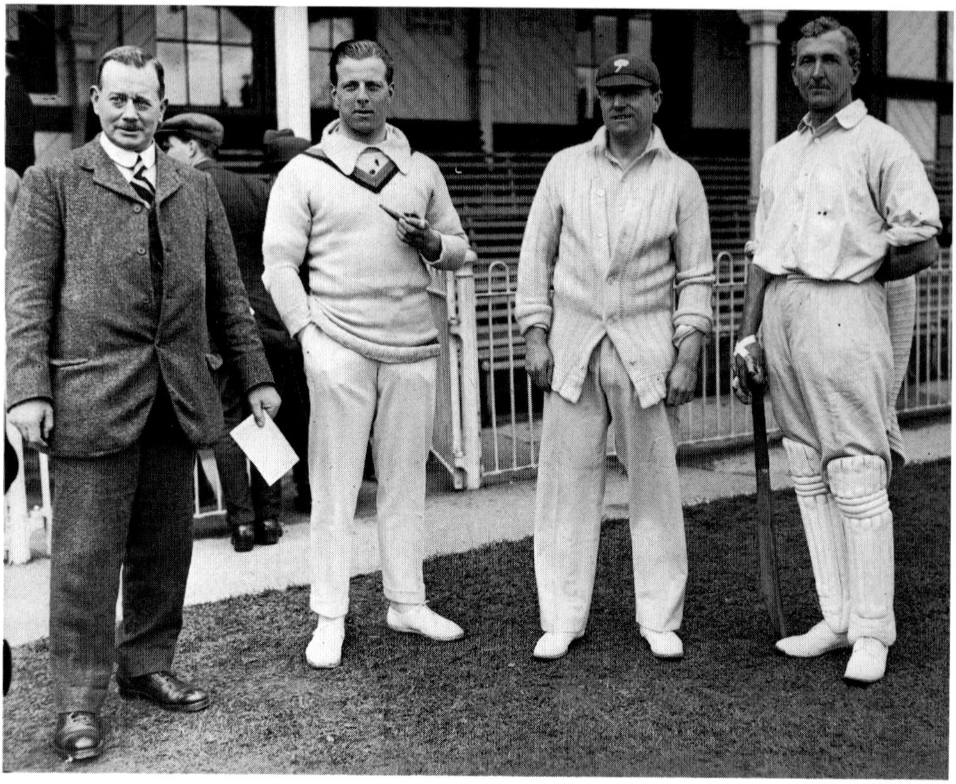

Above Hampshire colleagues Tennyson, Burton and Fry pictured in 1921. Lionel Lord Tennyson was the grandson of the poet, Alfred Lord Tennyson. (*BBC Hulton Picture Library*)

Right Fry and fellow Hampshire opener Brown stride out to the wicket in May 1921, with C.B., at the age of 49, keen to regain his England place. (*BBC Hulton Picture Library*)

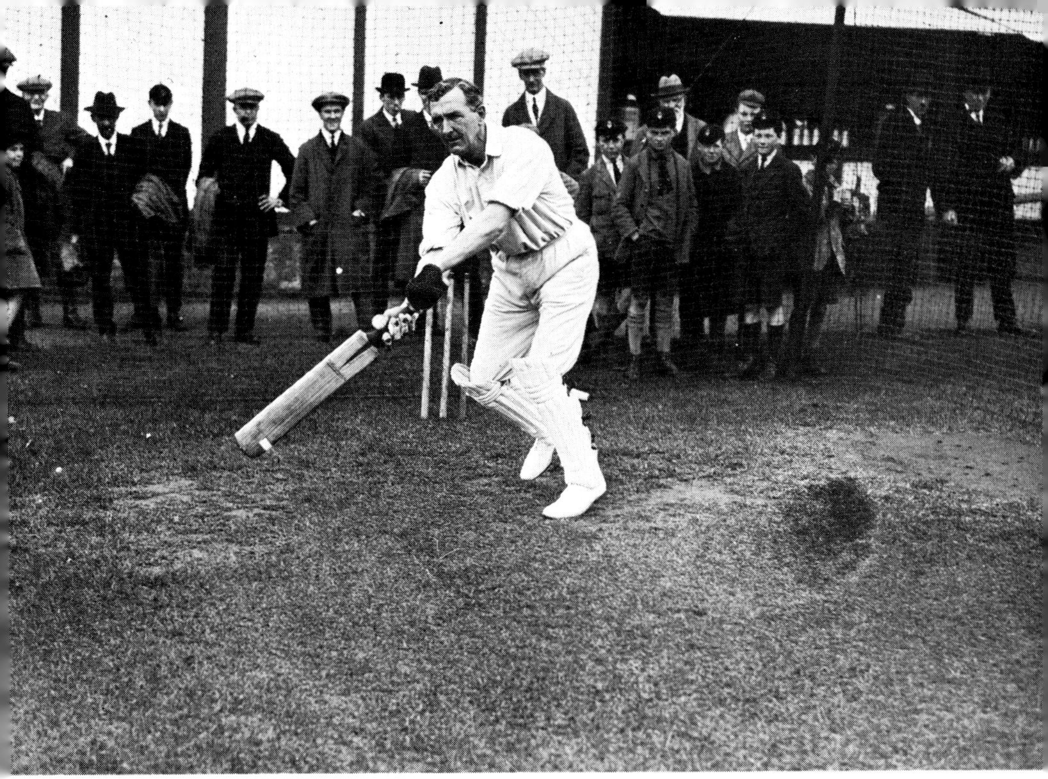

Above Even when practising in the nets C.B. Fry was a big draw. This was during his swansong season for Hampshire in 1921. (*BBC Hulton Picture Library*)

Below Fry rather lacked the common touch needed for successful electioneering, but here he is putting the point across during the campaign for the Banbury seat in 1923. (*BBC Hulton Picture Library*)

Right Exchange of gifts: C.B. marked his retirement from the training ship *Mercury* in 1950 by presenting the bat which produced six successive hundreds in 1901. The boys gave Fry an elegant statuette of himself. (*Press Association*)

Below The three ages of man: 82-year-old C.B. Fry launches himself into a cover drive at the County Ground, Southampton in 1954. Looking on are son Stephen and grandson Jonathan. (*Southern Newspapers PLC*)

rowdyism, he was perhaps the least affected.'

It was a verdict confirmed by the following week's edition of the *Luton News*, in which a letter from Fry to Mr C. Green, the Luton secretary, was quoted. After the game C.B. had received an official apology from the Luton directors, anxious to make it known that they were not condoning the behaviour of their fans. In his reply Fry said it was unnecessary for the directors to apologise since they could do nothing to control the spectators. He concluded: 'I am quite sure they were even more upset than anyone else at the annoyance to which I was subjected.'

Irrespective of the polarised accounts of Fry's dispute with Colvin and the aftermath, C.B. ultimately emerged with credit from a difficult situation and went on to play superbly for Southampton during the rest of November, reviving suggestions that he should be picked again for England the following spring. It was a train of thought which gathered popular momentum as Fry contributed immensely to Southampton's superb Cup run in 1902.

The formbook pointed to an early exit from the competition. The Saints were drawn to play Spurs, the Cup holders, in the first round. Tottenham had beaten Sheffield United after a replay in the 1901 final, their first match at Crystal Palace attracting an incredible 110,820 spectators. The game had added spice and significance because Spurs were attempting to break the stranglehold which teams from the Midlands and the North had had on the competition since 1882.

Spurs had home advantage for the original tie against Southampton on 25 January, but the Saints held them to a 1–1 draw and C.B. was nominated as the best player on the field. The replay finished in a 2–2 draw and it needed a third match, on neutral territory at Reading, to separate the sides. Southampton edged this one 2–1 to deny a Tottenham team which contained just two Englishmen, the remaining players being a selection of some of the best talent in the rest of Britain.

Fry recalled in *The Captain* that one Spurs supporter had given him a fair amount of stick in the first game: 'Why ain't yer playing cricket?' the fan had shouted to Fry. 'Why ain't yer playing for Sussex? Why ain't yer in Australia? Garn, why ain't yer brought G.O. Smith and Oakley and R.E. Foster; yer a cheat, Fry, that's what you are and no error.' C.B. told his young readers: 'But I wish him no evil. He was keen. He wanted the 'Spurs to win. So it was really a great compliment.'

Southampton also bagged notable scalps in the second round. Liverpool were the reigning league champions, but they proved no match for a buoyant Southampton team, who won 4–1. Fry enjoyed another excellent game, although it was his error which led to Liverpool's goal. In the quarter-finals the Saints were drawn to play at Bury, another highly demanding tie. This was a repeat of the 1900 Cup Final, which Bury had won 4–0, so there was a little revenge-seeking in the minds of the Southampton players. They got the desired result, winning 3–2, but it was an improbable victory in view of the way Bury dominated the match on their mud-heap of a pitch. The true quality of the Lancashire team was reflected in their 6–0 victory over Derby County in the final of 1903 FA Cup, which remains the biggest winning margin for a final in the history of the competition.

The critics were not over-impressed with Charles Fry's part in the game at Bury and there was a down-to-earth impression of his performance in the *Bury Times*: 'Fry, the amateur, to see whom no doubt large numbers of persons visited the ground, was as great a disappointment as the result of the match. Everyone expected to see one of the finest backs yet played on the Bury ground; but though he is speedy and recovers quickly, the fact that he has to recover so often bespeaks faulty play. Had a back without Fry's great name shown the same hesitancy and lack of tackling power, he would have been soundly condemned.'

Even the *Football Echo* saw fit to question C.B.'s approach to the game with these high-minded words: 'He gave one the impression of being a man who was a law unto himself on back play, and whose example it would be disastrous to copy.' There is little doubt that this one game, an isolated failure for Fry, significantly soured his chances of winning further England caps.

Southampton were back at Tottenham's ground for the semi-final, which saw them pitted against Nottingham Forest. Fry almost scored a rare goal with a powerful long-range shot in the first half, but it was Forest who took the lead after an hour. Southampton then justified C.B.'s assertion that they were not seen at their best until trailing by taking complete control in the last half hour and winding up impressive 3–1 winners.

There was a scare for Southampton during the build-up to the final against Sheffield United, the beaten finalists in 1901. Fry had succumbed to 'flu and was swiftly despatched to Brighton in the hope that the bracing sea air might buck him up. He was able to take his place in the side, although he was clearly not in tip-top condition, when the final was held at Crystal Palace on 19 April. The crowd of 76,914 paled in comparison with the attendance for the previous year's final, but now Spurs had broken the mould by winning the cup for the South the degree of interest was not quite as great.

There were three interesting characters in the Sheffield United team. Their goalkeeper was a mountainous figure, Billy Foulke, who managed to give opposing forwards the feeling that the goal he was defending had shrunk. He was 6 feet 2½ inches tall and weighed an astonishing 21 stone. Despite this apparent handicap he was, according to Fry, capable of great agility. At left half there was Ernest 'Nudger' Needham, sometimes referred to as football's answer to Ranji, while the centre forward was Alf Common, who three years later achieved immortality as the first footballer to be sold for £1,000 when he was transferred from Sunderland to Middlesbrough. Fry himself was the first amateur to appear in an FA Cup Final since the Wolves player, R. Topham, in 1893.

The two sides failed to produce a classic game—neither the first nor last time where a Cup Final has fallen victim of tension and over-enthusiastic tackling. Nevertheless, Southampton could count themselves very lucky to get another bite at the cherry. Common gave Sheffield the lead, but also went in for the sort of over-reaction which would, no doubt, nowadays earn him a charge of bringing the game into disrepute. He got so fed up with being barracked in the first half that he turned on a spectator whom he regarded as the prime offender, knocking his hat off. Common was advised that the incident could not be allowed to end in such an unsatisfactory manner and the second half was delayed while he sought out the offended spectator to shake his hand in apology.

Southampton's efforts at getting an equaliser grew increasingly desperate as the minutes ticked away, but in the final minute of the game their luck changed dramatically. The *Football Echo* said: 'In the last minute Wood netted amid a scene of undescribable enthusiasm. The referee, however, was doubtful, and consulted the linesman, after which he pointed to the centre.' It was a highly controversial goal, especially in view of the alleged confession by the goalscorer, Harry Wood, that he had been offside. No one had more cause to be delighted by the Saints' good fortune than Fry, whose failure to clear the ball from defence had led to Common's goal for United.

The other abiding memory of this first game between the sides was of the Sheffield supporters shouting 'What ho!' as Billy Foulke launched his bulky frame into a series of booming punts which soared deep into the Southampton half.

The replay, which was held a week later at the same venue, had more to offer the purists, even if it ended in disappointment for the Southampton players and fans. An early goal from Sheffield United, who had the advantage of a strong wind at their backs, set Southampton on their heels, but Fry was a week closer to full fitness now and they were denied further goals. In the second half only Foulke stood between Southampton and an equaliser, but they eventually levelled the scores through 'Jigger' Brown with fifteen minutes to go. It seemed as though Southampton were the side likely to score in the last period of the game, but United regained the lead through Barnes with five minutes left. C.B. almost turned into an unexpected goal-scoring hero for the Saints soon after, but he shot over the bar when well-placed: the Cup was on its way up north again.

When he had had time to digest the Cup defeat he wrote of United's never-say-die qualities and collective will which made them harder to beat than their technical merits would have suggested: 'Somehow you find that to beat them you have to play not as well as they do, nor a little better, but a great deal better. You cannot give a name to what it is in them that baulks you of your stride to victory, but it is there, some stumbling-block inherent in their play. Is it unitedness? Or is it Sheffieldness? Or a bit of both? Anyhow, it is there. There is a continual try about them from beginning to end, an unflagging resistance that becomes aggressive the instant you falter a step.'

Southampton were not accustomed to finishing football seasons as the bridesmaids, but they also had to concede the Southern League title to Portsmouth, finishing five points behind their south-coast neighbours.

Fry's career in professional football came to a rather quiet and undistinguished end during the 1902–3 season. Southampton, aware that C.B. would probably not be available for many of their league games, had brought in a new man, Robertson, to act as understudy. That was the intention, anyway, but due to a combination of circumstances he became something more than a stopgap. C.B., anxious for new scenery after fifteen years on defensive duties, made it clear that he would like to play at centre forward, just as he had done for Casuals on occasions while he was still at school. He started the season in his accustomed position of full back, giving a shaky performance in Southampton's 5–2 win at Reading, but he was eventually granted his wish by being included at centre forward, although he found it difficult to trap and control the ball. He was also none too delighted by the punishment which came his way from opposition defenders. The *Football Echo* said on 29 November: 'It is stated that C.B. Fry has discovered where the hardest knocks are received.–The question is being asked whether he will play centre forward again.' He then played against Spurs at inside left on 27 December, more in response to the team's needs than through personal preference, and again struggled.

It was then thought that C.B. would have little appetite for playing up front again, and Robertson had done so well as Fry's shadow at right back that he now kept the master out of the side on merit. The result, sadly, was a split with Southampton. Fry was still anxious to participate rather than spectate and he signed for Portsmouth in January 1903.

It was a brief and distinctly unsuccessful marriage. C.B. made his debut in Portsmouth's 4–0 win over Millwall on 20 January and was beginning to show his best form in Pompey's match with Bristol Rovers when the fates turned against him. He strained muscles in his left thigh and his leg had to be put in plaster. He was fit again in time for Portsmouth's FA Cup tie with Everton on 7 February, but this proved to be one of the unhappiest matches of his career. Portsmouth lost 5–0 and to make matters worse C.B. was laid out by a bad tackle. Writhing in agony, he had to leave the field, and although he later returned to the fray he was obviously still in great pain. His prime reason for joining Portsmouth had been to assist them in their Cup ventures and, with this avenue quickly closed off, Charles Fry's very brief career with Pompey came to a sad end. He had in fact already contemplated leaving the first-class game and his unhappy experiences at the start of 1903 merely confirmed his resolve.

13

IN HIS OWN WRITE

Charles Fry's first dalliance with journalism came while he was still at Oxford when he wrote for *Isis* on cricket, soccer and rugby under the various pen-names of Centurion, Spheroid and Pastor. The invitation to write about university sport was welcome as C.B. needed the income to supplement the minimal contribution from his father. The experience of writing about games in which he himself was involved proved useful: Fry managed to resist any temptation to glorify himself in these reports. However, it was not until three years after his departure from Oxford that C.B. began to think seriously about helping to finance his cricket career through journalism. It was not a path that had previously been trodden by sportsmen to any great extent.

He contributed an article to the first edition of the *Badminton Magazine* in August 1895, discussing wickets and groundsmen, and a year later his thoughts could be found in the *New Review* when he was asked to reflect on the 1896 season. Sham-amateurism was an obsession even then and Fry saw the whole controversy over payments to amateurs as injurious to the great game of cricket: 'As a class, the Professionals are hard-working and respectable. Many of them are most charming members of society. But to play a game from love of it is a different thing from making it a profession and a source of income. A strong leaven of Amateurism is absolutely necessary for the good of the game.' Fry's solution was to urge clubs to give amateurs 'liberal out-of-pocket expenses' so they would have no need to seek under-the-table payments.

At the same time Ranji's *Jubilee Book of Cricket*, which came out in 1897, was taking shape, and no secret was made of Fry's considerable contribution to this magnum opus. The two friends had the opportunity to mull over the shape of the book in the south of France where Ranji was recuperating after suffering from congestion of the lungs. The other key figure in the *Jubilee Book of Cricket* was A.J. Gaston, familiar to readers of the *Sussex Daily News* as 'Leather Hunter'.

The money Fry received for this venture enabled him to pay off the remainder of his Oxford debts and in July 1897 he wrote an article for the *Windsor Magazine* entitled 'Cricketers I Have Met'. It contained this lyrical description of cricket's unique qualities: 'Half the charm of playing cricket is that you knock up against men as they really are. There is something in the game that smothers pretence and affectation, and gives air to character. You cannot be a cricketer and stay in your shell, your inwardness must come out in your play . . . Cricket finds the truth more surely than wine does; so it speaks well for human kind that no pleasanter fellow is to be met than the typical cricketer.'

His observations on individual players were more significant in showing his talent for witty and imaginative description. The Surrey fast bowler Tom Richardson was 'something between a Pyrenean brigand and a smiling Neapolitan', while Richardson's county colleague Bobby Abel 'has the peculiar serious expression common to grooms and music-hall artists: one is never quite certain whether he has just lost a dear relative or is on the point of saying something very funny.' C.B.'s payment for such originality was a fifteen-guinea fee, handsome reward almost 100 years ago.

The real journalistic breakthrough came after he had ended his two-year stint at Charterhouse in the summer of 1898. The demands for his writing services had risen dramatically on the strength of the entertaining piece in the *Windsor Magazine* and he could now expect to generate a regular income through journalism.

He had no greater ally in this ambition than Sir George Newnes, whose plans for a new magazine 'for boys and old boys' presented Fry with a perfect outlet. The outcome was *The Captain* and when the editor, Warren Bell, wrote his editorial for the first edition in April 1899, he had clearly been delighted by C.B.'s opening contribution, an article entitled 'How to Train for Sports'. Bell, rejoicing in the pseudonym of 'The Old Fag', wrote: 'Here's the finest athlete Oxford ever turned out showing the soundness of his brain-piece by writing for No. 1. of *The Captain* as neat an article as you could wish to read. No padding–straightforward, nervous, clean English–thinks out an idea, expresses his views on it, and gets on to his next point in a way that all contributors to school magazines should mark and digest.'

Ten pounds accrued to Fry for his initial offering, but the fee was soon doubled as the reputation of *The Captain* ascended in concert with C.B.'s effortless grip on the young–and the not so young. Letters reached the offices of *The Captain* by the sackful and from all points of the globe. They sought Fry's advice on training, sporting equipment and health; yes, he was even something of a medical authority. He was given the honorary title of athletic editor, but his contributions were truly eclectic. Nevertheless, he stopped short of giving dangerously mischievous replies and was prepared to refer patients to higher authorities. He wrote to one correspondent in 1901: 'I fear you ought to consult a doctor, and ask him whether your heart is sound. Do this at once or you will regret it.'

The faithful lapped up any little piece of trivia about their hero, even revelations like this: 'My favourite drink between innings, it may amuse you to hear, is a mixture of soda water and stone ginger beer–ginger beer out of stone bottles, I mean.'

Rival concerns eyed the Newnes stable's number one asset covetously. It was rumoured that one publisher was willing to launch a new boy's magazine–if C.B. had been willing to desert *The Captain* and write exclusively for the new publication. Instead, Fry's links with *The Captain* were strengthened and Warren Bell was able to write at the start of 1902: 'By special arrangement, Mr C.B. Fry has undertaken to contribute to no magazine intended for boys or athletes except *The Captain*. Readers are requested to bear in mind that we have secured, especially for their benefit, the services of the first writer on athletics in the world.' Sir George Newnes agreed to pay Fry the handsome retainer of £800 a year. Under the agreement the *Strand Magazine*, another Newnes publication, also contained C.B.'s articles.

He weaved his spell in *The Captain* for almost six years, but was forced to quit in 1905 when *Fry's Magazine* was gathering momentum. He was succeeded as athletics editor by Pelham Warner. Fry made no secret of the satisfaction he had gained from *The Captain*.

It was, after all, a perfect amalgam of ideal and monetary reward to reach the young, to educate and to entertain. Hundreds of clubs wrote asking him to be their patron, president or vice-president. When he wasn't coming up with sparkling answers to readers' questions he was composing 'letters from a self-made batsman to his nephew'. They started 'Dear John' and were signed by Charles Burgess.

C.B. remembered his time on *The Captain* with no little pride: 'I consider that I wrote a lot of good articles for *The Captain* about how to do things; but though these were all right in their way, what I made my hit with was "Answers to Correspondents". I sometimes re-read the intelligent questions, real as well as imaginary, and the inspired answers with genuine appreciation. *The Captain* was, I suppose, the most successful boys' magazine that has ever appeared, and it lasted for many years; but it never persuaded advertisers that it was read by parents. Advertisers did not believe that boys are likely to buy such articles as soap and whisky. I have always thought that the disbelief of advertisers in the capacity of boys to absorb soap was the snag which eventually tripped up the career of *The Captain*.'

Volumes of *The Captain* are keenly sought to this day and not purely on the strength of C.B. Fry's contributions: a certain P.G. Wodehouse had some of his earliest work published in the magazine.

Fry also worked for the Manchester-based sports paper, *Athletic News*. J.J. Bentley was the editor when C.B. first worked for the paper, but he gave way to J.A.H. Catton. Fry recalled enjoying friendly relations with both men, but Jimmy Catton saw things a little differently. He was a diminutive figure and sensed a certain scorn on Fry's part when they first met. It was as if C.B. expected editors of sporting magazines to be prime physical specimens like himself.

Catton wrote in *Wickets and Goals*: 'As editor and contributor we got along very well—in spite of his scornful eyes. But one day Fry, who was fishing in the Orkney Islands, thought it right to telegraph the whole of his article at private rates. As the article might as well have been written and posted the previous Christmas we differed and parted.' C.B. confirmed the circumstances of the split, but maintained that it was Loch Boisdale in the Outer

Hebrides from where the article was telegraphed.

He could now afford the occasional setback. In 1899 he had put together the *Book of Cricket*, an assessment of the top players of the Golden Age. It started out as sixteen weekly instalments and was later made available in book form. A profile of Fry in *Tit-Bits* on 24 June 1899 made it clear that he had already established a considerable reputation in the world of newspapers and magazines: 'In addition to editing works of this sort (the *Book of Cricket*) and writing for magazines, Mr Fry's pen is constantly busy with notes and comments for London papers, country papers, and papers published "across the pond". He also describes the doings of our visitors for the Australian newspapers. Needless to say, every hour of his bustling day is occupied, and we may safely affirm that there is no man in the kingdom who combines work and play in a happier manner than the subject of our sketch.'

Lloyd's News and the *Westminster Gazette* also got in on the act, but Fry reached his largest public through the *Daily Express*, which started up in 1900 and quickly found a prominent place for his forthright views on cricket and football. He was loath to comment on his own triumphs with the bat, but his history-making sequence of six successive centuries at the end of the 1901 season demanded mention. It was manna from heaven for the *Express* as their resident superstar carried the world before him. For the most part, however, he was happier singing the praises of the unsung heroes of the county scene, especially his own colleagues at Sussex. He was also very much involved in getting stroke diagrams introduced to the paper.

A few years later he was taken on by the *Daily Chronicle*, and still he managed to be both participant and spectator. Wallis Myers wrote: 'This dual labour with bat and pen was exacting; to any man less endowed with energy and will-power it must have proved insupportable. Very often, if you broke into his hotel at ten o'clock, when other cricketers were at the play or the card-table, C.B. Fry, in a loose flannel shirt with the sleeves turned up, would be found in his bedroom turning out copy. A friend who went to dine with him after his fourth successive century in 1901 was astonished to find the hero of the hour expounding in the public lounge of the hotel the art of kicking an Association football. That night he did not retire until two o'clock.'

Between 1905 and 1906 Charles Fry and the Middlesex player George Beldam collaborated on two books which provide a graphic illustration of the individual qualities which made the Golden Age so special. The first was *Great Batsmen: Their Methods at a Glance*, complete with 600 photographs of all the finest players of the age. In the introduction C.B. was at pains to point out: 'Every picture is an actuality. The photographs from which the blocks were made were taken of the various batsmen while they were actually playing the various strokes, and every detail in the pictures is on the negative. Not a word of the text was written until finished prints of the photographs were studied and discussed.'

It was very much a labour of love for Beldam, who was a true pioneer in taking action photographs of sportsmen. The co-operation from players and counties was wholehearted even if the process baffled some of them. Fry wrote, 'When one kindly secretary inquired how long each exposure took and heard one-thousandth of a second, he remarked, "Oh well, then, you'll soon be through with our eleven–about one-hundredth of a second for the whole team." '

The first part of the book consisted of picture sequences of selected players, not because of their intrinsic quality but on the strength of the completeness of the portfolios. That was C.B.'s claim, anyway, but with W.G. Grace, Ranjitsinhji, Victor Trumper and Fry himself as the first four under the microscope there was just a hint of meritocracy.

Fry's most memorable contribution to *Great Batsmen* is in his precise summation of players' talents. This of Ranji–'When he is playing his strokes it is scarcely too much to say that his fingers play up and down the handle like a violin player on the strings of his instrument.' Of Trumper–'He has no style and yet he is all style.' And of Jessop–'The batsmen who does nearly everything a batsman ought not to do–with consummate success.'

Two of the photographs, of Ranji and Trumper jumping out to drive, have been used frequently in posthumous tribute, but there is a less well-known picture of Fry himself which truly reveals the all-round sportsman. He has stepped down the wicket to play an off-drive and the completion of the stroke resembles a perfect full follow-through to a golf shot.

The critics were well pleased with *Great Batsmen*. The *Sporting*

Life said: 'Of its kind the book is a masterpiece; it is the most precious gem that cricket literature has ever possessed.' The *Evening Standard* agreed, describing it as 'the best book about England's game yet published'.

The only qualm was about conflicting visual advice, a question of doctors disagreeing in practice even if they agreed in theory. When *Great Bowlers and Fielders* appeared a year later, Fry wrote: 'We trust it will not be brought up against the present book as a fault that it shows how very differently various bowlers grip the ball and swing their arms in action of delivering it: for the main idea of the book is to set forth such differences.'

The impression of movement in the bowling action was far harder for George Beldam to convey, but the 464 plates were mostly informative. Previous 'action' pictures were more reminiscent of stationary bowlers trying to assist batsmen with a line of vision to the sightscreen. The book was given added spice by the thoughts of F.R. Spofforth (*Great Bowlers* was dedicated to 'The Demon') on quick bowling, B.J.T. Bosanquet and R.O. Schwarz on the art of the googly, and Gilbert Jessop on fielding.

Both *Great Batsmen* and *Great Bowlers* are in great demand today, fetching £70 or more at auctions. It is hardly surprising when one considers that Beldam's photographs in the two books form the most complete pictorial record of the legendary greats of the Golden Age.

C.B. was not restricted to technical studies of cricket and when the serious Achilles tendon injury put him out of action in 1906, he and his wife decided to try their hands at a spot of fiction. The result was *A Mother's Son*, which came out in 1907 and after considerable urging was part-serialised in *Fry's Magazine*.

If *A Mother's Son* had been a simple collaboration between Charles and Beatrice Fry it would certainly have been a more satisfying book than it turned out to be, unbalanced by distinctly unhelpful editorial intervention. Fry himself admitted that there was 'far too much about God in this book'. It was not just the religious references which softened the blow of the hero's demise in the Boer War, but some unforgivably high-minded passages, which, even allowing for the spirit of the age, were over the top. For instance, there is this passage early in the book: 'So it came about that our youthful hero reached his seventh birthday high in the favour of Lord Matechley, and rejoiced his mother's heart by his manliness, and his promise of growing up a very strong and noble Englishman.'

There are strong echoes of Fry's own childhood in Mark Lovell. The character Clodd who ambushes the ball when he feels he has been unfairly dismissed at cricket becomes Glogg in *Life Worth Living*. And again the fag-fight which announced Fry's arrival at Repton is clearly the inspiration for a similar trial of strength for Mark Lovell at Minchester.

A Mother's Son has too many stiff upper lips to pull on the reader's heart-strings, but the determined Mrs Lovell, bringing up Mark single-handed after the death of her husband, is a dependable support. 'You will outgrow my bowling but you will never outgrow my love,' she promises Mark.

There is a disturbing absence of cause and effect in the book, as though whole chapters have been exorcised, and major matters are summed up in a minor manner. Mrs Lovell has a wonderfully matter-of-fact attitude to her son's all-round talents – 'I want him before the business of life really begins, to play for England at cricket, and if it is possible to ride in the Grand National.' He not only takes part in the National, but also wins it, and makes the most astonishing debut for England against Australia, before spilling the virtually impossible catch which would have tied the match.

Mark's realisation of amorous feelings towards the charming Madeleine, his wife-to-be, is reflected thus: 'The change was wrought by that harlequin of our human pantomime, light-toed and masked Circumstance with the wand of his fortune in his hand. As a young lion, thinking nothing at all of money, the girl had charmed and pleased and fascinated him; now, as the poor man, the man who must work for his living, the beautiful heiress swam in his firmament as a goddess, near enough for his admiration, but out of reach for his supplication.' Mary Lovell captures the same spirit of dreamland a little later in the book: 'Love is so pure and spiritual a thing that it transcends every mortal consideration.'

Mark's death at the front, a glorious exit when he outsprints a couple of colleagues in a vain quest for the enemy positions, is foreshadowed by a letter home in which he says: 'I feel sure that death is only a stoppage in the clockwork.'

The one short passage in *A Mother's Son* which seems to offer a brief insight into the mind of Charles Fry was this, referring to Mark Lovell: 'In truth like most men with fair intellects and remarkable physique, he was far prouder of his mental ability than of his athletic prowess.'

Despite the overall patchiness of the book there are vibrant descriptions of Test match cricket and hunting, and extracts have been used in compilations of cricket fiction. Fry's later writings for newspapers suggested that he would have been capable of an excellent novel, but subsequently he had neither the time nor the inclination.

Batsmanship, which first appeared in 1912 and was reprinted as late as 1930, returned to the guiding principles of successful strokeplay, and for readers who could cope with its academic seriousness it was a rewarding education. Fry presented batting as it had never been presented before–a critical amalgam of eye, judgment, timing, footwork and wristwork. This passage about footwork is typical: 'The real difficulty of batting is precisely this– to be in time in getting into that position which makes the stroke easy. Strokes are easy or difficult to assume in the space of time available. Hence the vital importance of all movements which lead up to the final position being made with the greatest possible rapidity, starting from the instant when the length and direction of the ball were judged. For the sake of simplicity I am assuming correct judgment. A great number of bad strokes are entirely due to the fact that the batsman launches his bat at the ball while he is tumbling tardily from his original position into that necessary to make the stroke.'

The disciples, Douglas Jardine among them, of Charles Fry's comprehensive philosophy of batting, felt that their eyes had been opened, but there were others who saw the book as a grave disservice to cricket. *The Times Literary Supplement* described it as 'an extraordinarily searching analysis', but went on to express doubts about the treatise:

Mr Fry's method of instruction, if it were generally followed, might turn out a percentage of 'Test' players incapable of getting out for less than a couple of hundred runs; but it

would suffocate under a fatal half-science a whole other
world of cricket vastly larger and (*pace* Mr Warner) a good
deal more important to the country's welfare than the one
which figures in the first-class averages.

Mr Fry has a reference which seems to show that the village
blacksmith as a cricketer has come within his ken; but if that
refreshing artist is to be preserved from extinction under a
paralytic self-consciousness, he must be kept clear of the least
taint of Mr Fry's doctrine . . . Few of the great exponents of
the art have needed to degrade it to a science.

C.B. himself confessed that he was 'childishly proud' of *Batsmanship*. 'In my heart I even believe it to be the only book on batting
which really explains the art.'

Few books by cricketers or about cricket have attracted more
praise than Fry's *Life Worth Living*, an autobiography which hit the
bookstalls in 1939. But then C.B. started out with certain advantages–the ability to translate his experiences into highly readable
prose, a memory and imagination to match and the raw material
for memoirs of infinite diversity. Fry insisted that if cricketers
were mice they would not have the brains to find their way back to
their holes, but he was a notable exception. Sir Donald Bradman
described *Life Worth Living* as 'possibly the finest of its type ever
written by a sportsman', and there have been glowing accolades
from many people with the job of both playing and writing about
cricket.

But it was not purely a cricket book and it was not a bona fide
autobiography. Appropriately subtitled 'Some Phases of an
Englishman', it began with a history lesson and a detailed
genealogy of the Fry family; it ended with a trip to Hollywood. In
between, the fantasies of that dream capital of the world lent
colour to his adventures, which, in broad outline, were genuine
enough. Some of the figures, the dates and the places were
confused, but that was a slight price to pay for C.B.'s kaleidoscopic
vision. It would have broken his flow unforgivably to check each
minor fact.

More significant were the episodes which were bypassed: there
were no embittered reflections from the failed politician and no
sharp retorts to the clowns who sought to prove that the Prince of

Athletes was nothing more than an ill-tempered *poseur* by embroiling him in controversy. There was no temptation to hit back for C.B. had nothing more than a gentle contempt for his detractors. So, *Life Worth Living* became a genial account of a well-meaning world and even the controversies seemed like baby waves on an essentially calm sea.

Denzil Batchelor played the faithful secretary, recalling in his *Life of Fry*:

> Charles wrote it, or more often than not, dictated it to me in his dressing gown and bedroom slippers in his flat at Gloucester Place. He adopted the advice on story-telling given to Alice on what was probably after all the right side of the Looking Glass: he began at the beginning, went on to the end, and then stopped. He never re-cast the book, and he hardly re-wrote a sentence.
>
> The result was an autobiography in the round: more than a picture of its author—a glimpse or a touch of the living man in three dimensions. It gave to the world all he had done, all he had seen, much of what he had enjoyed of the fun of the fair. In appreciating these things, you became a friend, though not, I think, an intimate of the man who told the story.

There was little love lost between C.B. and his agents, A.M. Heath, after *Life Worth Living* had appeared in 1939. He had been to see Heath in October 1938 and claimed that this was simply with a view to them acquiring serial rights for the book—it was through his own efforts that Eyre and Spottiswoode were secured as publishers. The agents interpreted the agreement differently, however, and when their expected percentage of Fry's royalties failed to materialise legal proceedings were initiated.

A proposed second edition of the book was a victim of the Blitz, but *Life Worth Living* still managed to sell about 11,000 copies and Fry was pleased to see that it was well received throughout the Empire, especially in India, where he had spent a lot of time in the 1920s.

In the summer of 1943 C.B. was asked to become director of the publishers Hollis and Carter, a position he was delighted to accept. He told the *Evening Standard*: 'I'm going as a director to offer them a lot of good advice and–I hope–draw some fees. Now I shall get to know–after being on the authors' side of the fence–what publishers do make out of books.' Christopher Hollis said in *Oxford in the Twenties* that 'He was the most genial and kindly of colleagues but it would be idle to pretend that he was a regular attendant at the office–there was no reason why he should have been–or that at board meetings his remarks confined themselves very strictly to the agenda nominally under discussion.' He preferred to regale his fellow-members of the board with tales of Albanian overtures at the League of Nations.

In fact, his experience on the other side of the publishing fence did nothing to convice him that the author received his just desserts. He wrote to the Society of Authors in March 1953 lamenting that 'The return on literary adventures has not succeeded in stepping itself up in consonance with the cost of living.'

It was more than a little ironic that Hollis and Carter should achieve a major coup by getting a reluctant Fry's tacit agreement to another book of reminiscences, only for the project to fall foul of his highly developed anxieties. He thought he should be paid some advance royalties and was loath to give the publishers control of serialisation. He wrote to the Society of Authors, pleading for their help and describing Hollis and Carter's proposed agreement as an 'absurdity'. His PS was: 'No one but a lunatic or a terrible tiro would accept an agreement like this.' That was at the end of February 1953. In the summer of 1954 C.B. was writing again to the Society to thank them for sending him a revised form of agreement, but the lapse had been no ally to the project and the reminiscences, which would have been enthusiastically received, never materialised.

FRY'S
MAGAZINE

Charles Fry's masterful contributions to *The Captain* and *Strand Magazine*, both in the Newnes publishing stable, put him in line for a greater challenge still. An attempt by Eustace Miles to introduce a magazine about physical culture helped to convince Sir George Newnes that something more wholesome should be promoted; and Fry was the man selected to lead the venture in 1904.

C.B.'s first assistant editor was Wallis Myers, who wrote about the frenetic preparations for the launch of *C.B. Fry's Magazine*: 'For months past he has been preparing the ground, throwing himself with almost super-human energy into the new venture. One picture crosses my mind. A huge sheet of white paper was fixed up with drawing-pins to the wall of a room in Southampton Street. It was divided off into squares, each square representing a page of the first number. As the various subjects for treatment were selected this space-value was regulated on the giant design. For hours he wrestled in his shirt-sleeves with the problem of make-up and proportion.'

Fry was a fairly experienced journalist, but he was a complete novice when it came to the production side. However, Sir George Newnes was confident that his protégé could pick up the knowledge quickly and so it proved. C.B. soon discovered that the flow of contributed items was unreliable and the only way to be certain of filling each month was to be prepared to write a staggering amount himself–a task for which he was admirably qualified.

Warren Bell gave readers of *The Captain* a graphic description of C.B. in his new domain, saying he reminded him of a 'tiger-cub trying to behave like a domesticated cat in a drawing room'. Bell went on:

Every now and then, after a spell of solid desk-work, he has to get up and pace his room with fevered steps. This is his vent for bottled-up energy. Then by way of throat and lung exercise he holds animated conversations through the speaking-tube with the Art-Editor. Here's a sample:

'Who-hoop! You there, Art-Ed.?'

'Aye, aye, sir.'

'Got that block of Jessop?'

'I thought he was a slogger, Mr Fry.'

'I mean the block of his picture.'

'Oh, I see. Aye, aye, sir.'

'Not so much "Aye, aye, sir." This isn't a war-ship. I say, look here, you know, are we getting to press in good time?'

'Aye, aye, sir.'

'It'll be no nose for you in a moment if you give me any more of those parrot answers. Got Stanley Wood's boxing picture yet?'

'What boxing picture?'

'Thunder—'

Here Mr Fry leaves the tube and ascends two flights of stairs in 3½ seconds, takes screen in Art-Editor's room in a bound (5ft 11½ ins.–office record) and finally descends stairs in two springs. Having thus let off steam he settles down to his desk again until another query sends him flying upstairs again.

'Yes,' said Mr Fry's gifted assistant-editor to me the other day, 'I guess it's a bit more placid editing the *Guardian* over the road there. Never mind—we're selling like hot cakes . . . have another cigar.'

Wallis Myers wrote:

The office of *Fry's Magazine* during the two years I knew it intimately, was one of the liveliest places in London. It was a workshop, a debating hall, an athletic academy and a restaurant rolled into one, the whole office pervaded by Mr Fry's vivifying personality. You never knew what was going to happen next. One day somebody came in and said that cricket was being played by an electric light over a swimming bath near Fleet Street. The discussion in hand came to a peremptory close, a cab was whistled up, and in ten minutes we had invaded St Bride's Institute. In a twinkling Mr Fry had taken the first bat that came to hand and was defying the bowlers.

As in sport so in journalism, Mr Fry is all-round and embracive. He is not an editor who sits tight before desk for regular hours. He does not pull down an American roll-top at six o'clock and go off to catch a train to the suburbs. He is not hemmed in with galley proofs and manuscripts, fretting and fuming at his staff. He rarely writes in the office. Most of his work there is done standing up or walking about. He has no pride, false or otherwise, with his staff. He will invade the Art Editor's sanctum with a brilliant cover idea. He will 'phone a tip to the advertisement manager. He will rush in, pipe in hand, to borrow a match from his assistant. He will send the office-boy out for a bag of sandwiches and pass half of them on to the messenger. He does not keep an emergency silk hat in a box. He will go off in a tweed suit and bowler to interview a Cabinet Minister. He will don his flannels, his football togs, or his running 'shorts' and spend a busy hour in the photographer's studio for the purpose of illustrating a 'how to' article he had in hand. The taxi-cab finds him a generous patron. Action is his watch-word; he must get there quickly. He would be the first man to drive his own aeroplane to the office, and if the porter on the roof expressed himself curious as to the mechanism, Mr Fry would probably take him for a trial trip.

Fry was quick to exploit the inherent privilege of his new position, and within the broad framework of *Fry's Magazine* as the champion of outdoor life he could vote for the status quo or, as was far more likely, play the heroic crusader in a rapidly changing world.

The first edition came out in 1904 and set a high-minded example, as though Fry was deliberately repressing his playful instinct. He wrote this about G.F. Watts's Physical Energy, a striking equestrian statue which had been twenty years in the making: 'As it stands it typifies the pause, the arrest, the interval between one act of supreme energy and the coming moment of continued action. It is the noble tribute of fulfilled and honourable age to the unfulfilled ambition of the once restless soul now steeped in the eternal peace of death.' A cast of the statue, destined for South Africa as a memorial to Cecil Rhodes' pioneering achievements, was placed in Kensington Gardens at the end of 1907.

There was also an intriguing comparison between the ruins of the Colosseum in Rome and the Crystal Palace, which was the venue for the FA Cup Final and capable of holding more than 100,000 people. The coffee-stalls outside the Colosseum, he said, were not that different from the coffee-stalls at Euston Station in the small hours of a Cup Final morning. But then England's gladiatorial arena operated on slightly different lines—'No splendid pomp here, no martyrdom, no death, no cruelty—just a hundred English thousands, and an English game evolved for the heart of the nation; merely a pastime—football. We cannot discover here the evils upon which the Italian sky smiled so blandly, nor the heroism. But it is a pleasant fancy to find in a strong and manly game, however modern, however faulty, traces of bravery and contempt of pain.'

It may have been speculation of this sort which put C.B. in mind of a campaign to introduce rifle-shooting as a bona fide sport in Britain. He regretted the absence of a sport with a martial element and, without seeking to undermine conventional military training, hoped to bring about a shot in the arm, as it were, for national defence. 'I would have every elementary school in the country furnished with a miniature range, and I would have a proper course of instruction and practice systematically carried out.' The message was driven home *ad nauseam*, but although C.B. claimed tremendous support for his idea, and the point was taken up by Lord Roberts, there is no clear evidence that his vision was realised.

There was an endless stream of visitors to the offices of the magazine. Cricketers like Ranji, W.G. Grace and George Beldam were always welcome and Wallis Myers recalled one occasion when Beldam came in, armed with action photographs of sportsmen. He launched into a dissertation on the relationship between

Fry's drives at cricket and J.H. Taylor's drives at golf. Myers takes up the story: 'Suddenly Beldam whipped off his over-coat and seized the poker. I dropped my pipe in momentary alarm. But he was only giving us a practical illustration of Taylor. Then Mr Fry took the poker, stood at an imaginary wicket, and knocked George Hirst with terrific force past mid-on. A discourse followed on the subtleties of wrist-work, stance and follow-through. It lasted quite a long time, and I do not think we did any more planning out that day.'

Inventors were keen to try out their new gadgets and games on Fry, knowing full well that his fertile brain would give them a fair audience and that if he liked their ideas he would take great pleasure in publicising new products and technological innovations.

C.B.'s talent for throwing his weight behind a novel, or seemingly novel, idea was revealed in the craze for a game called Diabolo, which enjoyed immense, if brief, popularity throughout most of Western Europe. In 1905 Fry was visited at the magazine offices by a French engineer, Gustave Phillipart, who had got hold of the implements for Diabolo from a game which had been in vogue almost a hundred years earlier in both France and England. The old game was variously called Le Diable, Le Bon Diable and Le Joyeux Diable, so the transition from this to Diabolo was no great departure, but the credit for the name went to C.B., although *The Times* said the title Diabolo (which they translated as double cone) had been in existence for as long as the game had been played.

Phillipart returned to his native Paris in 1905, with Fry's prediction that Diabolo would make its mark in England within two years ringing confidently in his ears. The French capital itself was gripped by 'Diabolo fever' and in 1907 Phillipart came back to Britain, accompanied by expert players, to promote the game in all its glory.

C.B., who was writing regular sporting columns for the *Daily Chronicle*, presented the history of the game and his involvement on 18 September describing himself as 'the godfather' of Diabolo. He maintained that he had delved into his classical background to come up with the name, the Greek verb *diaballein* meaning to throw across. Both he and Phillipart were convinced that the game, complete with variations, would be considered as a serious sport and not just a toy game. 'It ought to become a standard game, with tournaments and so on,' said Fry. Using the same gifts for instruction and explanation which later made *Batsmanship* such an essential work for cricketers, he wrote a book on Diabolo. It never sold immensely, but was at least flattered with translation into a number of tongues.

The *Daily Chronicle* was sufficiently smitten with the possibilities of the game to promote a Diabolo display at Earl's Court on 10 October 1907. A large crowd turned up and J.M. Barrie was among the interested spectators who watched the demonstrations of Real Diabolo and Diabolo Tennis. Fry said the display was 'a distinct success', but a high wind tended to catch the more ambitious throws and send them singing away into the crowd.

The double-headed tops with which the game was played could be caught or thrown by hand or with something resembling a skipping rope. *The Times* was sceptical about Diabolo's long-term appeal, but at least admitted that 'The high throw – 60 yards seems possible – is a great feature of Diabolo; it gives the same feeling of easy exhilaration which one gets from a late cut at cricket or a perfectly-executed golf drive.' Competitions were held at Crystal Palace at the end of October 1907, but despite the 'rampant craze' for Diabolo, *The Times* predicted its early demise: 'Even if it can be dignified with the name of "game" at all, it can never, however great the skill of the performer, be called a good game.'

Fry later admitted that Diabolo had never made the grade as the serious game he and Gustave Phillipart had so fondly envisaged. In May 1908 there was a hearing in the Chancery Division in London when Phillipart sought an injunction to prevent William Whiteley infringing a trade mark which he had registered in 1905. The dispute rested on whether Diabolo was an invented word and entitled to be considered as a trade mark or merely a name descriptive of an improved form of 'The Devil on Two Sticks.' It was claimed that the game had been christened Diabolo in the 1860s when it was played on board the frigate *Sutlej* in the Pacific. Phillipart was asked: 'Do you mean to say that you took the Greek word "Diaballo" and evolved from it "Diabolo"?' His reply was: 'It was not my invention myself, but with the assistance of my friend Mr Fry, who is a good Greek scholar. When we created the word "Diabolo", we had no idea of calling people's attention to the devil.'

It was hardly surprising that other businesses should want to grab a piece of the action: the worldwide sales of Diabolo in 1907 had amounted to £53,000. The imitators' hopes were fulfilled as Mr Justice Parker ruled that the word was not a valid trade mark. He added that although Diabolo was not current in the English language it still had an implicit reference to the devil. He need not have worried: the craze did not have lasting appeal and soon ceased to be a money-spinner.

There was much more long-term relevance in C.B.'s trip to Paris at the beginning of 1907 to see and interview Santos Dumont, the Brazilian-born pioneer of manned flight in Europe. The French were far more open-minded about the feasibility of man taking to the air, but C.B.'s article at least introduced the subject to a supremely sceptical British public. In November 1906 Dumont had flown more than 200 yards in his '14 bis', a contraption consisting of half-a-dozen box kites, and Fry was able to report: 'At last, thanks to Santos Dumont, once regarded as a fanatical exponent of the steerable balloon, the flying-machine has achieved a brilliant triumph which marks a step towards the conquest of the air of a kind entirely different from the limited success possible to the most perfect dirigible balloon.'

A £10,000 prize had been put up by *Le Matin* for the first person to make a convincing flight and this offer was matched by the *Daily Mail*, causing Dumont to suggest to Fry that he should use his contacts and own native ingenuity to launch a British challenge for the prize. Two years later all the fantasies about manned flight had turned into reality and C.B. was able to write in January 1909: 'I rather pride myself on having published in this magazine the first article that dared accept the aeroplane as a near possibility for the ordinary man, and the first article—by about a year—that declared the Wright brothers not an American mystery but genuine people with an efficient machine.' Already Fry's interest had gone a stage further—now he was singing the praises of the hydroplane!

It was during one of Fry's jaunts to the Continent that he became briefly involved with a Belgian scientist, Dr Tacquin, who suggested to C.B. that he should hang up his bat and go in for aeronautics instead. The same Dr Tacquin got into trouble when he tried to introduce trading links with the Sus district of Morocco, so it was probably just as well that Charles Fry remained nothing more than an enlightened spectator of the progress of manned flight.

Despite his close involvement with every aspect of the magazine's production—and Fry was quite happy to say a few sycophantic words about health-enhancing products if it helped to boost advertising revenue—C.B. remained suspicious of the integrity and motives of some of his journalistic brothers; but then he had some justification. At the end of 1906 he made some casually derogatory remarks about the game of football when he addressed a meeting at Walworth, little realising that a *Sporting Life* reporter was lurking in the audience.

The result was dynamite and in January 1907 he told *Fry's Magazine* readers that he had been represented as a 'virulent opponent of football, who told how football is honeycombed with drink and undermined by gambling, or words to that effect, with suitable sensational headlines. In fact, I was represented as having talked unmitigated nonsense.' At Fry's insistence the *Sporting Life* published his flat denial of the alleged crime, but they continued to defend the original report and claimed that even if this 'popular idol' had been attacked irrelevantly by a host of angry letter-writers, it proved that people had a genuine interest in English sport.

One American paper even rejoiced in the large, improbable headline: 'C.B. FRY, C.B. MURDERS A REFEREE.' This was subtitled with 'for surely the shock will kill John Lewis when he hears that C.B. says that football sometimes makes people thirsty.'

At the end of 1907 there was a fairly dignified slanging match between Fry and Sir Home Gordon, the same cricket writer who, as we have seen, consistently questioned C.B.'s right to a place in the England side. C.B. was always the champion of maligned cricketers and Gordon was forthright in his criticism of players in his review of the 1907 season for the *Badminton Magazine*. Fry's response was immediate and equally outspoken, with the result that Gordon took offence and demanded right of reply in *Fry's Magazine*. This was granted without condition, Gordon beginning: 'My reply is to an onslaught made not with the rapier of argument, but with the bludgeon of reckless virulence.' Although Fry allowed Gordon to use up some precious space in his magazine he did not fail to remember that the editor has the ultimate right of reply. He used that prerogative coolly to dismiss Gordon's revised line of argument. Subsequently the two men continued to beg to differ.

The character of *Fry's Magazine* was its master's voice, and he was not altogether reluctant to express his opinions on a myriad of topics. 'Straight Talk' was introduced early in the life of the magazine, later giving way to 'The Sportsman's View Point' and 'Expert Opinion'. In 1908, for instance, this section of *Fry's* regularly stretched to more than 10,000 words, and in the course of just two issues his interest was attracted to the safety razor ('the razor of the future'), men's fashion, hire purchase, the value of having a rub-down in the morning, map reading, clean accumulators, road improvements, phrenology and aeroplanes, oxygen as a stimulant, Esperanto and fish hooks.

The importance of C.B. to the magazine was amply illustrated when his contributions diminished in deference to his responsibilities to the training ship *Mercury*. The circulation, having hovered around 100,000 in the early days, making it the third most popular monthly publication, dropped off in sympathy. For a couple of years there was a complete absence of editorial direction and the situation was complicated further when Sir George Newnes died in the summer of 1910.

The publishers' new managing director, Lord Riddell, had different ideas about the running of *Fry's Magazine*, and with C.B. ceasing to edit it the venture was taken up by Fry's Magazine Ltd. in 1911. Fry himself was sufficiently appeased to write profile pieces on Winston Churchill, Edward Grey and Horatio Bottomley, as well as contributing a column called 'To My Mind', but *Fry's* was Fryless again for most of 1912 and 1913.

He got back into the swing with a series of articles about physical education, underlining his often expressed belief that brain and brawn could reside in the same person, but the new owners were beginning to acknowledge that something radical was needed to put *Fry's Magazine* back on its former pedestal.

The low-profile editor, Burton Baldry, owned up to the scant use of their prime asset when he wrote in April 1914 that Fry's

position and standing is unique in the annals of sport. His knowledge of sporting matters is unrivalled, and the benefit of his practical experience is an asset possessed by no other sporting magazine or weekly in the world.

Some three years ago Mr Fry was compelled, for private reasons, to relinquish any executive control in this magazine, but arrangements have now been completed whereby he will be enabled to renew his immediate connection with the magazine that bears his name, and to supervise the entire editorial policy, as well as to write regularly. The magazine, therefore, in future will bear the imprint of his personality, and readers will obtain the benefit of his opinions on matters covering the whole field of sport.

It was no secret that the magazine's decline had coincided with Fry's absence, but there was a new mood of optimism in the summer of 1914. The company had just brought out a book, *Success at Golf,* and they were also in the process of starting up a sister magazine, *The Sportswoman.* The circulation figure for May was significantly up and the editorial predicted a bright future: '*Fry's* is getting back on the rails it left nearly three years ago.'

A few months later, of course, the whole world's future was in jeopardy, and the call of patriotism forced the suspension of *Fry's Magazine* in September 1914. Burton Baldry issued the following statement by way of explanation:

In such a crisis as the present we must consider our country and its needs rather than our individual ambitions and aspirations. This is not a time for sport, even for the peculiarly German sport of butchering harmless citizens and sacking villages. National endeavour is diverted to other and more important channels. The matters that come within our scope must take a back place, even though in allocating them this back place we are depriving ourselves of our livelihood. There is work to be done, and even though the sword cannot edit *Fry's Magazine,* we lay down our pen with the assurance that it can be used to better advantage after the war is done.

However, the hope was forlorn. There would be no place for *Fry's* in the post-war world, as spiralling production costs, worries over advertising and the hangover effect from the editorial soul-searching made it a non-contender.

15

THE GOOD SHIP *MERCURY*

Charles Fry's future was shrouded in uncertainty when he left Oxford in 1895. His instinct would have taken him into first-class cricket, but we have already seen that he was in debt when he left the university and without parental backing could not begin to contemplate a full-time career in sport. The Indian Civil Service and the lure of a job in South Africa bypassed him and he reluctantly opted for an assistant master's post at Charterhouse in 1896. This enabled him to play cricket in the second half of the 1896 and 1897 seasons, but he was still not content and although he was starting to make useful money from newspaper and magazine articles the income at this stage was insufficient to subsidise cricketing travels.

The mists began to clear when C.B. came into contact with the training ship *Mercury*, nestling by the banks of the Hamble River in Hampshire. A shore community had sprung up in support of the training ship, which was moved from Binstead in 1892, and there was a house, chapel, theatre and playing fields. The man behind this quiet revolution was Charles Hoare, senior partner in his family's famous banking firm, who had founded the training ship in 1885. There were both similarities and stark differences between Hoare and C.B. Both had an astonishing variety of interests, the same love of the outdoors, the same high-velocity intellect. 'I never met his equal in all-round capability,' said Fry in *Life Worth Living*. Both had kindness in abundance, but whereas C.B.'s generosity was a natural extension of the ebullient side of his nature, Hoare's regard for his fellow-man sprang from a more austere base.

As a teenager Hoare had shown natural aptitude as a whip and drove the stagecoach from Sevenoaks to London. He retained a great interest in horses and hunting and from 1879 to 1885 was master of the Vale of White Horse Hounds, with whom C.B. also hunted, building stables and kennels at Cricklade. Like Fry he enjoyed shooting, fishing and motoring; and he was also a keen railway enthusiast. He played cricket for Kent and from 1905 until his death in 1908 was President of the Hampshire County Cricket Club. But there was more to Charles Hoare than outdoor zest. He was an art connoisseur and owned a remarkable collection of prints and old furniture. He was no mean artist himself and a capable architect, too, but the guiding force in his life was religion—a purer faith than C.B.'s mix of belief and superstition—and it was in the image of Catholicism that the training ship grew.

The motto of the *Mercury* could be found in the chapel, written boldly beneath the bronze crucifix on the wall: 'Dedicated to minds that can soar, that will rise and not be discouraged by obstacles or difficulties, that will chance and dare for what they love and know to be right. To co-operation, combination, dash, perseverance, and unselfishness, this building and its adjuncts are fearlessly dedicated for harmony, the good of mankind, and to hearts that can beat for others. Its ideal is Good Friday's Hero.'

Hoare's personal life, however, had taken a less than virtuous twist. Although married he had become romantically involved with Beatrice Holme Sumner, later to become Mrs Fry, and they had two children, Robin and Sybil. There was no chance of the Hoares' Catholic marriage ending in divorce, so another solution had to be found. This is where C.B. entered the equation and an arrangement was made whereby he would marry Beatrice Holme Sumner and in return Charles Hoare would help to subsidise Fry's full-time cricket career. This is not to say that the Frys felt no affection for each other, but it was an off-beat relationship—she was eight years older than him—and it was often said afterwards that she was more like a mother to him than a wife. C.B.'s 'Madame' had experienced the strictest of privileged upbringings, but, like C.B., there was a radical split in her personality. When running the *Mercury* she was a paragon of austerity, as hard on herself as she was on the boys, and she dressed in such a way that all hints of femininity were concealed and suppressed. She felt that women were automatically taken to be weaker than men, in both body and mind, and the only way she could challenge the stereotype was by being excessively masculine in her manner.

Once the arrangement had been made, C.B. was able to resign his mastership at Charterhouse and the marriage took place at St Pancras Parish Church on 4 June 1898, Fry classing his profession as journalist. There was no lengthy honeymoon, for five days after the wedding C.B. was playing for Sussex against Kent, delighted to be able to play full-time cricket at last.

The couple settled just a few miles away from Hamble at Glenbourne Manor in West End and in the garden C.B. worked on his batting technique. Mrs Fry was the bowler and the fielding was done by a versatile pair of Scotch terriers, Jane Brindle and John Sandy. Soon there was the patter of tiny Fry feet. Charis—and despite the evidence given on the birth certificate it has been rumoured that C.B. was not her father—was born just eight and a half months after the wedding. Then came Stephen and finally Faith. Both C.B. and Madame were dominant personalities, though in different ways, and the children found it difficult to establish their own identities. All three of the Fry children are now dead and both girls remained spinsters throughout their lives, although Charis came close to marriage on more than one occasion. Stephen, through taking jobs abroad, was able to escape the shadow of his father temporarily, but although he played cricket for Hampshire during the 1920s and even captained the side on occasions, little of the paternal talent had rubbed off. Stephen's son Charles completed a unique treble when he played for Hampshire just over twenty years ago, having also won his Blue at Oxford.

C.B.'s dual success as a cricketer and a journalist had brought the family a comfortable existence and after a few years Fry was able to finance his own career without assistance. However, the whole pattern of their lives changed when Charles Hoare died in 1908 at the age of sixty-one, leaving not only the *Mercury*, but also property in Kent, Lancashire and Monmouth.

Although Hoare's estate amounted to more than £234,000 there was no money allotted in his will for the continued running of the *Mercury*, which was left in the hands of trustees. They were directed to find a public body to take over the running of the ship and Hoare's valuable collection of model ships was to go to this body. The trustees were asked to provide funds for the work of the ship for no more than two years, but within a few months it became clear that there was not sufficient money to keep the *Mercury* ticking over. The trustees sought High Court permission to be relieved of their responsibilities and it was here that the Frys, hardly wealthy in spite of C.B.'s journalistic rewards, dived in with admirable disregard for the possibility that they might go down with the swiftly sinking ship. It was the clarity of Hoare's vision which motivated C.B. and made him think that the risk was justified. He wrote: 'I thought it worth while to put other things in life aside and offer to try and carry it on. The real reason why I did it was simple annoyance at the sheer stupidity of allowing such a work to die.'

There was an immediate need to raise money for the day-to-day running of the *Mercury* and the begging bowl was passed round. There were some sizeable donations from the wealthy and influential, but they were mainly dependent on small donations. There were agents in almost every village in Hampshire and in the space of six months £2,000 was raised, sufficient to convince the High Court that the training ship could get into the black and be considered as an educational charity.

Fry's cricketing connections came in useful. When R.E. Foster died in 1914 C.B. recalled in appreciation that when the *Mercury*'s need was at its greatest Foster had conducted a whip-round at the Stock Exchange and gathered the formidable sum of £250. Meanwhile, Fry himself had unconventional means of adding to the coffers and publicising the cause to a wider audience. For example, his close interest in the progress of manned flight, initially prompted by Santos Dumont's experiments in France and subsequently fuelled by the Wright brothers' dramatic success in America, encouraged him to take on a £10 wager with a fellow-sportsman in the New Forest. Fry maintained that planes would be ordered by private individuals before the start of 1910; he was proved correct and wrote in *Fry's Magazine* in January 1909: 'I have won the bet already, and am expecting shortly to pocket the £10 note, which I shall give to the Training Ship *Mercury*, which is the best training institution for boys in the empire, and needs subscriptions.'

With the *Mercury* having no assured source of income the Frys inherited an annual deficit of £4,500, but their success as fund-raisers, their careful housekeeping and the fact that they claimed nothing more than basic expenses, enabled them to discharge the debts and stay on an even keel. The *Mercury* was in debt again at the tail-end of the First World War, but a foundation fund was later established which meant in effect that the training ship could still be maintained when empty. Fry estimated that in the period from 1909 to the start of the Second World War he and Madame had put £24,000 into the ship.

In the light of the *Mercury*'s financial headaches the future of Charles Hoare's superb collection of ship models became crucial. There were around 200 in all, including some dating back to the middle of the seventeenth century and one model which had been owned by Lord Nelson. The collection had been rather conservatively valued at £3,000, but the major concern for the new honorary director was to confirm that the models classed as an appurtenance of the establishment rather than as part of Hoare's estate, as was maintained by the executors.

It seemed that C.B. was on a sticky wicket, but wisely he went to the trouble of providing six affidavits in the hope of persuading the High Court judge who would consider the matter. The affidavits were made possible by convincing submissions from high-ranking nautical types who stressed the importance of the collection and that the models should remain part of the training establishment.

The judge agreed, but it would have been rather opportunistic for C.B. to dispose of the collection while the decision and the reasons for it were fresh in the mind. Nevertheless, for the next twenty years it was a constant temptation to sell the ship models: there was little reticence among potential buyers and the figures mentioned became increasingly attractive. The first offer was £6,000 and the value rose steadily until in 1925 there was a bid of £20,000.

Still the temptation was resisted and there was general determination that the collection should both remain in Britain and be available for public inspection. Following the opening of the National Maritime Museum at Greenwich it became possible for both conditions to be met. Negotiations were opened and there was satisfaction all round when Sir James Caird paid £30,000 for the museum to receive the collection in 1929.

The *Mercury* adopted a different philosophy from other training ships, which often resembled borstals and could never hope to turn out the sort of boy who would be welcomed into the Navy and have a genuine chance of making it as an officer. As C.B. wrote in *Life Worth Living*: 'There were plenty of training-ships for the persistent truant and the young semi-delinquent, but if the well-behaved fifth son of the farm labourer wanted to get sea training, his only chance was to raid his father's employer's orchard. Moreover, while a boy who somehow or other had come on the rates was provided with a fine chance of sea training, the son of hard-working parents with not a penny to spare or to owe had practically no chance at all offered to him.'

Charles Hoare had devoted himself to providing training for boys of good character and the Frys saw no reason to change the emphasis. For C.B. in particular it was an engaging challenge to plead the case for the *Mercury* and to argue, by implication, that Britain had a strangely apathetic attitude to sea training in general. It was a topic which he pursued vigorously through correspondence with the Admiralty and education authorities and by speaking to countless gatherings.

Recognising that many parents of potentially excellent cadets were quite unable to afford to send their children to the *Mercury* he issued an empassioned plea for sea scholarships. The tenor of his message was presented with all the usual charm: 'We sing Rule Britannia very loudly—and sometimes in tune. Why not give some scholarships for sea training?' The appeal did not fall on totally deaf ears. Victor Alexander, education officer with Somerset County Council, was the first person to draft a scheme for free naval scholarships. More than thirty years later the self-same Victor Alexander was First Lord of the Admiralty and delighted to accept an invitation to present the prizes at the *Mercury*'s annual celebration of excellence in 1942.

Not surprisingly, this innovation of sea scholarships, allied to the already high reputation of the *Mercury*, meant that applications flooded in from the length and breadth of Britain, and as C.B. revealed in an article for the *Sunday Graphic* in 1947, he had a novel way of selecting likely lads:

The main trouble was that parents applied from all over the

United Kingdom, many of them far away. Distance and expense more often than not precluded interview. And one had to know.

What did I do? I simply insisted that with application papers should be sent the mother's photograph. And if I liked the look of the mother I decided in favour of the son. And it worked.

Of course I took other information into account. Still I did find my device (or say invention, because I am rather proud of it) a wonderfully valuable guide.

Intuitively, like a poet, I put my money on the mother . . . and it worked. So write me down as a natural champion of mothers.

In the same article he pointed to the damaging confusion that could result where children were expected to observe different codes of conduct in their homes and in institutions. More significantly he demonstrated that he and his wife had a subtle appreciation of the most effective means of enforcing discipline. Some misguided mothers, he said, were inclined to regard it 'as a species of tyranny arbitrarily imposed to make people do what they do not want to do under pain of penalty. That is a cardinal error. Discipline is nothing whatever but unselfishness organised and directed. Indiscipline is a baleful form of selfishness. Just that.'

It has to be pointed out that C.B.'s day-to-day involvement with the *Mercury* waned as year succeeded year, so he had limited experience in putting the theory into practice. One has only to look at the diversions which he created for himself between the two wars to realise that his role became increasingly peripheral. The *Mercury* has been described, not without a grain of truth, as his plaything.

There is no doubt that a part of C.B. believed in the theory behind the *Mercury*, and no one could better express as a spokesman the ingredients which made it tick, but he was more like a commentator, privileged to watch the training ship at work, than a true participant. Make no mistake, there was something of the Devil's advocate in Fry's supposed views. The honorary director preached the value of discipline and an ordered, uncluttered lifestyle, but as an individual he insisted on being right and if his views clashed with the official line, then the voice of authority was clearly misguided. He was oblivious to the apparent contradiction.

My assessment of C.B.'s role on the *Mercury* is not simply the result of personal deduction. There have been dissenting voices, but the majority of cadets and staff I have spoken to have naturally settled on the word 'figurehead' as an apt description of his involvement. This may sound like indictment, but Fry himself made little attempt to suggest that he was the driving force behind the *Mercury*'s smooth-running engine. That accolade was reserved, both by him and by other observers, for his remarkable wife.

She was blessed with administrative qualities which he so patently lacked–and was much more prepared to translate principles into reality. The twinkle in C.B.'s eye as he conducted divisions on a Sunday rather gave the game away. He had never lost, and never would lose, his sense of mischief, but those outward hints of humanity were absent from his wife.

The ceremonial side of his job was very appealing to Fry, who liked to dress up in his naval uniform, even if the titles he was given were only honorary. On the outbreak of the First World War he was given an honorary commission as lieutenant in the Royal Naval Reserve, in September 1916 he was promoted to commander and finally, after the end of the Second World War, he rose to the honorary rank of captain. He was once asked by a colonel why he didn't put up any of his service ribbons. He replied to this effect: 'Because I'm not entitled to any, Colonel. No one in pre-service training is. But I'm very proud of my blank blue-black chest–it shows I have done nothing wrong from the Boer War up to date.' Mrs Fry was awarded the OBE for her tireless efforts during the First World War.

Shortly after C.B. had been made an honorary captain he was asked by an acquaintance: 'Why are you now only a captain? You used to be a commander.' C.B. said: 'I guess their Lordships of the Admiralty thought I had grown too big for my boats.'

Notwithstanding the jokes there is no doubt that Fry took his commissions very seriously. He confessed towards the end of his life that part of him would have liked to join the Navy as a small boy and become an admiral, but as R.C. Robertson-Glasgow pointed out, 'In his uniform of Captain, R.N.R., he looks like six admirals, and, probably to preserve symmetry of figure, carries his tobacco-pouch in his cap.'

He could also be very covetous of his title, honorary or not. During the 1936–7 tour of Australia a dinner was given to the Oxbridge graduates in the England party in one of the state capitals. When Fry entered the dining room he found that his place had been marked with a card inscribed Mr C.B. Fry. He felt so offended that he left the room and did not return.

That spontaneous reaction was the real C.B. He had turned out generation after generation of recruits for the Navy—over 1,000 *Mercury* boys fought in the First World War alone—but he himself was unable to serve his country. During the First World War he had been tied to the *Mercury* and by the time the next war came along he was too old to contribute. Since there was no place for him in active service in 1942 Fry volunteered, at the age of seventy, to go down the coal-mines as a Bevin Boy, but that suggestion too was taken with a pinch of salt.

It is easy to assume that Mrs Fry was a complete ogre, so concerned with presenting a tough persona that she seemed to be devoid of feeling. The attractive young woman went on to do a convincing male impersonation. She dressed in an unflattering suit, complete with tie and voluminous skirt and the obligatory hat. Her only concession to eccentricity was socks that often did not match. Her gruff manner and ultra-strict régime frightened many of the boys who were in her charge, but she earned their respect by mucking in and demonstrating that there was method in the apparent madness. When C.B. was fighting the Oxford by-election in 1924 he said of the *Mercury*: 'The instructional side is easy. The difficulty is to give the boys a proper environment—shall I say, a garden to grow in? It is my wife who cultivates that garden, and she gets up every day at five in the morning. She is a positive genius at the work.'

He underlined the same points in an interview which appeared in the *Daily Mirror* in 1937, also bemoaning the fact that whereas everyone wanted to talk to him about cricket he was just longing to tell them what a wonderful institution the *Mercury* was. He also explained to the *Mirror* reporter that there were no ordinary lines or canings at Hamble. If a boy was brought to Mrs Fry and told he was not reliable he would burst into tears rather than meet her stern glances.

Early in the Frys' reign on the *Mercury*, C.B. decided to remind the Admiralty of a promise they had made to Charles Hoare, to loan the gunboat *Magpie* as an extension to the establishment. Fry then discovered that the *Magpie* was lying less than a mile away and had become the rendezvous for Admiralty intelligence personnel. In any case it was suggested that they might instead adopt an old frigate then based at Bristol, but although C.B. travelled west and promptly accepted the offer there was no further progress made on the deal.

The next candidate was the HMS *President*, a drill-ship which was in London's West India docks. Since the upper deck had already been adapted for training purposes and there was bounteous accommodation Fry saw it as a definite asset to the Hamble set-up, but by now he had come to accept the inevitable delay, if not ultimate disappointment.

There was no movement on the deal until a snap inspection a few years later. The visiting party was composed of a number of VIP's, headed by Winston Churchill, then First Lord of the Admiralty. With him was his brother, Jack, Admiral Hood, and Fry's old friend from Oxford days, F.E. Smith, now Lord Birkenhead. They were suitably impressed by the parade which was arranged in double-quick time, while Winston Churchill left his mark on C.B. by asking a string of highly intelligent and informed questions about the training ship.

As a parting shot Churchill asked if there was anything the Admiralty could do for the *Mercury*. It may have been intended as no more than a pleasantry, but Fry wasted no time in jogging memories about the *President*. The result was that the ship began its journey from London and got as far as Chatham in Kent, but no further. It took another visit from Winston Churchill a year later for the *President* to be towed as far as Portsmouth and finally the last few miles were completed. In view of the protracted negotiations over its transfer it was appropriate that the *President* should be instantly accepted as part of the family.

This was just before the outbreak of the First World War, by which time the Frys had established a pattern that was the envy of other training institutions. Boys who saw out their time at the *Mercury* were readily accepted by both the Royal Navy and the Merchant Service. They were justifiably regarded as highly dependable, self-reliant and capable of taking charge in situations where others would flounder. The emphasis was on character-building and everything attempted and achieved on the *Mercury* stemmed from that fundamental aim. It was a startling success: the Admiralty made a capitation payment of £25 for every boy who passed out as an advance-class cadet. When the Frys took over there were no more than four or five joining the Navy as advance-class boys each year. Within two years 55 of the 60 boys entering the Navy were advance class. This outstanding record endured, with upwards of 90 per cent of *Mercury* boys meeting advance-class requirements, compared with little more than ten per cent from other establishments. To achieve the necessary standard they had to shine academically, as well as qualifying in seamanship, rifle drill, signals and swimming. Equally important, in view of the *Mercury*'s struggles to make ends meet, was the annual income of more than £1,000 generated if upwards of 40 boys were regarded as advance class material.

Charles Fry always took immense pleasure in results achieved by unconventional means and the *Mercury* had something unusual to offer in the shape of compulsory music teaching, an innovation for which Mrs Fry must take much of the credit, although it fell neatly into line with C.B.'s devotion to the Greek ideal. Every boy who joined the training ship was required to take up a musical instrument and although natural aptitude varied enormously, the introduction of music as an integral part of the timetable was of definite value. In *Life Worth Living* Fry wrote:

> Every boy goes to his hour of practice and theory of music just as he goes to his hours of mathematics, seamanship, signals, physical training, and gunnery. He does not regard music as an accomplishment. He accepts it as part of his training. The effect is that the training has had a standard fine art incorporated in its routine.
>
> During my thirty years at the *Mercury* I have seen it proved that music has a remarkable educational value: in this sense, that you can see dull boys growing intelligent under its influence. This is not a matter of supposition. I have noted any number of cases where, the moment a boy began to improve in music, he also began to improve in all other

subjects, especially in mathematics. I have also noticed that in the examinations at the end of the year more prizes in all subjects go to the best musicians in the picked band than in any other direction. In most establishments the band boys are trained separately to be entered in army bands.

The *Mercury*'s private theatre was a remarkable feature of the shore establishment: Mrs Fry even sold a string of pearls to finance the building and equipping of the theatre, which was modelled on the Wagnerian auditorium at Bayreuth. For a long time it was described as 'the theatre that nobody knows', but all that changed in 1927 when the first public performances on a paying basis were given. The major impetus behind this was Stephen Fry, who, quite apart from being a capable musician, was also a stage producer and had a modern vision of the presentation of music.

The *Daily Express* wrote on 10 October: 'Mr Fry's (Stephen's) view is that at ordinary recitals one's attention is distracted by the piano itself, its maker's name pasted across it, and by other members of the audience. The audience at the Wagner Theatre at Hamble will sit in a dark auditorium, and the pianist will be a silhouette against a suffusion of tonic colour.'

Stephen himself had written a three-act symbolic play, *The Everlasting Choice*, complete with Wagnerian music, for the theatre's public debut, and C.B. displayed his skills of articulation as a reader of poetry, interpreting Walter de la Mare's 'The Listeners' and 'The Midlands' by John Drinkwater. *The Everlasting Choice* was invested with much of the spirit of the *Mercury* itself as it symbolised the adventures of the Soul on two roads—that of ease and selfishness and that of high endeavour and self-sacrifice that 'endures to the end'.

It is worth pointing out that the *Mercury* band were of a consistently high standard despite the obvious problems of rapidly changing personnel. They were even featured on BBC Radio's 'Bandsmen of To-morrow' feature in August 1943, bandmaster Eric McGavin telling the *Southern Daily Echo*: 'It is no easy task to keep a standard with the demand for boys for the Royal Navy and the Merchant Navy. My solo cornet player sailed from England three days before the BBC recording, and my present band have been together barely twelve weeks!'

The overall reputation of the *Mercury* as a training establishment was emphasised by the visits of two royal guests at the end of the 1920s. On 15 December 1927 the Prince of Wales, destined to reign briefly as Edward VIII, came to Hamble for the speech day. It was a big occasion, not just for everyone involved with the training ship, but also for the villagers who rushed out into the streets to catch a brief glimpse of the royal visitor. The *Southern Daily Echo* reported: 'Perhaps even more conscious than the boys of the honour the Prince was conferring upon the establishment was Commander C.B. Fry.'

The Prince was suitably impressed by the aura of discipline and efficiency and said, 'I congratulate Commander and Mrs Fry and all who have been responsible for so many years now in training well over 2,000 boys, giving them such a wonderful opening, such a fine foundation for their future, whether it be in the Royal Navy or in the merchant service, or even in jobs ashore.' He recalled his own days as a naval cadet and said how much he had hated long speeches. 'I did not get a prize,' he said, 'but I did get extra leave, so I have asked Commander Fry to give you two extra days at the end of your summer leave.'

The Prince was treated to an impressive selection of musical items by the band, including the prelude to Wagner's *Parsifal*, and *The Everlasting Choice* was given another airing. Quite a family benefit this: Faith Fry was Lady of the Prologue in her brother's play and also showed her considerable talent as a violinist.

Two years later the Duke of York, the future George VI, was invited to do the honours at the *Mercury* speech day. He had been given an excellent report on the establishment by his brother, and in the absence of C.B. (who had returned from India the previous winter suffering from mental illness and was now mainly based in London) the Duke was shown round by Mrs Fry. He told the boys: '*Mercury* prepares and fully qualifies you for the great battle of life. Having shown you the way, she can do no more; the rest is left to you, and I know you will not fail.'

At the end of 1935, when the *Mercury* had reached its Golden Jubilee, King George V relayed a message of congratulations from Windsor Castle: 'His Majesty feels that in this jubilee year of the *Mercury*'s existence you and Mrs Fry must feel rewarded by the success of your efforts.' C.B. responded: 'I have devoted the past 27

years to the *Mercury* and I feel that I have done something–
something more than knocking up a few ducks on the cricket field.'

Mrs Fry had got used to C.B. grabbing the headlines, but at the
end of May 1928 she had been subjected to a little flattering
attention herself. The root cause was a meeting of the Southampton Master Mariners' Club, 'The Cachalot', where one of the
subjects under discussion was the feasibility and desirability of
women becoming master mariners. It was a suggestion that Capt.
W.V.J. Clarke, DSC, refused to take seriously, saying: 'When I think
of this I cannot help casting my mind back to the half-deck. If
women became master mariners then it might as well be called the
better half-deck. I also think that there would be a bigger run on
paint. I can imagine them going to the bosun for lipstick.' A less
chauvinistic view was advanced by Commander Rupert Jones,
who cited Beatrice Fry as the prime example of a woman who
would not be found wanting in such a responsible position. 'She
used to lead the boys over the masthead. She set a wonderful
standard,' said Commander Jones. Despite his open-mindedness,
however, 'The Cachalot' voted by a resounding 33 votes to two
against the proposal.

Mrs Fry was asked by the *Evening News* if she felt she could have
become a master mariner. 'I am sure I would have succeeded had I
tried,' she said, 'and I would have enjoyed trying.' The *Daily
Chronicle* brought up the question of mutiny and the likelihood of
sea-sickness. Mrs Fry's reply was: 'There would be no fear of
mutiny if a woman were in command. As for sea-sickness, a
woman is no more liable to sea-sickness than is a man.' There was
also loyal support from C.B., who explained that the job of master
mariner soon sorted out the men (or the women) from the boys (or
the girls)–'You cannot cheat the sea; you cannot cheat the winds
and the waves. There is no way of getting round the things that
happen at sea, except by being competent to deal with them . . . If
men think that a woman can conduct a ship safely they will
certainly serve under her.'

If anyone needed confirmation of the resilience and self-reliance
associated with all connected with the *Mercury* there was ample
proof in their reaction to disaster in 1930. While the *Mercury* slept
on the night of 4 May fire broke out near the boiler-room and
quickly spread to other parts of the shore establishment. The

alarm was given by Charis Fry, who fortuitously awoke and through her bedroom window saw a 'mass of flames' coming from the boiler-house and bathroom. The blaze took hold with frightening speed because most of the buildings were made of wood with corrugated iron roofs.

Three fire brigades were alerted and called to the scene, but it was no simple mission for the Hamble brigade because sewage pipes were being laid in the High Street and they could not get their equipment through. In desperation they made a bumpy detour across fields to get to the fire.

Meanwhile the training ship had been plunged into darkness by the fusing of the light line from the shore, but there was not the first hint of panic among the *Mercury* boys, who reacted exactly as if they were taking part in a fire drill. Each one knew his responsibilities and the cardinal rule of fire-fighting—no talking—was rigorously obeyed. 'The boys lived up to their training and tradition', said one of the *Mercury* officers. 'They assembled and paraded out of their dormitories as though it were an ordinary fire drill. After they were all clear they did everything possible in helping to prevent the fire from spreading. One or two received cuts on the hand in assisting to remove furniture from rooms that were threatened.'

The youngsters also cut down dangerous trees and even took hoses to help out the hard-pressed firemen. Some of them appeared at the morning parade complete with the wounds of battle, but there were no complaints. The raging furnace took two-and-a-half hours to control, with flames leaping sixty feet into the air, and at first light the full extent of the damage became clear. Two school-rooms, the bathroom, boiler-room, dining hall, officers' sitting room and wireless room were all destroyed, as well as valuable oil paintings and other items of historical value. The damage was conservatively estimated at £4,000, but as Mrs Fry lamented, the disaster struck deeper than that: 'We have absolutely lost some of our most useful property,' she said. 'We feel like a bird that has lost its wing.'

Somehow the indomitable *Mercury* spirit saw the establishment through the crisis. The theatre became a temporary dining-room and they also managed to come up with emergency washing facilities. The messages of sympathy and support flooded in from all over the country, including one from the Duke of York.

In December 1930 Rear-Admiral M.E. Dunbar-Nasmith, VC, was the guest of honour at the *Mercury* speech day and he took the opportunity to reflect on the fire: 'You were faced with a situation which would have caused 99 schools out of 100 to close their doors, and send their pupils home. The truly gallant effort made on the part of Mrs Fry, the staff, and you boys, which enabled you to carry on, is worthy of the highest praise.'

By then the rebuilding programme was well under way and a year after the fire had ripped the heart out of the *Mercury* a superior set of rooms had replaced the buildings destroyed in the blaze.

Looking back over forty years, and much longer in some cases, there are common strands to the recollections of *Mercury* old boys. They think back to the overwhelming toughness of the régime, they remember Mrs Fry as the real boss and in most cases they feel that the discomfort and rigorous discipline were justified. It was a case of being told, or coming to realise afterwards, that the medicine had to taste unpleasant if it was going to do any good.

It was no handicap to be a talented sportsman, especially in C.B.'s eyes, and Reg Sinfield, the *Mercury* boy who went on to play cricket for England, was particularly blessed in this respect. He was on the ship during the first two years of the First World War and it was no coincidence that he was made leading hand. 'If you were a sportsman with C.B. and Mrs Fry, you were made,' he said. One of his privileges was to cycle into Netley each morning to buy newspapers and magazines. On Fridays he was kept busy doing the shopping, armed with the extraordinarily detailed lists that Mrs Fry compiled.

According to Reg Sinfield there were distinct differences between C.B. and Mrs Fry in their attitude to discipline: 'Although he was a disciplinarian he was very fair, but with her everything had to go like clockwork. I think she was too much of a disciplinarian and there were complaints from parents. People found C.B. a bit stand-offish, but I think he was just a bit reserved.'

C.B. had a highly practical approach to punishment. When Sinfield had got involved in a brawl with another boy the honorary director hauled them along to the gym, handed the two offenders boxing gloves and told them to sort out their differences under

Marquis of Queensberry rules.

Fry also had a novel way of employing Reg Sinfield for a spot of net practice: 'He took us for maths and he always used to ask me the hard questions, which I got wrong of course. The penalty was that I had to go and bowl at him in the nets. He used to ask for some half-volleys outside the off stump, then some straight half-volleys and then some on the leg stump.'

In later years Sinfield came back to play for the *Mercury* side during cricket week and the training-ship team, already boasting reliable performers in C.B. and Stephen Fry, were often strengthened by illustrious guest players like Ranji's nephew, Duleepsinhji, and the Nawab of Pataudi.

As a coach of young cricketers Fry tended to presuppose basic coordination and a good eye, qualities which were not necessarily evident. He was impatient for results and although his uncanny grasp of all aspects of batsmanship could be communicated successfully to the quick and willing learner, he overawed less capable performers. Nevertheless, there were original images which stuck in the mind. Peter Whitlock remembers being told by Fry that the head was balanced on the body like a billiard ball at the end of a cue.

There was something rather more sinister in the punishments, uncomfortably close to sadism, which were an integral part of life on the *Mercury*. Undoubtedly the original impetus came from Mrs Fry, but there were also instructors who abused the emphasis on discipline and took perverse pleasure in the suffering of the youngsters.

It was quite understandable that efforts should be made to ensure that the boys were proficient in swimming, but Reg Sinfield remembered an instructor who ducked the ones who were slower to pick up the skill. He earned a rebuke from C.B., but responded by imposing even stricter discipline and penalties. It was not unheard-of for boys to be made to swim round the training ship at four or five o'clock in the morning, even when the water temperature was dangerously low.

Punishments were severe and varied and they could not be easily forgotten by the punished. Richard Robinson, whose father was closely involved with the *Mercury*, wrote in explanation of Mrs Fry's approach: 'She was a little alarming to a small boy. I remember meeting her at a time when she was coming under a lot of criticism from parents and others for her harshness, the fact that boys were being made to go barefooted through the summer, on gravel paths. I had gone there with a message from my father. Mrs Fry was talking to a parent on the verandah. She turned to the woman. "Look at that boy," she said. "He's come a mile barefooted." Then she added, "And he likes it." It was gruffly spoken, but I am sure there was warmth there, and approval.'

James Darby, who was on the *Mercury* during Charles Fry's period of mental illness at the start of the 1930s, recalled:

Misdemeanours were recorded in a book and a cross was marked against our number. The list of crosses was read out every week in the Mess Hall by Mr McGavin. The cadets had a saying, 'Ten thousand times ten thousand the cross list is read and Bandy (Mr McGavin) in his temper sent all the messes out.' Cadets collecting many crosses would probably lose their good conduct badges, allowance of tuck and so on. I did not get many crosses, so I am vague about punishments inflicted, but they were harsh. I do recall a boy being strapped to the vaulting horse on the verandah of the cricket pavilion. His back was bared and he was caned severely which brought out wheels and welts. I do not remember if his back was bleeding, but all the cadets had to watch this act of cruelty.

Discipline became less heavy-handed in recognition of more liberated times, but instructors could still adopt a vigorous approach. Rex Mudway was on the *Mercury* from 1943–5 and remembered in particular Chief Officer Fraser: 'He could be very handy with his fists towards us, but even so he was quite well liked probably because if you were hit it was deserved. Some sailors off a landing craft moored near to us saw him in action one day and they used to keep a close eye on him until their ship left for the Normandy landings.'

The emotive word which a lot of *Mercury* old boys have used to describe their time on the training ship is 'hell', yet they have largely managed to avoid the emotional scars which one might associate with over-zealous punishment. Ian Dodd, a cadet from 1941–2, said he did not find the discipline excessive, adding: 'In fact in my own case, I found that when I joined His Majesty's Forces after leaving the *Mercury* it was like going into a holiday camp, because I had completed all my basic training at the *Mercury* and so I was, so to speak, inured to the discipline in H.M. Forces.'

The relationship between the *Mercury* and Hamble was carefully monitored and restricted by the Frys. Villagers who were seen as being higher up the social scale were invited to occasions at the training ship, but the boys' contact with the community outside was severely limited. C.B. himself liked to play the part of the local squire, riding into the village on his horse. He would stop outside the post office and get someone to tend the beast while he went in to complete his business.

Quite a few of the villagers depended on the training ship for employment and this was one good reason why a veil of secrecy was passed over the relationship between Charles Hoare and Beatrice Fry to be. It would make lively gossip column material now, but in late Victorian times the scandal would have been all the greater.

Most of the family were involved with the running of the *Mercury*, especially between the wars. Robin Hoare, one of Mrs Fry's children by the *Mercury* founder, was the exception. He won the DSO in the First World War and then went into fish farming. Sybil, on the other hand, was very much involved and ran the office. She was a miserable spinster, decidedly unpopular and inspired more fear than her mother. Faith Fry was of similar disposition, but there was much more warmth about Charis, who worked hard and suffered a lot from headaches. After C.B. was ejected as director in 1950 she became principal of Queen Alexandra's House, an institution for British and foreign students in London. Both Charis and Faith became chief officers in the Women's Royal Naval Service during the Second World War—'I have to address them as "Ma'am," ' said C.B.

The end of the Frys' joint reign on the *Mercury* came suddenly with Mrs Fry's death in 1946 at the age of eighty-two. On 12 April her left leg gave way while she was climbing stairs on the training ship and three days later she was taken into the Royal South Hants and Soton Hospital. A fracture of the left femur was diagnosed and on 23 April she died. An inquest the following day established that the cause of death was 'hypostatic pneumonia due to myocardial degeneration and fracture of the left femur.'

C.B.'s response to his Madame's death was stoic. Within the framework of marriage they had retained determined independence and, ironically, it was after they took on the running of the *Mercury* that the periods of separation became more frequent. Nevertheless, they had been together for forty-eight years and Fry's casual replies to words of sympathy were no indication of his true feelings.

Denzil Batchelor wrote in his *Life of Fry*: 'I went down to her memorial service, and Charles wrung me by the hand and said, to hide his emotion, "Look, I'll show you an infallible way to play a googly." He had picked up a cricket bat and was demonstrating imperiously, when the chapel bell rang. "Never mind, we'll finish afterwards." ' Christopher Hollis recalled sending a letter of condolence to C.B. 'He replied, "Dear Christopher, it is quite all right," and went on to complain about his income tax.'

The world at large was soon assured that C.B. had no intention of surrounding himself in a cocoon of private grief. Just a month after his wife had died Fry's name was appearing once again in the letters' column of *The Times*, bemoaning the widespread criticism of the modern breed of bowlers.

He still found it hard to decide whether he was a rebel or a tyrant. In 1948 he wrote the introduction to *Boys Will Be Boys* by Ernest Sackville Turner, a book about Bloods and Penny Dreadfuls—magazines which boys read purely for recreation. 'Silly cinema, cretinous croon-words have a deleterious effect,' he wrote in *Boys Will Be Boys*. 'The cinema of the baser sort and the moronic verbosity of the crooner, are ten times worse than any Blood could be.' His message was that anything which undermined discipline was bad and the sermon was also given in the *Sunday Chronicle* in May 1948, with only the odd word altered:

I would institute severe legal penalties against such deleterious stuff. Irreverence and indiscipline are great weaknesses in present-day outlook and behaviour. They are dangerous faults.

Bad literature, bad cinema, bad art of all sorts has a most deleterious effect.

The evil they do is this–they have a large influence in fixing in the mind of youth crude and inappropriate attitudes, i.e. tendencies to respond to situations.

The result of these artificial low-grade fixations is deplorable. General taste is vitiated. Youth and maiden are induced to substitute the world of blood, cinema, crooner for the real world.

They become functionally unable to face things as they are. They project their stock attitudes, absorbed from these primitive and under-bred sources into their world of everyday life. They accept these second-hand and third-rate values.

The previous year had seen the Ministry of Education carry out a full inspection of the *Mercury*. It emerged with flying colours, but it was now classed as a secondary school and the training ship's curriculum was expected to take in more formal education in the classroom, at the expense of practical skills.

C.B. felt estranged from the new climate, but he was still reluctant to throw in the towel when it was decided in 1950 that he would have to resign and make way for a younger, fitter man. Fry announced his resignation at the end of May 1950 and the management committee required him to quit the house by 1 July. He was understandably hurt by the sudden turn of events. He admitted that he had been ill for most of the time during the previous two years, but he was on his way back to full fitness when the bombshell struck.

He was to get a pension of £400 a year and was expected to supplement his income with royalties from *Life Worth Living* and the occasional newspaper article, although by now he was no longer in demand as a journalist. His successor, to be called Captain Superintendent, was Commander Matthew Bradby, a former tea planter and principal of an approved school at Heswall. He was to be paid £800 per annum.

It was initially suggested that C.B. should stay on in Hamble village, but he thought that it would not be fair to Commander Bradby if he stayed on the patch. He considered returning to Brighton, the scene of his cricketing triumphs with Sussex, but finally opted for a flat in London's Golders Green, to the evident surprise of his family. His destination could even have been

Scotland: a hotel owner from Ayrshire read about C.B.'s plight and offered him the use of a twelve-room house. Fry was suitably touched, but at least the Moreland Court flat, which he referred to as a 'rabbit hutch', had the advantage of being within ten minutes' drive of Lord's.

Under Commander Bradby's leadership the *Mercury* attempted to move into line with the modern world. More schoolmasters were employed and they ceased to wear uniform, so a dividing line was created between studies and seamanship training. The personal interest of Commander Bradby was reflected in a revival of the *Mercury*'s theatrical traditions and cadets successfully came to terms with the introduction of GCE examinations.

When Commander Bradby was forced to retire prematurely because of ill health in 1960 he was succeeded by R.F. Hoyle, who attempted to strengthen the training ship's educational base still further. The results were quite good: in 1960 *Mercury* cadets gained a total of 48 'O' Level passes, which rose to 126 in 1967, and some even went on to take 'A' Levels and were accepted at the Britannia Royal Naval College in Dartmouth.

This in itself was not enough to guarantee the *Mercury*'s survival. Only a handful of boys were joining the Royal Navy each year. The majority were going into the Merchant Navy and although some shipping companies were delighted to take on *Mercury* boys, circumstances legislated against the ship.

Sharply rising costs brought about an inevitable increase in fees, which fewer and fewer parents felt they could afford. At the same time education authorities were questioning the value of pre-sea training as opposed to ordinary secondary school education and they were reluctant to hand out training grants. The *Mercury* could boast with some justification that boys received a better education there than at ordinary schools, but this was ignored. In 1964-5 there had been a record number of 167 cadets, but at the end of 1967 this had fallen to 120. The unavoidable financial fact of life was that the *Mercury* needed a minimum of 150 cadets to break even and the trustees saw no option but to close the ship down in 1968.

However, some people who were involved with the *Mercury* refuse to accept that it needed to be closed. The feelings of regret were heightened when the bulldozers moved in and the shore establishment was ingloriously laid to rest. In its place an uninspiring housing estate was placed and the only memorials are street names—Fry Close, Mercury Gardens and St Agatha's Road, named after the chapel. When the chapel was knocked down Alan Hooker paid £5 for a lorry-load of stones which he turned into a wall in front of his home in Satchell Lane, Hamble. Part of the training ship lives on, but as Alan Hooker so evocatively said: 'The *Mercury* died with the Frys.'

16

POLITICS — HOME AND ABROAD

The legendary partnership between Charles Fry and Ranjitsinhji was renewed in unexpected circumstances as the League of Nations took their first hesitant steps towards establishing a framework for peace and international co-operation after the First World War. Ranji was asked to represent the ruling Princes on the Indian delegation to Geneva and he sought out his old sparring partner as his assistant. Thus when members of the British and Dominion delegations met up with their French counterparts in Paris on 12 November 1920, en route for Geneva, the *Daily News* wrote: 'One interesting and unexpected figure in the party is Mr C.B. Fry . . . the Jam Sahib evidently taking the very proper view that the man who is good at cricket is good at anything.'

There was great confusion at Paris because the British Embassy had neglected to reserve places on the train, but after vigorous protestations from C.B. the Geneva-bound party succeeded in sharing accommodation with fellow delegations. It was an early test for the spirit of international co-operation!

Things ran no more smoothly during the first few days in Switzerland. Ranji found himself cramped for room at the Hotel de la Paix and at a dinner given by the British minister, Theo Russell, Ranji was upset because he was not given precedence over representatives from the Dominions. When he wrote to complain about the arrangement there was some suggestion that Fry had put him up to it, but Ranji maintained that although he personally did not care about who was called into dinner first there was an important principle at stake.

The rumpus was compounded at a banquet given by Sir Eric Drummond, Secretary to the League, who made an attempt to get round the earlier confusion by placing delegates in alphabetical order. Unfortunately the plan backfired when Ranji found he had been allotted the same seat as a Central American delegate. He threatened to walk out and only remained after Sir Eric Drummond had begged him not to be so hasty.

However, there were further recriminations and it was felt in British diplomatic circles that Ranji had only reacted because of the urgings of C.B., who was thought to rate his position as the Jam Sahib's assistant particularly highly.

The matter was soon forgotten, but C.B. continued to relish his role as Ranji's right-hand man and he was vested with more authority than anyone in his position had a right to expect. Three years after his arrival at Geneva, Fry was sufficiently *au fait* with the complex workings of the League to write the *Key-Book of the League of Nations* for Hodder and Stoughton. It was about as dry as a desert, more the C.B. of *Great Batsmen* and *Batsmanship* than the *Evening Standard*'s free-flowing columnist of the 1930s. He included a mass of diagrams and charts explaining the subtle interplay between the various organisations within the League. There was just the occasional hint of emotional commitment from this fresh-faced harbinger of optimism: 'What does the Covenant, with its aims and objects, and its various provisions, tell us? It tells of a spirit superior to all national and class interests — the Spirit of Humanity — emerging serene and dominant from the slaughter-pit of universal war, constant in its purpose of building up a new world from the ruins of the old.'

History's verdict on the League of Nations has been a cynical one, reflecting the naivety of the highly capable people who tried to make it work, but there was clearly a refreshing honesty and single-minded devotion among the delegates who formed the League's first assembly in 1920.

Charles Fry was only able to make speeches himself in committee, but due to Ranji's illness during the first session he had the opportunity to shine as substitute delegate on the finance committee. He was also on the second committee of the Assembly, dealing with organisations of the League under the categories of economics, external finance, transit, health etc. In 1923 it was Fry, together with the French and Czechoslovakian delegates, who was mainly responsible for obtaining a reduction of 1,600,000 gold francs in the 1924 budget without interfering with the League's important activities.

Fry and Ranji quickly discovered when they arrived in Geneva that their cricketing fame was not too esoteric to be recognised by their new colleagues. 'Nothing surprised me more at Geneva,' wrote Fry later, 'than that all the Delegates from all over the world knew both of us as cricketers. Indeed, in our first week or two, this allocation of our value was rather embarrassing.'

According to Fry the only other delegate who could rival Ranji's magnificent hospitality was Paderewski, the brilliant Polish pianist/politician. Meanwhile, as C.B. pointed out, there was definite purpose to Ranji's dinners and banquets: 'Ranjitsinhji considered that he could do good work, since he had the means to do so, by bringing all the Delegations into social contact; and he was desirous of proving to the representatives of the nations that Indians in general, and particularly the Indian Princes, were very different from the mistaken notions commonly entertained of them. He certainly succeeded. He did big work for India at Geneva; no delegate was better known or better liked.'

C.B. recalled the incredible spreads which greeted guests when Paderewski offered Sunday dinners at his villa in Morges. Other fellow-movers during Fry's time at the League were Eduard Benes, the great Czechoslovakian statesman, the former French prime minister, Viviani, and the taciturn Japanese delegate, Baron Hayashi, who was only inspired to break his silence when C.B. was engaged in keen argument with Sir Arthur Priestley about Arab horses.

Charles Fry attended the first, third and fourth assemblies, in 1920, 1922 and 1923 respectively. There was glamour and prestige attached to the work, of course, but he also described it as the hardest he experienced in his whole life–a more formidable challenge than scoring centuries during the day then writing about them for *Daily Express* readers in the early years of the century.

He was also employed by Ranji as resident speech-writer and in this role C.B.'s big moment came in 1923. On 27 August an Italian General and four members of his staff were shot while engaged in determining the Greek-Albanian border. The Italian dictator Mussolini took this as a gross insult and followed up an ultimatum to Greece by bombarding and occupying the Greek island of Corfu.

The Greeks appealed to the League of Nations and Ranji was asked to make a speech on behalf of the British Empire, declaring that the matter was within the competence of the League. A hastily-written speech, composed by C.B., was duly delivered and noted – though it should be pointed out that the actual pressure on the Italians to withdraw came from the Council of Ambassadors in Paris. A month after the Corfu incident had flared up Mussolini agreed to evacuate the island, but he had reason to be pleased with the eventual outcome. The Greeks were ordered to accept the bulk of Italy's demands, including payment of a sizeable indemnity.

If there was one brief chapter in his life which appealed to Charles Fry's sense of the romantic and unusual, it was the suggestion, during his time at Geneva, that he should become King of Albania. It may never be established beyond all doubt that the offer was genuine, but the bulk of opinion has favoured the veracity of the tale. He himself merely claimed that he 'received a specific and definite invitation to become King of Albania, but in the indirect manner which so often characterises any affair in which an eminent Indian is concerned it amounts to this – that I was well in the running for the billet.'

During the 1920 session of the League, Ranji was visited by a member of the Albanian delegation, a Christian bishop who bore a striking resemblance to W.G. Grace and had apparently been empowered with the task of finding a likely lad at Geneva. The blueprint was given as an English country gentleman with £10,000 a year with which to boost the state coffers. The effect of the bishop's initial overtures to Ranji was that he asked C.B. whether he would have any interest in such an exotic succession. Fry's response was enthusiastic and an interview as arranged at the Hotel de la Paix, with the 'heir' to the throne borrowing some lavish Indian hospitality to give the impression that he was a suitable candidate. The desired effect was achieved and the whisky-drinking bishop was given no cause to doubt Fry's credentials.

This is how he described the rather inconclusive end to the episode:

How long I remained as the first candidate in the field for the crown of Albania beyond the first fortnight I do not know. If I had really pressed Ranji to promote me, it is quite on the cards that I should have been King of Albania yesterday, if not to-day. Nor would Mussolini have disposed of me as easily as he did of King Zog. Remember Corfu!

After about a fortnight I could see that the prospect either of losing my services or of having to find the £10,000 a year was beginning to weigh down the balance in Ranji's mind against my elevation. When he casually laid stress upon the inconvenience of having to live in a lonely castle on an island, and perhaps of a bullet in the ribs, I could see at once that his lively affection for me had decided him against the adventure. At any rate, for some reason or other the proposal gradually faded out, in the way that so many projects fade out in Geneva—and in India.

The discussion was revived in 1972 when Alan Gibson wrote a piece in *The Times*, celebrating the centenary of C.B.'s birth. The former Australian cricketer, Jack Fingleton, described the story as a 'Furphey'. Ranji's nephew, Duleepsinhji, had been Indian High Commissioner in Australia, and told Fingleton that Ranji had simply been playing a joke on his great friend. The ruse had worked so well, he said, that Ranji had sustained the charade to avoid hurting Fry's feelings. The converse of this was a suggestion made to Gibson that C.B. had realised his leg was being pulled, but played along with the joke because he did not want to embarrass Ranji.

Perhaps the most authoritative viewpoint in the revived debate was that of Professor Rushbrook Williams, who was very close to the centre of the action, taking over from Charles Fry as Ranji's assistant and adviser at Geneva. He emphasised that the initial offer had been made and, more importantly, it *had* come from the Albanian bishop and not Ranji.

C.B. may have been thwarted in his regal ambitions, but his political education at Geneva was still the impetus to his efforts at becoming a Liberal MP. To him the League of Nations appeared to be 'Liberalism internationalised.' He told a meeting in Banbury Town Hall on 22 October 1923:

Most of the nonsense talked about the League is nonsense.

Just as the members of a cricket club join with the intention of keeping the rules so the nations contract to keep the rules of the League. If you understand that you have grasped the object of the League.

I can testify as a witness that in the League you have the best the world can give to cure the ills we are screaming about. There is no League of Nations if by that is meant a super-state, but it is a great international institution embodying the principles of peace, security and co-operation, which are international equivalents of freedom, justice and brotherhood . . . I want to see the women of England build the Assembly Hall which is needed at Geneva, and the men be persuaded by the women that the League is an effective instrument. The voice you can create in England will have a great influence.

However, no voice was loud enough to compensate for the absence of the USA from the League and, to a lesser extent, the temporary membership of Germany and Russia. In *Life Worth Living*, which was published as the opening salvos were fired in the Second World War, C.B. reflected sadly: 'There is not the slightest doubt that there was the fullest intention on all hands to build up the League into a successful solution of all the difficulties of the world with fair dues to friend and foe alike. The mistakes and miscalculations which in after years have been cast in the teeth of the League did not arise from any foolish and unpractical conceptions at the start. The truth is that presently some of the members began to refuse to play tennis, and others never did like tennis at all as a game.'

In retrospect he could still bask in the memory of his adventures at Geneva: 'If a grandchild ever asks me what I did after the Great War (I mean the 1914 Great War), I shall tell him that I composed a speech which turned Mussolini out of Corfu and ran prominently in the race for the Kingship of Albania.'

The 1920s, for Fry, were days to savour. For half the year at least, Hamble became a distant port. The two friends carved out a privileged routine for themselves, wintering in India and spending the summer months on Ranji's estate at Ballynahinch in Ireland.

Fry first went out to India in the autumn of 1921, accompanied by the Maharajah of Patiala. He was keen to examine at first hand the preoccupations and personality of a nation he had grown to know politically through his involvement with the League of Nations at Geneva. It did not take him long to discover that there were two truths in India—the native truth and the version according to the British Empire. It was generally expected that the British visiting India would inherit the British version, complete with its innate arrogance and paternalism which merged into condescension.

C.B. was privy, however, to the internal truth, even if he was sheltered to a degree from the trials of the natives. He saw a nation plagued by insecurity, in search of its identity. More was the shame, then, that he was never returned to Parliament, where he would have expressed a balanced, enlightened opinion on the need for constitutional reform. If the House of Commons had possessed a few more alert minds, devoid of damaging preconceptions, they could hardly have failed to produce an earlier solution.

During his first stay in India, Fry was due to dine at the Royal Bombay Yacht Club, but when he discovered that Ranji would under no circumstances be admitted, because of a rule strictly barring Indians, he swiftly withdrew. He could not condone a system which made random distinctions on élitist or racist grounds.

Ranji was accustomed to being treated like a royal, his popularity and status in direct contrast to his state of Nawanagar, which in Indian terms was of modest dimensions. Equivalent in size to Kent, Sussex and Surrey combined, it had a population of around 400,000 towards the end of the Jam Sahib's reign.

When Ranji was installed on the throne in 1907 he inherited a state which was virtually bankrupt and riddled with corruption. The new ruler's charm helped to persuade the Gaikwad of Baroda to lend money, but Ranji had a tougher job in ridding Nawanagar of its curious collection of parasites. An institution of eunuchs had established themselves and acquired large tracts of land by gift, in return for their invaluable function of frightening away evil spirits on ceremonial occasions. Ranji took back the eunuchs' land and also that of the girls who had attracted the passing fancy of the previous ruler. He was in genuine risk of being poisoned because some of those who had been dispossessed of their land were distinctly displeased with Ranji.

He had other critical problems to concern himself with in the early years of his reign. The capital town, Jamnagar, was infested with mangy dogs, many of them suffering from rabies. Malaria, cholera and plague were wiping out large numbers of people and the population was actually decreasing, so Ranji ordered that houses should be pulled down and rebuilt with proper sanitary facilities. New drains were put in, the streets were lit and the dogs were ejected. Irrigation reservoirs were also built, harbours were laid down and docks, railways and roads were built. Ranji's charismatic initiative helped to increase the state's revenue by 300 per cent.

The royal coffers were suitably stocked, although Ranji's hospitality was not quite as extravagant as some newspapers liked to claim. At the end of 1927, for instance, the *Daily Herald* carried a story claiming that the Jam Sahib had spent £200,000 entertaining the Viceroy. C.B. challenged the figure, which was obviously overstated, but the very suggestion gave some clue to the lavish entertainment which Indian Princes doled out to their guests.

Ranji wanted Fry to throw in his lot with Nawanagar and dangled a lucrative carrot in the hope that C.B. would become one of his ministers. But although he had broken away from the *Mercury* to a degree he could not sever the connection completely and he became instead an honoured guest, who wrote speeches for Ranji, accompanied him to meetings and social gatherings and took on various secretarial duties. It was as well that the agreement was never put on a formal footing. C.B., as an Englishman in the Indian's court, was in an invidious position, and the British in India were inclined to view him as a potential spanner in the works, impossible to gag and more than likely to see the natives' point of view.

When he appeared on 'Frankly Speaking' on BBC Radio in 1953, C.B. recalled: 'I was always rated as pro-Indian and rather hunted by the English bigwigs of the time. But I knew as anyone with the brains of a louse would that the only way of being pro-British then was to be pro-Indian in the right way. Well, I got into trouble. The Indian was against us more socially than politically, and really what the Indians wanted was that their face should be saved, and not feel that they were an inferior nation ruled by aliens.'

According to Fry the Indians felt cheated because the British made bold noises about home rule, but having tempted with this vision of independence they took no steps to bring about the transfer of power.

C.B. made half-a-dozen trips to India between 1921 and 1928 and while he was content to be a backroom boy he was still keen to influence the thinking of politicians at home who had it within their power to initiate change. When Lord Birkenhead became Secretary of State for India in 1924 Fry put the case for the Indian States to him and Birkenhead's parliamentary secretary, Sir Warden Chilcott, was despatched to India on a fact- and opinion-finding mission. It was partly on the strength of Chilcott's visit that the Butler and Simon Commissions came into being.

Fry remarked later in life that Ranji treated him like an amateur KC or QC and their mutual respect and friendship influenced the attitude of the other Indian Princes towards him. Instead of treating him with a mixture of affection and suspicion they looked upon the English visitor as a relation of Ranji's, a brother even. Ranji himself was the perfect host, with a hospitality that bordered on the proverbial. He had an uncanny gift for seemingly spontaneous organisation and Fry was accustomed to being woken up with the news that a shooting expedition had been decided upon. It was not always obvious at the time, but considerable planning had gone into these arrangements. However, there was no need to concern guests with shopping lists.

The Maharajah of Bikaner, another generous host, offered excellent sport for his fellow Indian potentates, their visitors and notables from British India. At Gujner there were not only ducks to shoot at, but also Imperial Sandgrouse, an imposing sight as they swooped fleetingly down to the lake.

In *Life Worth Living*, C.B. recalled some of the Maharajah's guests and a curious form of sport in which they participated with great enthusiasm: 'Sometimes in the evenings at Gujner, the Prince of Wales, Lord Cromer, Admiral Sir Lionel Halsey and I played vigorous games of billiard fives. This is a devastating game. I remember H.R.H. wrestling heavily with the Admiral underneath the billiard table for possession of the ball. Once the Prince drove a ball so hard that it leaped off a cushion onto the wall and made a round hole. The next evening the Maharajah discovered that some careful house-wallah had filled up the hole with plaster. The Maharajah's eye never misses a detail. He had the hole regouged. Why obliterate the traces of a royal guest?'

Lord Reading was one of four Viceroys with whom Fry came into contact. Lord Hardinge and Lord Chelmsford both cut more impressive figures, which was more important than it should have been, while Lord Willingdon, Fry said, achieved the remarkable feat of winning the friendship and respect of all classes of Indian people.

He was also privileged to see Mahatma Gandhi and wrote in 1940 that 'This little man is a brilliant talker and a paramount politician. What is more, he deals with an awkward argument just as Ranji used to deal with a fast bowler–he glances it to leg. Indeed, to see him sitting cross-legged on the ground at Ahmadabad in apparent poverty and few clothes on, with his protruding ears and steel spectacles, and to be suddenly involved in a stream of rather highbrow English worthy of an English professor, is startling.'

Ranji's state of Nawanagar lacked fishing, but it could offer exotic sport in the form of panther-hunting and C.B. was happy to follow a line of pursuit which had started with the humble prey of sparrows in the wilds of Kent almost fifty years earlier. It worked in Fry's favour that on the first occasion he stayed with Ranji in Nawanagar he was the only guest, for he was taken to the Burdar Hills, well-known panther territory.

Patience was the key word. Before nightfall Ranji and Fry had to be ensconced in a tower in the jungle so that they could observe the nocturnal movements. The groundwork was done by a dozen *shikaris* and goat-herds, who tried to avoid becoming human sacrifices but ran severe risks in persuading the panthers out into the open. The panther senses that when the goats are driven home its evening meal beckons and it is not put off by a carbide arc-light which it takes to be a full moon. After a long wait the panther was attracted by the plaintive cry of the tethered goat and came to investigate. Ranji was instantly aware of its proximity and told C.B. to prepare for the kill. However, it became clear when the animal homed in on the goat that it was a female and Fry

chivalrously refused to shoot. A sharp sound from Ranji made the
panther take flight, but C.B. was assured that either she or her
male partner would be back soon. The male failed to make an
appearance and at the end of a long night the hunting party were
forced to concede temporary defeat.

Ranji was determined that his guest would not be denied and
the ritual was repeated on six more nights. On each occasion,
however, either a lady appeared or no panther showed up, and C.B.
rejected Ranji's suggestion that he should bury his principles and
take a pot at a lady. Eventually a daylight victim was found and
there was an extraordinary scene as the villagers of Mopi Top
warmed to the task of setting the panther up for the kill. The
shikaris threw stones at it and Fry waited for the moment of truth.
'Suddenly there was a silence. The panther was under way. View
halloos might have caused him to break back. I saw a creature like
a yellow maggot threading the bed of the nullah towards us. He
crept slowly along, with his white belly scraping the ground. Very
different from the tall, ghostlike panthers of the night jungle. They
were feline greyhounds. This fellow, until he stood up fifty yards
away and began to lope, was a huge dachshund-mastiff. As he went
by, just after he was past me, I had an easy shot and bowled him
over.'

As mentioned earlier, Nawanagar could not cater adequately for
the fisherman. C.B. ventured into Kashmir for a spot of trout-
fishing, but the rarefied atmosphere was not sympathetic to
Ranji's asthma and he had to look elsewhere for sport. Holidaying
in Ireland the two men discovered that there was splendid salmon
and sea-trout fishing at Ballynahinch Castle in Connemara. They
were hooked. Ranji, not content with renting his holiday home,
bought the property instead and he and C.B. enjoyed idyllic
summers in the 1920s seeking out the bounteous fish. Fry recalled
catching no less than sixty salmon in the space of three weeks,
including a 29-pounder which led him a merry dance downstream
before succumbing.

The weighty concerns of state were largely forgotten on these
Irish sojourns, but the two men could not escape their fame
entirely and during one visit they were invited to Dublin as the
guests of the Government. At a banquet their presence was noted
by the prominent Irish politician, Tim Healy, who was delighted

that they had chosen the waters of Ballynahinch in preference to more glamorous haunts at the far corners of the earth. C.B.'s classical background came in handy: the banquet was being held to mark the Tailtean Games, an Irish version of the Olympic Games, and Fry marked the occasion with thirty effortlessly delivered lines from Aristophanes' *Frogs*.

In 1908 Charles Fry was asked whether he would consider standing for Parliament. He showed instinctive interest and nominated Oxford City as the seat he would most like to fight; but there were still runs to be scored and a training ship to be resuscitated: politics could wait.

He was already an experienced speaker when that suggestion was made. The sporting superstar had been in demand for years and when *Fry's Magazine* started up in 1904 he was quickly bombarded with invitations to expand in print on the trenchant views which he soon had already made public. Wallis Myers wrote of Fry the orator:

> In speech, as in action, there is about him the note of intensity; but while he is voluble he is always fluent, while he is independent he is always relevant. Never by any chance does he talk by the clock. The graceful decision of movement in his gestures, and the absence of stress and effort proclaim him to be a man accustomed to exercise and the open air. Were he compelled to speak from his seat, with hands and head motionless, one can well believe the utterance would lose much of its persuasiveness and charm; for he must up and be doing. Indeed, when he rises at a dinner-table, instead of speaking with his back to the chair, and his hands resting on the table, he will nimbly step back and use the top of the chair as a kind of forum on which to emphasise his points.

Fry's political ambitions were rekindled at the end of the First World War. He was in the twilight of his cricket career and having succeeded in putting the *Mercury* on a sound footing he was ready for a fresh challenge. He felt great affinity with the newly-formed League of Nations and further motivation was provided by Ranji, who was keen to see a group of MPs with a sympathetic under-standing of the Indian question.

Narrow-minded detractors have suggested that C.B.'s successes were ultimately outweighed by his failure to find an immortal niche. What would have happened if Fry had taken 150 of the votes which went to his Conservative opponent in the 1923 election at Banbury? His combination of ingenuity, brain power and asser-tiveness would surely have taken the House of Commons by storm. Prime Minister perhaps? Cabinet minister at the very least? But he would never have warmed to the discipline of party politics. He was essentially an independent and although he responded to Liberal overtures when the opportunity beckoned, the affection did not endure. There was natural empathy between the Liberal party and the League of Nations, but his thoughts were those of an original, pursuing every problem and issue from first cause. Undoubtedly he would have been the MP who ignored the three-line whip, the maverick who sensed the emergence of a power-seeking faction but rejected its advances. The rebel in Fry went unexorcised with age. He may sometimes have exaggerated the shock which his actions engendered in others, but he had a predilection and a shining talent for argument which would have marked him out as a rare jewel in the political arena. His achievements in other areas left little doubt that he had the single-mindedness to confront any challenge with the intensity of a head-hunter, but politics had a more complex ring. The ambition and lust for power which characterise so many politicians were not in Fry's make-up.

In 1919 Fry came curiously close to standing as Labour candi-date for Horsham and Worthing. The confusion first arose when he attended a League of Nations meeting at Chichester and on the spur of the moment made a speech on the humbug of condemning the League before a study had been made of its aims. Labour activists asked him to oppose Lord Winterton and he agreed on the understanding that they found the strongest Tory district and he would address a meeting there. After he had spoken at the meeting someone came up to him and said: 'You are a Liberal.' He replied: 'I'm sorry. I simply told you what I think.' Another candidate was found.

Rumours connected C.B.'s name with the Horsham and Worthing seat again in 1922 and by now the locals were clearer about his political allegiance: it was suggested that he should represent the joint Labour and Liberal interest. However, a more attractive proposition had come up in the shape of Brighton, one of the few constituencies where two members were elected, and Fry was confirmed as Liberal candidate at the beginning of November, which disappointed more than one local Liberal party. It must be said that the Liberals were in decline, and while Fry was the sole party representative at Brighton there were two formidable Conservatives in opposition, one of whom, Major George Tyron, had been made Minister of Pensions in a Cabinet reshuffle just two weeks before the election.

Fry and his wife caught a train from London's Victoria Station on 2 November and at Brighton they were met by an enthusiastic band of party workers and press who were given an immediate taste of Fry the ingenuous political novice. He was asked what he proposed to do and C.B. replied with characteristic enthusiasm and less typical self-effacement: 'Whatever you think best. You can do just what you like with me.'

The Frys' first step was to take up residence at the Hotel Metropole and on that same evening there was a message of encouragement from Sir John Simon, C.B.'s colleague at Wadham, who himself was just being readmitted to the political mainstream after defeat at the 1918 General Election. Simon's wire carried the sporting allusion which became the trademark of so many messages of goodwill to Fry. It read: 'Bravo. Feel confident you will make top score. Every good wish – From your old friend, John Simon.'

It was Fry's reply the following day which revealed his inexperience in matters of electioneering and set him up for ridicule from his rivals for the seat. His message to Simon was: 'I sincerely hope we shall join hands soon in the great game where the stakes are a happier England, with social and political justice.' He received a stern-faced reminder that the welfare of the nation was not comparable to cricket and that betting should not be allowed to enter the equation.

It was unquestionably a *faux pas* on Fry's part, but the voting public warmed to his openness and humour. His Tory rivals were more *au fait* with local and national issues and they knew when it was prudent to remain tight-lipped. C.B. had the international string to his bow, but he preferred to cover gaps in his knowledge with circuitous answers, often embroidered with rich humour, and was even honest enough to plead ignorance when questioners probed a weak spot.

Run-drenched afternoons at Hove were brought into sweet relief by the arrival of Ranji and his entourage. Ranji was often present at Fry's pre-election meetings in Brighton and while he refused to align himself with a political camp, also attending Conservative meetings to preserve the illusion of impartiality, his presence could only add weight and charisma to Fry's campaign. Pressmen were assured that only one car had been made available for Fry, but there appeared to be a whole fleet bearing the royal arms of the Jam Sahib. 'Even I feel like a prince when I ride in one of them,' said the Liberal agent.

When C.B. wasn't travelling in motorised style he was playing the part of the open-air man. He cantered round the streets of Brighton in riding breeches, top-boots and spurs and showed himself off to the electorate. When a crowd gathered he would address them from the natural dais of the saddle.

On 3 November Fry made his opening speech at the North Road Lecture Hall, the rapturous welcome announcing the wave of enthusiasm which he whisked up wherever he spoke during the campaign. He told audiences that if there was any town he regarded as home it was Brighton. 'I spent as a small boy a lot of time in Brighton and whenever I came here I always had a bilious attack on the first day.'

His inflated view of the League of Nations was revealed when he said he had come through 'the greatest Arc de Triomphe in the annals of time'. He was a Liberal, he said, because Liberals represented progress. He wanted politics to be honest and free of catchphrases. This had special significance because Fry had shown utter contempt for Conservative claims that he had borrowed their slogan 'Don't be misled'. It was inconceivable, he maintained, that he should associate himself with a negative concept.

A couple of sharp exchanges with questioners showed how Fry's sense of humour could easily be construed as flippancy. The *Sussex Daily News* wrote: 'Replying to a lady, who asked if he thought so much land should be kept for the "sacred pheasant" he said:

"When a pheasant is on the wing and I have a gun, I find it very difficult to treat it as a sacred bird." Answering another inquirer he said he considered 'undesirable aliens extremely undesirable.'

Harry Wheater, the Independent Conservative candidate who was championing the anti-waste cause, clearly did not rate Fry as a genuine prospect for election at the start of the campaign. He said he was his friend, but felt he was not as serious and earnest as he might have been when confronted with issues of great import.

Nevertheless, during the fortnight leading up to the election the Conservative candidates and supporters could not fail to notice, with increasing concern, the success of the Fry guide to conversion – the show-business appeal of his glittering past allied to an endearingly straight bat. Ranji's mere presence was a tremendous plus-mark, while the famous singer Clara Butt, a friend of the Frys, gave musical support to the cause.

C.B. was left in no doubt that he had the backing of the Liberal hierarchy. Lord Gladstone, perhaps unwittingly, gave a genuine indicator to Fry's politics when he sent him a telegram which read: 'On behalf of the Liberal Party I heartily wish you success. If real Liberalism is to have its way in the new Parliament we must have true Liberals like you.' Three years before his death Fry threw more light on his curious relationship with the Liberals. In a radio interview he said: 'I told Asquith I wasn't a Liberal. I was an Independent. He said, never mind, you be independent and we'll see if we can get you to vote Liberal when we get you into Parliament.'

Gladstone was both right and considerably wide of the mark. Fry was capable of a spring-cleaning exercise in any party, but Gladstone would have more faithfully captured the man's appeal if he had distinguished between the manifesto scholars who simply relayed the Liberal line and the free-thinkers like Fry who were liberal in its all-embracing sense.

But such distinctions were irrelevant to the people of Brighton and the ecstatic local Liberals who spoke of the greatest support for Liberalism in the town since 1905. One policy statement particularly appealing to Brightonians was Fry's declaration that he was in sympathy with full divorce facilities for men and women.

However, he confessed to a lunchtime gathering of railwaymen at York Hill that he didn't feel completely at home fighting elections: 'I am not used to oratory,' he said. 'I would much rather be playing football.'

There were no sophisticated opinion polls in 1922, but as polling day approached there was a definite feeling in the town that C.B. might threaten the Tory stranglehold. D-Day was on 15 November, and the Frys were joined by their son Stephen for the announcement of the results the following day. The majority of the second Conservative over Fry, just 4,785 votes, was seen as a minor miracle. At the previous election the two Tory candidates had finished almost 24,000 votes clear of their two Labour opponents.

Anyone attending the after-match receptions, without prior knowledge of the results, would have been convinced that Fry had booked his passage to Westminster. This was clear indication that he had exceeded all reasonable expectations by capturing 22,059 votes. He told buoyant Liberal supporters that the two weeks leading up to the election had been among the happiest days of his life, and although he had been beaten he had the consolation of knowing that he had polled more votes than any other Liberal candidate at the General Election.

Fry's exultant rearguard action at Brighton was not forgotten: he was quickly marked down in the Liberal form book as one to watch and encourage. In time-honoured tradition the party hierarchy wanted to reward C.B.'s near-miraculous showing on the south coast with a more realistic opportunity for election.

Another General Election loomed at the end of 1923 and early in November the *Oxford Chronicle*, an unashamed Liberal mouthpiece, announced that C.B. was a strong tip for the Banbury seat. There were similarities to Brighton, since Banbury was close enough to Oxford for voters to be fully aware of the all-round swathe Fry had cut through university life in the 1890s and his subsequent sporting triumphs. The Conservative candidate, Major Edmondson, had won in 1922 with a majority of almost 5,000, but it was widely felt that the electorate were inherently Liberal in their sympathies. The prospect was that Labour would not fight the seat, leaving the way open for the Liberal choice to sweep up the Progressive vote.

That was the scenario anyway, with the prospect of Fry being the Liberal nominee. Another term with the League of Nations had only boosted his political credibility and he had already announced his arrival in Oxford by speaking to the Oxford International Assembly about reparations, the current controversy about how much Germany should be made to pay for their promotion of the First World War. A lively discussion was envisaged between Fry and Count Bernstorff, the First Secretary of the German Embassy in London, but C.B.'s fellow-speaker was forced to pull out at the last minute because of a heavy cold. He might not have relished the confrontation in the peak of health. In Bernstorff's absence Charles Fry introduced the various quaint equations which were being put forward in an effort to arrive at the Germans' bill. The American President, Woodrow Wilson, emerged with the sum of A (damage from air) plus B (sea damage) plus L (land damage) equalling R (reparations). Others, said Fry, had complicated the equation by introducing the factor H (honourable understanding), which could be divided into the damage total to produce a more agreeable figure.

In the 'Out and About' column in the *Oxford Chronicle* on 9 November there was this vote of confidence: 'The Liberals of North Oxfordshire will be particularly fortunate if, as now seems likely, they secure Mr C.B. Fry as their candidate at the coming election. Mr Fry's Liberalism is of a very robust school, and I should say that his general views would be quite acceptable to the majority of those who voted for a Labour candidate at the last election.' In a leading article in the same issue the note of confidence was endorsed: 'North Oxon is one of those constituencies where the prevailing sentiment is undoubtedly Liberal and democratic, and where victory is assured for a Liberal candidate who can knit together Progressive voters in his support . . .'

Harold Early, who had been introduced as a Liberal candidate at a late stage in the 1922 campaign, was magnanimity itself in his appreciation of his illustrious successor. 'His name and fame will sweep through the Division like a prairie fire,' he said. He cited the *Mercury* as positive proof that Charles Fry was not one of the hard-hearted school of Oxford academics—'Fry really cares about things . . . I love the Banbury Division, but if there's any man I would gladly hand it over to, it's Charles Fry.'

The *Oxford Times* showed a certain right-wing bias by writing of C.B.: 'He might be a good candidate for a seaport town, but, so far as our County Division is concerned, we cannot rate him higher than a superior carpet-bagger.'

On 12 November local Liberals packed Banbury Town Hall and made it perfectly plain that Fry was the man they wanted. One veteran supporter described the show of enthusiasm as the 'most remarkable since 1885'. C.B. had told them: 'This piece of England caught my eye when I saw the fields and I thought of hunting. I do some hunting. However, that isn't politics, but if I fight this constituency we are going to unfurl here the proudest banner you can float in politics – to spread the standard of Liberalism.'

Fry was suitably flattered by the confidence in him as a potential candidate, but made it plain that both he and the top brass in the party wanted to ensure that this time he had a one-way ticket to the House of Commons. He told the town hall meeting that he was going to see Lord Gladstone the following morning. 'What he wants to know from me is that I am not going to stand for a constituency that is not going to shoot me in. There is very little doubt about this constituency.'

Harold Early interpreted the fatally optimistic mood of the adoption meeting when he said they would be the envy of every division in the country if they managed to secure Fry as a candidate. Sure enough he telegraphed his acceptance of the nomination on 14 November and the following night he was addressing his first meeting in the three-week build-up to the election.

It had been thought that there would be a straight fight between Charles Fry and the Conservative MP, Major Edmondson, with the majority of the 6,463 voters who had supported the Labour man, Captain Bennett, at the last election expected to transfer their vote to the Liberal nominee. Unfortunately for Fry, and the Liberal organisers who had viewed the Banbury seat as a banker, there was an unexpected turn of events as Captain Bennett announced that he was going to defy doctors' orders by standing again. Liberals saw it as a petty exercise in revenge for the run-up to the 1922 election in Banbury when the boot had been on the other foot. Then it was Labour who had made their intentions clear early in the campaign and Harold Early had taken his place on stage when the rehearsals were nearing completion. Labour supporters, however, were adamant that their views could not be fully represented by Liberal policy. The two parties were united in their opposition to Protectionism, but there was a definite feeling among Labour disciples that the Liberal Party did not have the same appetite for change in society.

Nevertheless, Captain Bennett's decision to stand was roundly condemned by the *Chronicle* as a 'futile demonstration'. They pointed out that there could be only two outcomes – either C.B. would see off both Labour and Conservative, or the Progressive vote would be split between the Labour and Liberal candidates, in which case Major Edmondson would be returned again and Protectionism would inadvertently be endorsed. In any case, the *Chronicle* pointed out rather myopically, there was no point in Bennett standing because he had no chance of winning. That much was beyond dispute and Fry gained an influential ally in Haman Porter, the Oxford district organiser of the agricultural section of the Workers' Union. Porter urged all workers to give Fry their vote on the grounds that it would prevent the Tory man getting in.

The recriminations were in vain and the smooth passage which Fry and his supporters had expected turned into an unbearably nerve-wracking campaign. By the day of the election C.B. was 'done to a turn'. In fact, he was so shattered by the exertions of the previous three weeks that he was too ill to attend the declaration and had to be represented by his agent and the ever-faithful Harold Early. C.B. initially collapsed with nervous exhaustion and after being laid up in the Randolph Hotel he was taken back to Hampshire to gather strength for the post mortems. Major Edmondson, boasting just four votes more than his 1922 return of 12,491, had clung on to the seat, just 224 ahead of Fry. The prognostications about Captain Bennett's chances proved correct as he captured just 2,500 votes and lost his deposit.

Labour's ill-timed and ill-considered intervention attracted a great deal of post-election criticism, but it was also suggested in the *Oxford Chronicle* that Fry might well have won the day if had spent a bit more time in the area and spoken to more people face-to-face. Fry returned after the weekend to thank Liberal supporters and promise them that he would be back for more. One meeting on 11 December showed that C.B. had not lost his sense of humour. The *Banbury Advertiser* reported: 'Having been handed a large box of Banbury cakes Commander Fry humorously remarked that that was not the first time he had taken the cake, but he would not handicap his opponents by saying that before the election. He was not a Prohibitionist and liked anybody who wanted to have a Banbury cake to have one.'

Harold Early was asked to look back on the campaign for the *Oxford Chronicle* and reported that following his recuperation Fry was once again 'bantering, vigorous and confident'. He concluded: 'May I sum up by saying that the general feeling of Liberals hereabouts is reflected in the answer C.B. Fry wired to his supporters on Friday afternoon: "We shall have better luck next time." '

While Charles Fry was cursing his luck at Banbury he was also able to reflect on what might have been if he had opted for one of the four other constituencies which would have valued his services, including Brighton and Southampton.

There had been a far happier outcome for Liberalism in Oxford itself. The exceptionally popular Frank Gray, who had won the seat from the Tories in 1922, regained the seat in a two-cornered fight with the Conservative candidate, Captain R.C. Bourne, his majority this time being 2,693. However, his joy was not to last long and Gray's demise signalled what was to be C.B.'s final attempt to become an MP.

Frank Gray was a lawyer with the common touch, at his best when fighting cases where the human element took priority over the legal principle. He had a curious selection of friends and he admired resourcefulness, to whatever dubious ends it might be applied. His father, Walter, had been a Conservative MP, but the younger Gray was an ardent supporter of Free Trade. He had become involved with politics through his friendship with W.R. Morris, the motor vehicle pioneer. The two fell out very publicly as Morris, whose initial success as a businessman owed much to Free Trade, became a committed Protectionist. The feud came to a head as the 1923 election loomed and it looked as though Morris would be the Tory candidate, but illness prevented his direct involvement. However, it did not rule out some merciless heckling from Morris's supporters at meetings where Gray was speaking.

Gray's success in the 1923 election confirmed the charisma which had won him the Oxford seat the previous year. Charles Fenby in *The Other Oxford* explained his infallible technique for winning votes: 'After he had given up his legal practice in 1920, Frank had an enormous fund of energy to draw on and he launched a campaign during which he called at every house in Oxford and made friends with everybody who was willing to be a friend. He had an obvious gift for making quick, superficial friendships through banter and a genuine curiosity about other people and he was soon at home even with people who received him with surliness or even hostility.'

Unfortunately Gray's golden touch as a politician was not matched by some of the people who lent their support to his 1923 campaign. The depressing revelation came when the deadline approached for submitting expenses' schedules. Officially Gray had overspent by just £2, but the actual figure was much higher. His agent, J.C. Johnstone, who had been Private Gray's captain during the war, failed to come to terms with the strict requirements of his role. Inevitably there was a petition to unseat Gray and a week-long hearing at County Hall in Oxford at the start of May 1924 exposed the wide network of irregularities without isolating every incident.

The *Oxford Chronicle* loomed large in the controversy. The editor at the time, Percy Linaker, was also joint secretary of the local Liberal Association and on the eve of the election a special edition of the *Chronicle* had been brought out, free of charge, devoted almost entirely to Gray's candidature. The *Chronicle*'s coverage of the petition hearing amounted to around 25,000 words and Johnstone was found guilty of corrupt practices. Although Gray was cleared on the same charge there was no way in which the petition could fail. It was extraordinary that an astute lawyer like Gray should have had no knowledge of the bungling going on all around him, but at least with his personal honour intact he had the motivation to give his wholehearted support to the person whom Liberals hoped would succeed him as MP.

On 16 May, two days after the petition had been decided, C.B. was addressing the Oxford Liberal Association at the Reform Club and after a weekend of consideration he accepted the invitation to stand at the by-election on 5 June. But once again the equation was unbalanced by the selection of a Labour candidate, Kenneth Lindsay, to take on Fry and the Conservative nominee.

To the popular press it was the Battle of the Blues. Charles Fry's sporting exploits at Oxford needed no amplification, but Captain Bourne had the unique record of stroking Oxford to four successive University Boat Races between 1909 and 1912, while Kenneth Lindsay was a soccer Blue. A leader in the *Oxford Chronicle* on 23 May pointed out that Fry was in fact something more than an athletic legend: 'Commander Fry is no shallow partizan, to whom politics is a game of "ins and outs", but a man anxious to serve in Parliament.' That quest was given added vigour by the endorsement of the Gray family, Frank throwing himself into the election campaign with the zest of someone determined to exorcise the ghost of his own disappointment.

The Times referred to this as a very important election and quoted Tory supremos as saying the sole issue would be motor cars and the importance of Protection in producing a healthy car industry in Britain. However, they soon broadened their outlook, choosing to hammer the Liberals for their mistake in putting Labour into office.

Fry's opening public meeting at the British Schoolroom in Cowley Road on 22 May served notice that the glorious wit which had eased him through the last two elections was still very much in evidence. His message of benevolence was: 'Do all the good you can, in all the ways you can, by all the means you can, to all the folks you can.' He said he had retained his account at the Old Bank and the manager would vouch for his financial stability; and he refuted the suggestion that he still had undergraduate debts to pay off. These had been discharged twenty-seven years earlier and solely through money earned by his own efforts. He also quashed rumours that Ranji was coming over from India, saying the Jam Sahib would no more take part in the election than he would chop off the hand of one of his subjects with his own sword.

But if there was no Ranji there was the enthusiastic Frank Holme Sumner, Fry's brother-in-law, who charmed crowds with his own brand of eccentricity. At a meeting in Summertown on 24 May he called on the audience to get down to work for the cause— to 'draw their swords and strip to the waist, like pirate kings'. However, he had second thoughts about the image and suggested instead that people should 'take off their coats to it—or at least roll up the sleeves of their jumpers'.

C.B. himself was in excellent form at the same meeting. The

Oxford Chronicle said: 'Commander C.B. Fry was received with applause and laughter when he said he was supposed by many people to be a bird who laid duck's eggs in the summer, but as a matter of fact he had done quite a lot of other things as well.' When the lights were switched on midway through the meeting Fry remarked, much to the amusement of the audience: 'Liberalism is its own light.'

At the end of his speech C.B. was asked whether he was in favour of private enterprise or mass production in the building of houses. He replied that he was in favour of using every means to get houses built. Every way was a good way.

He had an endearing talent for off-beat replies – not the standard, evasive responses of politicians determined to preserve the illusion of omniscience, more the quick-fire patter of a stand-up comedian; and always there was an inventive turn of phrase to mark him out as an original. At a mass meeting in the town hall on 28 May he said: 'Liberalism has principles and always stands by them, but it is not a cinema show policy, which changes from day to day.' At a previous gathering he was advocating equal rights for women and foresaw a women's police force. 'I believe women in politics will save the country,' he proclaimed boldly. There is still difference of opinion on whether he was proved wrong or right.

Christopher Hollis said of Fry, in *Oxford in the Twenties*, that 'He was not a conventionally well-informed candidate. He had his own technique. They asked him why was there unemployment in England but none in France. He replied gaily, "I have no idea – no idea whatsoever, bowled me middle stump – neck and crop. By the way what does neck and crop mean?" They cheered him to the echo as lustily as if he had given a properly considered answer.'

Professor Gilbert Murray, whose own efforts to capture the Oxford University seat for the Liberals were singularly unsuccessful, gave a glowing reference to Fry as the campaign reached its final stages: 'If Oxford is looking for a man of practical statesmanship and distinguished record, a man with knowledge of India and the Navy, of education, and of progressive international politics, it is Fry first and the rest nowhere at all.'

Fry and Gray pursued a breathless programme right to the end. On 4 June, the day before the election, the two men addressed no less than fourteen open-air meetings. In *46 Not Out*, R.C. Robertson-Glasgow recalled of Fry: 'When, for the sake of oratory, he hopped from the bonnet to the roof of his car, a spectator shouted, "Well, he hasn't forgotten how to jump." '

There were moments of frustration, however, as the *Oxford Times* reported:

> An election comedy amused everyone who turned up for meetings at the junction of the Kingston and Hayfield Roads. At seven o'clock in the evening Mr Fry was to address a meeting and Captain Bourne was to be at the same spot an hour later. But it was not until twenty minutes to eight that the Liberal candidate arrived to find Captain Bourne's platform—a steam wagon—on the opposite side blowing off steam. Mr Fry was as much amused as the audience, but the driver shut off steam when the meeting commenced. 'Now that the Conservative steam has been shut off we'll commence,' said the candidate amid laughter, but before he had uttered half-a-dozen sentences two dogs took an intense dislike to each other. They made their quarrel known to such an extent that speech-making had to wait until the arguments of the canine interrupters had ceased. Then the meeting proceeded.

The final campaign meeting was held in the town hall, with a letter from Liberal leader Herbert Asquith to Fry evoking a storm of applause. It read: 'I sincerely hope that after the splendid services rendered by Mr Frank Gray, Oxford City will not fail to return you as a sincere and courageous Liberal to continue his work for sane and practicable reform.' Fry himself complained that the only criticism his opponents could level at him was lack of oratory. He retorted that distinguished oratory was not a prime requirement when it came to pointing out the failings of Protectionism. His final slogan was: 'Vote Gray's way and Thursday will be Fry's day.'

But it was not to be, and there was a depressing sense of *déjà vu* about his defeat, with the 2,769 votes won by Kenneth Lindsay more than accounting for the differential between Bourne's share of 10,079 and Fry's total of 8,237. The *Oxford Chronicle* gave a circuitous account of his reaction when the results were announced at the town hall: 'He did not deny that personally, although he hoped he was capable of accepting a defeat in the manner one ought to accept it, he did not deny that so great a privilege as that enjoyed by Captain Bourne had been denied to him.'

He wore a tired smile as he did the traditional rounds of the party strongholds, referring to himself and Frank Gray as 'two brothers in adversity'. Addressing the East Oxford Liberal Club he said the problem with three-cornered contests was that one finger tended to become a thumb—difficult to handle. There was a message of condolence from Asquith, but it could do little to assuage the self-pity.

There were signs of general distress in the Liberal Party and their local image was obviously not enhanced by the circumstances of Frank Gray's dismissal, but according to Ivor Davies in *Trial by Ballot*, Charles Fry was not the right tactical choice. Referring to Fry as 'versatile but unapproachable' Davies added: 'He was not Frank Gray's successor. That was all that was wrong with him. He was a different type and lacked the essential human appeal.' He maintained that the Liberals should have opted for someone with no connection with the university. Fry may have 'outblued' his rivals, but Captain Bourne had the advantage of having spent more than half his life in and around Oxford. A similar note was sounded in an *Oxford Times* editorial: 'It was the general opinion that Mr C.B. Fry was rather overshadowed by the personality of Mr Frank Gray.'

There was pale consolation for C.B. in the knowledge that they would invite him back if he was willing to have another stab at the seat, but the glitter had all but rubbed off for Fry: he did not relish a repeat performance. When the Labour Government fell in the autumn of 1924, prompting yet another General Election, he was taken unawares and simply did not have the time he demanded before making up his mind whether to stand again. From the outset he had told Oxford Liberals that he would not make a snap decision, but the 'rush election' left them no choice but to opt for someone else, and the distinguished physician, Dr R.O. Moon, stepped into the breach, only to see Captain Bourne increase his majority to over 5,000. The *Oxford Chronicle* offered this explanation for C.B.'s hesitancy: 'He had fought three forlorn hopes and

did not see his way clear to standing again.' They also repri-
manded *The Observer*, who had blithely jumped the gun on 12
October by announcing Fry's candidature.

There was another curious turn of events a few days later. On 17
October, with the election only twelve days away, the *Sussex Daily
News* reported that the Brighton and Hove Liberals were willing to
back Fry as an Independent candidate. They had just been told by
their first choice, Margaret Hardy, that she was not prepared to
stand at this election, although she might get involved at a later
date.

On 18 October *The Times* reported that Fry would be standing,
but the *Daily News* had the correct news on the same day: 'At a
special meeting of the Brighton and Hove Liberal Association, held
at 116 Western Road, Brighton, last night, a telegram was read
from Mr C.B. Fry. With sincere regret and with thanks for the
affection of Brighton, he had finally decided that he could not, at
the eleventh hour, accept the honour of standing as a candidate at
the General Election.'

The rumour of his standing as an Independent rather foreshadowed Fry's drift away from his already tenuous affection for
the Liberal cause. Christopher Hollis said that in Fry's final years
he 'became very critical of Liberals whom he considered–rightly
enough–to be in a general way unathletic and indifferent to the
rhythm and proper balance of ballroom dancing on which the
well-being of the soul, he had by then come to learn, was primarily
dependent.'

In view of his politics and previous disappointments it came as
something of a surprise when the *Daily Mirror* announced on 12
November 1926 that, 'Mr C.B. Fry has not yet done with politics.
He is to make another attempt to enter Parliament, and I hear that
he will be adopted as Liberal candidate for the Horncastle Division
of Lincolnshire.' It was true that he had visited Skegness the
previous weekend and conferred with committees of various
Liberal organisations, but in fact, after meeting local workers in
Hornchurch itself, he decided not to put his reputation on the line
once again.

C.B.'s opinions, especially his devotion to free enterprise, were
more in tune with Conservative policy than the other two major
parties and almost ten years later he could be found pledging his

support for a Conservative candidate at the Wavertree by-election in Liverpool. Initially Fry sent National Tory James Platt a message of good wishes, then on 4 February he was due to address a meeting on Platt's behalf, but was shouted down by hecklers. 'I would like to take 150 of you to Australia with the next England team to show the Australians how to barrack,' he shouted above the tumult, but the crowd allowed him to say little else. Randolph Churchill was standing as a freelance Conservative, and his father was in Liverpool to offer support, but it was the Labour candidate, J.J. Cleary, who carried the day.

Later still C.B. teased Oxford University Liberals with the idea that he might make one last bid to join the Parliamentary ranks, but even if he had made it to the House of Commons he would have struggled to convince some of his fellow MPs that he should be taken seriously as a politician. Lord Caldecote was Attorney-General when Fry was fighting Brighton and during the campaign he went down to speak. 'If you want a good cricketer, elect Fry,' he advised, 'but if you want a man of business, don't.' Fry's retort was: 'I have yet to learn that a total inability to play cricket is a proof of business ability, even in an attorney.' Lord Caldecote replied: 'Fry does not know I played for the Houses of Parliament.' However, there was no doubt who had the last word: 'I did know,' said Fry. 'I bowled him out.'

In the odd moment of wistful reflection about his failure to make the Commons C.B. might have remembered what he wrote in his own magazine in 1906: 'We spent an afternoon recently at the House of Commons, and in addition to many reflections which it would be impertinent to relate in this place, we were much struck by the worn-out, fagged and lifeless appearance of many of the members.' There was an absence of air and 'vivifying sunlight'. Charles Fry would never properly have felt at home in an atmosphere of that kind.

17

RETURN OF THE EXILE

In 1934 Charles Fry was reborn. It is not an unforgivably dramatic way of describing his emergence from five years of disorientating darkness. He had been out to India for the last time in 1928, acting as Sir Leslie Scott's assistant while he prepared the Indian Princes' case for the Statutory Commission. Towards the end of the trip, which was to be his last to India, C.B. developed paranoiac symptoms, believing that he was being chased by natives who were out to steal his personal documents. He returned home, but familiar surroundings did nothing to ease his mental distress.

It soon became obvious that Mrs Fry would be unable to cope with the joint demands of the *Mercury* and a sick husband. Nor could the family finances cope with an extended stay in a home. However, the ever-generous Ranji stepped in to relieve the monetary burden and Anne Bradley was employed as a nurse for C.B. Having seen him through these troubled years she was not forgotten and when Mrs Fry died in 1946 she returned to C.B.'s life as his housekeeper and looked after him during his final few years in the flat at Hampstead. C.B. left Miss Bradley £200 in his will 'in acknowledgement of her kindness to me during an illness some years ago and afterwards'.

Fry's behaviour was distinctly strange during his years of exile, which were mostly spent in London. At one point when he was staying in Brighton he was supposed to have gone for a walk along the beach early in the morning and suddenly shed all his clothes, trotting around stark naked. At Hamble he was seen casting his fishing-rod out of his bedroom window, and waltzing with an invisible partner. He also had a tendency to mount his horse facing the wrong way and to dress eccentrically, a trait which endured beyond his recovery from mental illness.

Alan Hooker, who had the job of looking after C.B.'s Bentley at Hamble, recalled that the owner suddenly decided he wanted to sell the car. Mr Hooker put petrol in the car, which was taken out for a run to make sure that the engine still purred. He was then instructed to put the Bentley back on its blocks because Fry had changed his mind about selling it, though soon, in fact, a new home had been found for the aristocratic car.

On 14 February 1934 the *Evening Standard* greeted C.B.'s attendance at the annual dinner of the Worshipful Company of Carpenters with this paragraph: 'Among other distinguished cricketers there will be no more interesting figure than Mr C.B. Fry, who has been in retirement owing to ill health for some years, and is now making his first public appearance.' The following day the *Standard* reported that C.B. was 'full of delight at his return to the world', adding that 'He was the life and soul of the group among whom he was sitting. His pungent comments on current topics showed that he had not lost his touch with affairs during his exile.'

It was just a week later when C.B.'s son Stephen was married to Gladys Yvonne Blunt, daughter of Mr and Mrs Bernard Blunt, of New Jersey, at The Sanctuary, Knightsbridge. C.B.'s first grandchild was born the following year, but died in infancy. However, there were three more grandsons to follow, Jonathan, Charles and Stephen, who all revived the Fry tradition at Repton. Their father helped to set up the Palestine Broadcasting Service in the mid-1930s and also worked in New York, but after the war the family settled at the Master Builder's House Hotel at Buckler's Hard, beside the River Beaulieu in Hampshire. Stephen Fry followed in his father's footsteps by standing as a Liberal candidate at Southampton in 1950, but he met the same fate as C.B. and even lost his deposit.

Two months after the wedding C.B.'s monocle was peering perceptively at another season of cricket. Fry the journalist had been taken on by the *Evening Standard* as a snappy columnist, to follow the fortunes of the Australian tourists. He was initially unhappy about the prospect of being overshadowed by Douglas Jardine, fresh from presiding over the calculated destruction which was the bodyline series; but the *Standard* had separate roles in mind for these two sage authorities. Jardine would write exclusively on the Test series, while Fry's brief was to contribute a column based on the American model – all chopped sentences, full of vivid images, the odd epigram and the more-than-occasional classical allusion.

The *Evening Standard* were sufficiently proud of the Jardine signing to announce it to the world on the front page of the paper on 19 April. Jardine meanwhile was bagging his last catch on a game-hunting expedition in India. They were more reticent about C.B., but soon started blowing the trumpet for him when 'C.B. Fry Says' proved to be a smash hit with their readers.

The Australians steamed into Southampton on the Orient liner *Orford* – Bruce Harris having kept readers in touch with on-deck trivia – and made predictable noises about the cricket prevailing over the politics which had become entwined with the sport when Don Bradman's blood was sought in Australia just over a year earlier.

Fry admitted subsequently, with uncharacteristic modesty, that he had not been the first choice for the role of *Standard* columnist. His friend, E.V. Lucas, was the man they had hoped would bring an extra-sporting appeal to bear, but Fry proved to be an inspired stand-in and his efforts at reaching the nursemaid in Wimbledon, that embodiment of a cricketing indifferent, were notably success-ful. His pen may have rusted a little through lack of use, but by the time his chauffeur drove him up to Worcester for the traditional opening to the tour the adrenalin was flowing freely and there was no mistaking the relish with which the 62-year-old Fry approached this unexpectedly exciting twist to his career.

E.W. Swanton, who was just starting out on his own career as a cricket writer, was handling the straight reporting for the *Evening Standard*. He wrote of C.B. in *Sort of a Cricket Person*:

I have no clearer memory of him than the first morning of that game at Worcester. The press-box then was in the little stand behind the bowler's arm at the New Road end, and here we were installed with Brooks, the chauffeur, stationed just below, at ground-level and within reach, handy for the dispensing of champagne from the large hamper in his charge ... That spring morning, seeing Bradman and the Australians for the first time, writing away ceaselessly in a large script of endless octavo sheets, conversing amusingly the while, refreshing himself modestly from time to time and offering hospitality to all and sundry, he was in wonderful fettle. By lunch he had concocted nearer two thousand words than one of crisp, staccato stuff, epigrammatic and brilliant, and as it went on cascading over the wire caused the office to cry out for mercy. They already had more than they could carry! He was the only man I ever knew who could write and talk simultaneously on two different subjects.

Those first words which eased *Standard* readers into C.B.'s beguiling flow of impressions were: 'Full of people, all talking. No interest in Bradman's broken shoe-lace at Suez. Or Woodfull's fall on the deck at Crete. It's just the age-old love of cricket and expectations.'

Bradman's appetite for runs had been unaffected by the traumas of the previous Ashes series and a double century against Worcestershire announced his genius to Charles Fry, whose praise was glowing: 'Bradman has a gem of a body for batsmanship, conformation perfect; hence perfect poise. A bundle, beautifully shaped, of what the Greeks called harmony.' And so it continued, a masterly assessment of the unique qualities which made up the greatest run-getter in the history of the game. Fry had nothing but secondhand information to go on before that day at Worcester, as he saw Bradman performing for the first time, but he was helped by a succinct verdict from his wife, who had told him: 'He's a little man, with fairy feet, who watches the ball.'

The asides were mercifully tolerated by the *Standard* sub-editors and the mention of Madame as critic prompted Fry to recall an exchange with Billy Murdoch, the Australian who had been his captain during his early years with Sussex. ' "Your wife writes your articles, doesn't she, Charles?" To which me: "Billy, you're behind the times. She makes all my runs too." '

On the same day as he sang Bradman's praises to the skies C.B. also revealed his gift for subtle taunting. 'I've told several people here all about cricket. Percy Perrin, for example, and Harry Foster. Both are argumentative, and happen to be good judges. But they'll read these notes and profit by them.'

The honeymoon was going splendidly for both C.B. and his new employers. The potent mix of astute observation and youthful vitality brought immediate reaction. 'His first appearance as a cricket columnist on the *Evening Standard* last night was a sensation,' the paper boasted, and followed up the next day with: 'Everyone is reading C.B. Fry. His analysis of Bradman was the most brilliant ever written.'

The rejoicing went far beyond the walls of the *Evening Standard* offices. Trevor Wignall wrote in the *Daily Express*: 'I sat very close to Mr Fry in the Press seats at Worcester, and I could not help but marvel at his boyish enthusiasm, his earnest satisfaction when something good was done, and his agility. Only infrequently did he take the trouble to walk out of his place and down the short flight of steps . . . His more usual custom was to climb over the table and then take a 6-ft leap . . . There were times when I feared for his limbs, but the man I had last seen captaining England at the Oval was as nimble as ever . . . Welcome back to the fold and the craft, sir.'

There was no deception in the majestic start to Fry's comeback innings and there was complete justification in 'The Londoner's Diary's' impression of his first seven days as *Standard* scribe: 'In one week Mr Fry has achieved a rare reputation in cricket journalism. His articles are being read by those who take little interest in the game.'

It did not take him long to coin the soubriquet 'The Don', and Bradman himself has confirmed that it was Fry's invention. But just occasionally C.B. submerged himself in riddles. He wrote of Bradman during the Fourth Test at Leeds that he was 'a sublimated plodder who plods so excellently that plod is just not the word.' More often than not, though, his images were inspired, like this description of the great Australian: 'He smashes with a sort of sardonic smile in his strokes.'

C.B. walked the delicate tightrope between snobbish contempt and mock superiority. Take this comment on accommodation during the Australians' game at Cambridge: 'Australians seem to be quite nice people. We, the élite, stay at the famous Bull. The actual players are at the University Arms.'

Even in the hour of triumph for C.B. there were cruel reminders that misfortune is always waiting to pounce. At the end of August 1934 his younger daughter Faith was involved in an accident where a five-year-old girl was killed, but at least the inquest showed that Faith Fry was blameless. And the following June C.B. had half-a-dozen gold and silver medals stolen from his flat in Ashburn Gardens, Kensington. They were all trophies from his record-breaking days as an athlete at Oxford. The medals had been carefully selected from a case which contained many others worth less. The value of the stolen medals was £100, but C.B. pointed out to reporters that the sentimental value of the medals was far more important than their actual worth.

He rode these personal storms and continued to sell thousands of papers for the *Standard*. His musings were always provocative and when the Australians toured again in 1938 his popularity was reflected in Test Match reports stretching to 2,000 words or more. There was charm in the controversy which he promoted, in his mild rebukes and subtle taunts.

He was quite capable of stirring up an entire nation, however, and some of his comments that summer were unsympathetically received in Australia. The wounds were opened during the First Test at Trent Bridge when C.B. referred to the Australians as 'South Sea Islanders' and was highly critical of the tourists' reluctance to open the game up once Stan McCabe's magnificent innings of 232 had made defeat highly unlikely:

> We must remember that in Australia they think their boys invincible; and defeat on the cricket field a national disaster . . . The Australians are grand sportsmen but in terms of their own conception of sport; to which, of course, they are fully entitled.

The letters rolled in to the *Evening Standard*, who quickly initiated 'the trial of C.B. Fry'. One correspondent called his contributions 'tripe'. Another said: 'Your cricket commentator appears to think that the Australians acted unsportingly, but it must be generally conceded that Mr C.B. Fry himself easily surpasses our visitors in that particular trait.' A third wrote: 'Aren't you always right, Mr C.B. Fry? And can't you report cricket without always saying so; and can't you use three words where one would do?'

Fry then revealed a curious obsession with the educational background of the Australian players, pointing out that only a couple had benefited from public-school training. At another time he used the occupations of the Australians in ordinary life to preface their names. Don Bradman says he remembers no animosity resulting from these references, but Jack Fingleton, in *Cricket Crisis*, suggested that a little more charity would not have gone amiss: not everyone could scale the upper echelons of the education system like C.B.

On 18 June Fry entered the witness box to conduct his own defence, a marvellously coherent piece, from which this extract is drawn:

> Either you know what the game of cricket is, or you do not. If you do not your opinion does not count: if you do, you cannot accept the dictum, explicitly or tacitly advanced by my opponents; namely, that in cricket the end justifies the means.
>
> It is a lie that cricket is a business; it is not; it is a field-game with old traditions and a code of conduct.
>
> I do not like the general public attitude to cricket in Australia. It is hectic and cocky.
>
> I beg leave to retain my own views on the ethics of the game I love.
>
> I beg leave to remain an Englishman.

There was another reason for the Trent Bridge Test to be etched in Charles Fry's mind: Reg Sinfield, a cadet on the *Mercury* during the early parts of the First World War, was at last selected for England at the age of thirty-seven. C.B. described him as a 'peculiar' bowler – he dealt in a brand of slow medium off-breaks – but there was no hiding his pride: 'So my boy, Reginald Sinfield, wears his England cap, and I am ever so glad. A splendid fellow and he looks it.'

Fry's delight was compounded when Sinfield grabbed the prized wicket of Don Bradman in the first innings, but he was only twelfth man for the Second Test at Lord's and his brief England career was over.

Sinfield, still coaching at Colston's School in Bristol at the age of over eighty, remembers C.B. visiting his home in order to get tips for the England side. Reg was out, but his wife wasted no time in advancing her man's claims: 'I couldn't agree more, Mrs Sinfield,' said Fry. 'I've been telling them that for years.' When Reg got back he was anxious to know whether his wife had offered their illustrious guest a drink. She assured him that half a bottle of whisky had disappeared during C.B.'s visit!

Fry's recommendations were normally treated with due respect, but in Reg Sinfield's case his connection with C.B. may have actually worked against him. 'I wasn't popular at Lord's because he wasn't popular,' he said. This theory was borne out by previous disappointments: Sinfield's legendary Gloucestershire colleague Wally Hammond had given him to understand that he was a certainty for the 1936–7 trip to Australia, but in the end he was overlooked.

One person with a vague impression of Sinfield's merits was Aubrey Smith, the former Sussex and England player, who achieved even greater fame and fortune as an actor in Hollywood. He was among C.B.'s party staying at The George in Grantham during the Trent Bridge Test. In *Babbled of Green Fields*, Denzil Batchelor said that Aubrey Smith was asked how he rated Reg Sinfield as a bowler. 'Aubrey massaged his jowl. "Yes," he rumbled at last in his basso profundo; then, after deep thought and more massage, he added firmly: "And no." He could not be induced to elaborate further.'

When Charles Fry was not disapproving of the modern habit of chewing gum on the cricket field he was conjuring up concise, highly visual images of the cricketing heroes: 'The Don is fully flannelled and gripped behind the glass door of the Australian dressing-room, in the shade. It will be a bushman's luck if he is called on before lunch . . . He has emerged on to the balcony, pale but cheerful of smile. He is a spirited Don.'

C.B. was encouraged to branch out by the *Evening Standard*, and he had a chance to comment on sports in which he had previously taken nothing more than a peripheral interest. As Denzil Batchelor wrote in his *Life of Fry*:

The new sports, the games about which he knew nothing, always interested Charles more than the game at which he had spent years of his youth, dazzling the spectators. It was only very rarely that he could be persuaded to watch modern soccer players: one such occasion being when England played and beat the Rest of Europe. Charles's visit was primarily made to make a close-quarters' inspection of Stanley Matthews' sleight-of-foot in action. My major memory of the occasion is that after the game the lift to the directors' box chose to levitate between the earth and the upper element, like Mahomet's coffin. One or two ladies showed a disposition to hysteria. The officials caused champagne to be passed through the bars to sustain those of us who had not touched a drop since halftime and Charles wrote 'C.B. Fry Says' against the wall of the lift.

When Don Bradman went back to Australia after the 1938 tour to England he embarked on a run of high scores which enabled him to equal C.B.'s six successive centuries in 1901. There were high hopes that Bradman would create a new record, but the sequence ended abruptly when he was dismissed for 5 in a match against Victoria at the end of February 1939. Fry despatched brief condolences in a telegram, then wrote at greater length, saying: 'You have succeeded in endowing me with an hour or two of semi-posthumous fame.'

In the early part of the Second World War C.B. was engaged by the *Sunday Express*, as 'captain' of their sports team. He also put together the 'Londoner's Log' on a couple of occasions as stand-in for Lord Castlerosse. But, as Laddie Lucas mentioned in *Five Up*, there was a clash of strong personalities between C.B. and the editor: 'Charles, a proud man, met his match in Gordon. After the third (vain) attempt at gaining editorial satisfaction for his copy he strode back across the news room, resplendent with monocle, spotted bow tie, light grey suit, black and white shoes and all, and sat down at my desk, nonplussed. "Moral for life," he said. "Never argue; but never give in." '

18

AUDIENCE WITH HITLER

If *Life Worth Living* had been concocted after the Second World War, C.B. might have chosen to inter one chapter which may have seemed defensible when it was written in 1939, but subsequently loomed as an alarming expression of sympathy with a savage régime. It was hardly a warts-and-all autobiography–Fry's mental distress, election setbacks and occasional sporting failures were neatly bypassed–so the story of his meeting with Hitler and brief acquaintance with the Third Reich could equally have been lost in the mists of time.

At the start of 1934 Hitler was convinced that the British would make better friends than enemies and through von Schirach, the head of the Youth Movement, an attempt was made to contact the Boy Scouts' authorities in Britain. The Germans felt, quite reasonably, that good relations between the two countries could only be encouraged by greater understanding and ties among the young people.

This approach failed to bear fruit and via a chance meeting with a German lady at the Junior Army and Navy Club, C.B. was adopted as a potential healer of wounds. It was suggested that he go over to Germany to see the Nazi leaders and discuss the problems, but he emphasised that he would not make the trip to Berlin unless he was allowed to see the man at the top.

It was eventually confirmed that Hitler would grant Fry an audience and arrangements were made for him to travel out to Germany in the middle of April 1934. He briefed himself by talking to leaders of the Boy Scout movement and also got in touch with his Wadham friend, John Simon, who was Foreign Secretary at the time, and the Ambassador in Berlin, Sir Eric Phipps.

His first few days in Germany were spent as guest of the Propaganda Department. He had discussions with von Schirach and witnessed Hitler at his rabble-rousing best when the Nazi leader addressed landworkers on the occasion of the official opening of the great eastern motor-road.

Fry's early impressions of Nazi Germany, recounted here from *Life Worth Living*, were chillingly suggestible:

> If the Propaganda Ministry had thought it well that a humble person like myself should be impressed with what Germany of the early Nazi régime was like, they certainly succeeded. There was no question that the people were devoted to the Fuehrer, and there was no question that the world of the fields and valleys round Munich was a world of work, simple-minded and disciplined. I cannot refrain from saying that the atmosphere of effective discipline strongly appealed to me. No one was running about doing what he was not wanted to do; everybody knew his allotted place and went there when called. Remember that this was the spring of 1934.

A meeting with Rudolph Hess did nothing to poison Fry's favourable impression of this rehabilitated Germany and he was convinced 'that Herr Hitler and his men genuinely wished to be friends with us'. The Germans in turn, whether or not they had belligerent designs at this stage, naturally saw C.B. as a valuable ally in England. His fingers had been plunged wholeheartedly into many pies and at his athletic peak he was precisely the sort of person Hitler would have vaunted to the skies as a glowing example of the master race . . . if he had been German.

Meanwhile, Fry's suggestion that a liaison committee be set up in England to look into possible co-operation between the youth movements of the two countries was well received in Berlin, though not by Alfred Spender, the Liberal and former editor of the *Westminster Gazette*, who was strongly opposed to the Nazi régime and scarcely relished the prospect of being on the committee.

The smooth marriage between gainful employment and full social life appealed greatly to C.B., who made this unflattering comparison between London and Berlin: 'There was a complete absence of the lounge-lizard type of youth, who looks as if he would break in two in the middle, so frequently seen in the entertainment resorts of London. Nor did one see the sort of girl who looks as if she were presenting herself to the late hours of the night as the whole object of her existence. Indeed, Berlin of 1934 gave me the feeling of a world swept clean by a fresh wind which had left it stimulated, energetic, and ready to work without losing its capacity to enjoy itself.'

Fry's long-awaited audience with Hitler came a couple of days before the end of his stay in Germany. The interpreter for the meeting at the Reich Chancellery was von Ribbentrop. Fry made a point of inviting him to stay in England and said he would take him to Lord's. He told von Ribbentrop that the best means of securing friendly relations between their two countries was for the Germans to take up cricket!

This was C.B.'s recollection of his entry into Hitler's office: 'In front of us at the end of a long, lofty, narrow room, as it were almost on the horizon, I saw Herr Hitler at a desk in his light brown tunic. He sprang to attention on the instant and gave me the Nazi salute, which I returned still framed in the doorway. He then took two steps forward and halted to let me start; as I stepped off he stepped off, and kept in precise step with me, so that we met precisely in the middle of the room.'

The two men talked (for once C.B. played second fiddle in a conversation) for more than an hour. Hitler outlined the constituents of his vision of a new Germany and the country's problems – the Communist threat, antagonism from the Jews – and emphasised the need for rearmament. He was impressed by Fry's idea of 'rapprochement' between the youth of Germany and England. C.B. referred to Hitler's 'innate dignity', but history gave a sinister edge to this appraisal: 'I was attracted by him. He looked fresh and fit, and, as I say, notably alert. He was quiet and courteous and simple. He treated everything that occurred in the conversation with an apt precision that cut out all waste. A characteristic I noted was the economical consecutiveness of his mind. He gave the impression of effective grip.'

The barbarous excesses of the Second World War have given a prejudiced slant to any discussions of the theoretical merits of Hitler's pre-war policies. The rekindling of national pride and self-respect, highly effective in its way, has become immersed in its own perverted manipulation. Charles Fry remained convinced, however, that you could separate the good from the evil in such a system and achieve something worthwhile. Ultimately he favoured the notion of a corporate ideal, where the training of the young emphasised discipline rather than goodwill and children's minds were keyed in to the needs and aims of the state. He recognised the value of good deeds, but only where they reflected an overall purpose. He wrote in *Life Worth Living*, which was published just after the outbreak of war in September 1939:

> The German Youth Scheme is a definitely coherent State method of producing the citizens it wants. We have not any such definite State methods. We may get our own results successfully in our own different way. We say we like liberty. But if we are to achieve a rival efficiency, then we must persuade ourselves to organise a machinery for inter-relating our scattered and excellent activities and societies of youth.
> This would be a desirable development. Communism and all its corollaries are a turgid curse of mankind. Whatever storms the Germans have ridden into, they did face and outride that storm: a tremendous feat of national character.
> The fact that we have come to look upon the Nazi system as hostile and dangerous to our interests does not prove that the means whereby Germany has reformed herself into such a capacity are not worth our close attention. Whether we like it or not, we do not enhance our own national virtues, however great, by inserting a national ostrich head into a national sand in order to pretend that random voluntariness can obtain the same results as organised discipline.

There were no obvious signs of contrition a year later, when hostilities were well underway. This is what readers of the 'Londoner's Log' in the *Sunday Express* were told by C.B. on 15 September 1940:

> There is nothing subtly deceptive about Hitler; he is not a humbug; he means what he says at the time and he speaks out frankly enough what he has in mind.
> But he perpetrates quick changes of attitude and goes back

on himself because he is a fanatic with one idea – the resurgence and dominance of Germany – and anything he has said or promised if it obstructs that purpose simply ceases to stand. He is like the Prophet Mahomet, had the Prophet, instead of preaching the one God and the Koran, preached the sheer power and dominance of his own people.

Wicked and monstrous he may be in our view. But any one who jeers at him as a small man or a paranoiac is a fool. Neither is he a neurotic nor an hysteric. He may at times act like one. But then he is, like many another crowd compeller, a consummate actor. He has what the Greeks called 'hypocrasy,' meaning the power of assuming a character necessary to the situation and sustaining it before the audience.

You may detest this man for what he has done and what he leads others to do. But the practice of laughing at him as a small man is mistaken.

What he has worked with is the congenital and cultivated belief of the Germans that they are the one people who can make War pay. They have been in the game since the time of Julius Caesar.

This being so, they are all on for invading us – if they can.

When talking about this episode in his life Fry was apt to embellish the original story. He claimed he had told Hitler that it would be sheer folly to contemplate invading England and that he had advanced cricket as a significant addition to the sporting and social fabric of Germany. In later years C.B. greeted the Cold War with similar advice for the Russians and doubtless if he had acceded to the Albanian throne that nation would now form a cricketing oasis in the Communist desert.

But some people chose to take Fry's original thoughts on Hitler's Germany at face value, without qualification, and they resented his stance. Towards the end of his life there was mounting astonishment as successive Honours Lists failed to include his name. Warner, Hobbs, Bradman and Hutton received their titles, but C.B. was granted nothing more than the honorary naval rank of Captain. His bold opinions did not always commend him and his versatility made it hard to categorise his contribution, but above all, perhaps, that visit to Germany in the spring of 1934 struck his name off the list of possibles.

If so, it was a shamelessly myopic verdict. Fry was as capable as anyone of distinguishing between the malevolent dogma and the positive application of principles. Following the 1936 Olympic Games in Berlin, C.B. was invited to the German Embassy in London to watch the private film of the event. It was not the celebration of Nazidom which left a lasting impression, but the glorious rhythm of the American Negro Jesse Owens as he winged his way to victory in the 100m, 200m and long jump.

In a radio interview towards the end of his life Fry confessed: 'People who knew the Germans before 1934 wouldn't ever have believed that they'd do the things they did.' The Night of the Long Knives, Hitler's brutal elimination of possible rivals, came at the end of June, just three months after Fry's visit. Fewer people were left in doubt about the severity of his methods after this. However, C.B. clearly was not convinced that Fascism had to be synonymous with evil. He showed interest in another imperfect form of the doctrine, that supported by Oswald Mosley and his British Union of Fascists, which had been set up in 1932. Recently revealed documents have shown that Fry attended a get-together of British Fascists in 1934 as a guest, but there is no indication that his interest was anything more than academic. He may well have sympathised with Mosley's ideals, but his politics at this stage were more in tune with right-wing Conservatives.

19

DOWN UNDER

At the age of sixty-four Charles Fry finally made the trip which had eluded him so frustratingly thirty years before. This was no unexpected call-up for the England touring side to Australia–his berth was courtesy of the *Evening Standard*, Mrs Fry having long since proved that the training ship *Mercury* could function without him. It was a poignant journey for C.B., whose status as a player could only have been enhanced if he had been able to take on the Australians on their home patch, free from the distractions which cut into his seasons in England.

Fry boarded the SS *Orion* at Toulon, bearing gifts for the English touring party. He had brought with him seventeen hats or helmets with reinforced steel brims, intended to provide effective protection from the sun (there was an inordinate amount of rain during the tour). They could also legislate for batsmen's survival if the Australians had any reciprocal arrangement in mind after the bodyline tour.

Bruce Harris, who was also covering the tour for the *Evening Standard*, said in his book *The 1937 Australian Test Tour* that Fry 'was a sort of universal companion to passengers who liked to listen to him' on the *Orion*, while Neville Cardus, yet another member of the glittering *Standard* team, remembered that, 'Every morning Fry held court amongst the deck-chairs on the *Orion*, as she ploughed patiently through the seas. He dressed differently every day; sometimes with topee and short leather trousers, as though about to trace the source of the Amazon; or in scaled green sort of costume which made him look like a deep-sea monster; or in a bath towel worn like a toga. One day, to tease him, I said: "Good morning, Charles. No hemlock yet? Give us your ideas about the Iambic." In full spate came forth a swift survey of the origin and development of the Iambic, with quotations from all periods and writers, every sentence ending with "you see what I mean" or "however." ' According to Cardus, C.B. 'talked all the way to Australia and all the way across Australia and all the way back home.' Fry was not amused. He claimed that Cardus had not sat on the same deck going out and went home in a different ship and by a different route!

Nevertheless, a certain weariness may be detected on Cardus's part, underlined by a couple of stories which have circulated about the tour. The English cricketers and journalists were in Melbourne on Armistice Day and they were in the lounge of the Windsor Hotel, about to attend a reception, when the sirens announced the two minutes' silence. Cardus recalled in *Autobiography*: 'We all stood side by side and Fry was next to me. "This'll irk you, Charles." He nearly died, but he checked his retort. I think this was one of the most severely disciplined acts of his career.'

Then there was a lunch in Sydney where Fry launched into one of his more rambling speeches. Ian Peebles wrote in *Spinner's Yarn*: 'Neville Cardus made the devastating reply to such a harangue in saying that for years they had known all about C.B. Fry, now they all knew about Fry B.C. This brought about a pause, if not a complete rift, in their friendship.'

There was so much more that C.B. wanted to do in Australia than just renew acquaintances with old adversaries and watch cricket. He was richly interested in the physical qualities of the places he visited and the diverse sub-cultures which were woven into a nation. 'Everywhere I went in Australia', he wrote in *Life Worth Living*, 'I was pursued by the feeling that, magnificent as are the five great cities, one was not actually seeing the real Australia. One wanted to be away in the real life of Australia, the stations, the sheep-runs and the cattle country, the illimitable cornfields, and perhaps the mines. One knew all the time that the life of the cities was only there at all because of wool, kine, corn, and gold. Primary products. The kind of men who made Australia are still there somewhere, though they are pretty well taxed out of existence. But nowhere more acutely than in Brisbane did one hanker after the wider world away from the walls; Queensland spreads out into so vast a land of bush and pasture, and even away up to the sugar plantations and tropical products of the north.'

The claustrophobic overtones in that description of Brisbane were certainly evident in his behaviour and in what he wrote for *Evening Standard* readers back home after the first day's play in the opening Test: 'I might see more if three pillars and a floppy awning, the size of a marquee, were not interrupting my view. A truly awful seat they have allotted to us.'

It was bad enough for C.B. to be denied access to the pavilion, an honour happily accorded to him at the other Test centres in Australia. He was, after all, a former England captain and the senior member present of the MCC. Fry was so moved by this shoddy treatment that he ejected Bruce Harris's typewriter from the press box. E.W. Swanton gathered that it was thrown out, but Jack Fingleton recalled that C.B. proved his enduring worth as a footballer by kicking it out. In any event it was a rare show of temper from Fry, who, in his journalistic hat anyway, was the epitome of genial good humour.

His impressions of Sydney suggested that the writer was altogether more relaxed in his surroundings: 'Sydney at last, after forty years of hearsay. The great circus is mottled green and brown after the draught. The mowing machine has marked concentric rings from the white picket fence to the middle oblong of burnished soil. On the wicket the stands seem to frown down upon one like giant eyebrows, with speckled, elongated pupils observing sternly below them. The famous democratic mounds are patchy with parched grass.'

Following the Sydney Test, England were two up in the series with three to play, seemingly in sight of a famous triumph, but the fates had been with them and the heavens had opened on the Australians rather than on the tourists, who were presumed to be responsible for the un-Antipodean weather. Don Bradman had failed to score in two of his four innings: it was not without reason that Gubby Allen and his men saw an imminent backlash.

At Melbourne, C.B. spent quite a lot of time with Hugh Trumble, who was secretary of the club. The press box itself boasted a splendid array of erstwhile cricketing talent. For England there was Fry and Jack Hobbs, while Mailey, McCartney, Woodfull and Ponsford were the Australian voices of experience. C.B. refused to let the English weather depress him—or anyone else. Dressed in a highly individual mixture of jodphurs, topee, muffler and drill coat, he found his way into the Ladies' Stand and gave an impromptu demonstration of strokeplay with the aid of an umbrella.

After the Third Test, which resulted in the simplest of victories for Australia, the English party enjoyed a brief interlude in Tasmania and Charles Fry continued to entertain and seek after entertainment. Denzil Batchelor entered their hotel 'to find him lying at full length in the foyer, demonstrating to Stanley Worthington that it was possible by a series of catalyptic jerks to reach a catch in the slips even after one had measured one's length on the ground.'

C.B. and Bruce Harris were motoring from Launceston to Hobart for the latest match on the tour when they stopped at a chalet 3,000 feet up, above the Great Lake. Harris wrote in his account of the tour:

In we stepped. Commander C.B. Fry, majestically monocled, called for hock with which to celebrate the lofty occasion. We were told that there was no licence; one had been sought, but had not been granted.

'Better ring up Joe Darling about it,' I suggested. Mr Darling, once cricket opponent of the Commander, is now a member of the Legislative Council of Tasmania.

Commander Fry is a man of action. 'I will,' he said, 'here and now.' So it came to pass, five minutes later, that Mr Darling, 100 miles away in Hobart, heard for the first time for 30 years a once-familiar voice declaring itself as follows:

'This is Charles Fry speaking. I want to know why it is that the Rainbow Chalet up here has not got a licence. Here we have travelled 12,000 miles to this delectable spot and we cannot drink your health or that of Tasmania. What about it? If you cannot do anything about it I shall have to ring up the Prime Minister!'

Mr Darling roared with laughter at the semi-serious joke. The laughter dissolved into a gargle and then into silence. Some imp of teetotalism apparently had cut the wire, and the conversation had to be continued at Hobart. Commander Fry spent a day with his old opponent on his sheep station, and

was shown there the sport of hare and rabbit shooting by
night from the front seat of a lorry driven cross-country.

According to Denzil Batchelor, however, the prey was larger and
altogether more entertaining–kangaroo.

And so on to Adelaide where Don Bradman repeated his feat in
the Third Test by scoring a double century and the series was
poised at 2–2. C.B. was at his most terse: 'The Don made a speech.
So did Allen. The crowd called for Fleetwood, but he was in his
bath. The lettuces at Adelaide are superlative.'

The Australian spectators failed to draw such glowing tributes
from Fry, who wrote during the decisive Fifth Test at Melbourne:
'Australia holds some long suits, but reverence is not one of them.
Boys pass round inside the picket fence with loads of bottles then
throw them out upon the sacred greensward. Old England ought to
be able to beat such iconoclasm.

'Before this match is over, I hope to see one non-striker on our
side back up once. After it, I hope to see English cricket start all
over again from the beginning, under the conduct of someone who
knows the principles of the game.'

The iconoclasts caught England on a drying wicket and won the
final Test by the proverbial street. Fry emerged from his patriotic
distress to say: 'Here is my hand, Australia.'

There were aspects of the tour which he had not relished, but he
had enjoyed himself whenever possible. He went racing during the
tourists' game with Queensland–his report for the *Evening Standard* was based on information he picked up from the commentary
which was relayed to the race course.

There was no ambivalence in his heart when the circus moved
on to New Zealand and there was fishing to delight even a much
travelled angler like C.B., who wrote glowingly of the experience:
'Perhaps it is not worth while travelling thirteen thousand miles
for the winter sports in the South Island, but it is certainly worth
while to travel that distance for the fishing in the North Island.
There is nothing like the long blue lake at Taupo, with its
innumerable lively rivers, anywhere else in the world. And there is
no fish as well worth pursuit as the rainbow trout of the region.'

It was not only trout which made New Zealand memorable–
'There is no pipe tobacco ever invented at all in the same class as

the Number Three Bulldog Toasted Navy Cut, which one can obtain in New Zealand, but which, owing to the annoyance of the proprietor with the Labour Government for interfering with the working hours of his employees, he refuses to export.'

Fry's notion that he could emulate Aubrey Smith and take Hollywood by storm was fuelled by a month's stay in the movie capital on the way back from New Zealand. Staying at Sir Aubrey's villa in Beverly Hills, C.B. was bewitched and enchanted, and for once he was content to be merely a spectator, on the sets of *Prisoner of Zenda* and the Marlene Dietrich film, *Angel*.

Aubrey Smith and Ronald Colman had brought cricket to Hollywood and C.B. was happy to play while he was there, but it was the versatility and rude health of the place which appealed to him and gave him a lyrical finale to his autobiography: 'You can fish for trout in the hills, learn rodeo on the locations, ride in the Row before breakfast, obtain rather better lawn tennis than anywhere else, play golf and bathe to your heart's content. So far as I saw, it is a world of wholesome, happy youth, middle age, and age. Artificiality may be hiding its head somewhere, but certainly it does not intrude.

'The sunshine and the climate!'

'Even on the threshold of make-believe, life can be worth living.'

This was not the innocent picture which Charles Fry carried with him to the land of make-believe. He later saw Hollywood spoonfeeding the post-war young with gift-wrapped artificiality; he sensed that ruinous change was in the air.

20

LAUD
OF THE
DANCE

When Charles Fry decided to enrol as a dancing student in 1934 it recalled a piece which he wrote in 1903 for Gilbert Jessop. It was on 'Training for Cricket' and included this 'quaint suggestion': 'Probably the idea may amuse you, but I really believe that outside correct batting practice nothing would be more conducive to the acquirement of skill in batting than cultivation of the art of step-dancing. Why? Simply because the fundamental requisites in batting are balance and quickness of foot.'

He saw no reason to change this view and wrote to the editor of *The Captain*, saying: 'I would have every boy taught dancing, not merely the social sort, but step-dancing; because English people walk so badly, are so bad with their feet as a rule–and English boys are absurdly self-conscious in matters of, so called, deportment.' Nevertheless, it was thirty years later before he decided to give ballroom dancing his own formal attention. C.B.'s first visit to Josephine Bradley's dancing school in London is remembered in Miss Bradley's autobiography, *Dancing Through Life*:

> One day, when I was seated at my secretary's desk, trying, in a few spare minutes, to attend to an accumulation of business matters, I became aware that someone large, dynamic, enveloped in an overcoat and floating scarves–it was wintertime–had approached me and was requesting, in a very charming voice, that its owner should be taught to dance.
>
> I saw before me as fine a specimen of manhood as one would wish to meet. He was not a young man, but he emanated the buoyancy and enthusiasm that one generally

associates with youth. Also, he exhibited none of the timidity which, for some strange reason, always seems to afflict a prospective male pupil when he comes to arrange about dancing lessons.

I consulted my appointment book, in order to fix dates and hours, and then asked what name I should enter.

'Fry,' he answered.

'What initial, please?' I enquired, in as good an imitation of my secretary's politely efficient manner as I could muster.

'C.B.,' responded the applicant.

The two initials together made a kind of dent in my mind, and without stopping to think I remarked:

'You play some game, don't you? Oh, of course, I know, you play football.'

My future pupil smiled genially at me.

'I used to, now and again,' he replied.

It was the start of a firm friendship between C.B. and Josephine Bradley; and he could not have chosen a better teacher. She was a brilliant dancer and had won the world foxtrot championship with her American partner, G.K. 'Andy' Anderson. Josephine Bradley had been on the first committee of the Ballroom Branch of the Imperial Society of Teachers of Dancing, formed ten years earlier. A whole new glossary evolved to describe the techniques and movements of ballroom dancing as opposed to ballet, but the emphasis was very much on natural movement.

Miss Bradley said the first aim of *Dancing Through Life* was 'to promote a sense of closer community between the teachers of the art'. The second aim was 'to bring to a wider public an apprecia-tion of ball-room dancing as an art having a scientific basis, which seeks to bring into play all the muscles of the feet and body that impart ease and grace of movement, not only in the figures of the dance but in the street and in the drawing-room, and as a recreation which conduces to a more shapely figure and improved health and which can be indulged at seasons and at times that preclude the enjoyment of exercise in the open air.'

Fry's philosophy was right in line with this belief: he not only felt that a sense of rhythm was a significant factor in the success of any sportsman, but also preached that mastery of the basic mechanics of movement – the ability to walk correctly with head held high – bred confidence. He had written in his own magazine in 1905 that 'dancing springs from the soul. The thing is to get hold of this lost and natural art of dancing, and train it up in the way it should go. It's a wasted talent.'

C.B. was also an avid student of human physique, very much after the Greek ideal. In an age where men could comment on male beauty without being condemned as dangerous perverts he was able to write in *Fry's Magazine*: 'The human body, as it was meant to be, and as we so often see it nowadays, is a glorious thing. And I hope that its beautiful fitness and strength will be worshipped, and striven after more and more.' He admired the lithe, athletic individual far more than the sort of person who saw body-building as an end in itself. The not-so-enlightened 1980s finds it difficult to talk about human beauty in a general sense and C.B.'s remarks seem to take on a sinister shade today.

Fry was actually taught to dance by Mollie Boote, who was one of Josephine Bradley's assistants and an excellent dancer herself. He was privileged in being able to take both women out and some of their twinkle-toed brilliance rubbed off on the ever-enthusiastic C.B. Almost fifty years after their first meeting Josephine Bradley remembered that 'C.B. got intensely interested in natural movement, he was very intelligent to teach and we turned him into quite a proficient social dancer. I don't think he had any particular gift: he was more interested in the techniques of dancing. I have no particular recollection of him having a fantastic sense of rhythm, but both Mollie Boote and I were very good dancers and that must have helped him. He was very well known and he had money, so if he took a woman out he took her to nice places, bought her a good dinner and amused her.'

C.B. was also the motivating force behind Josephine Bradley's autobiography – 'I was travelling to a lot of different countries and he was always wanting me to tell him something amusing about my trips. I remember I had just come back from Holland and told him of my exploits and he said, "You know, Jo, you ought to write a book on your life." He got the publishers for me and did everything.'

C.B. had dominated the odd dance-floor before he met Josephine Bradley, of course, but as a less polished performer. Dame Rachel

Crowdy coincided with C.B. at the League of Nations in Geneva. She was one of the guests when Fry was featured on *This Is Your Life* at the end of 1955 and described him as one of the finest dancers she had partnered, with this minor proviso: 'He was inclined to take such long and imperious strides that his partners found it very hard on stockings.'

At the grand old age of eighty-two he was still trying to defy the rigours of time. There was this item in the *Evening Standard* on 12 June 1954: 'Veteran cricketer C.B. Fry went dancing last night at the Royal and Merchant Navies' ball at the Dorchester. "It is the first time I have danced for more than six years," he said. "I practised in the bedroom to my wireless this morning, but I kept tripping over the carpet. I'm finding it much easier now with pretty girls to watch".'

It had been hoped that Fry would use his powers of persuasion and influence to bring about a recruitment drive for ballroom dancing, but the message did not get through to sportsmen, who have continued to opt for more conventional forms of training. Nevertheless, the Imperial Society of Teachers of Dancing have retained a quote from C.B., in which he said that training as a dancer during his active sporting days would have made him a 20 per cent better stylist as a cricketer, footballer, runner and jumper, not to mention riding and shooting.

In a radio interview Denzil Batchelor said about C.B.'s obsession with poise: 'He will tell you how he notices when an Englishman in evening clothes enters a ballroom, nine times out of ten he puts his fingers up to straighten his white dress tie. From boyhood he set himself not to be that type of man.'

21

ON THE AIRWAVES

The *Evening Standard* was not alone in recognising that the reborn Charles Fry had a real contribution to make and in the final twenty years of his life he became quite a darling of the airwaves. The BBC enjoyed a classic love/hate relationship with him. He automatically regarded his fees for each broadcast as inadequate and had a running battle with the organisation to get his expenses demands met. After all, Brown's Hotel was not prepared to put him up for free when he came to London especially to record a programme. Conversely, the BBC were apt to regard him as a luxury performer. He certainly made for splendid radio and would have provided superb television viewing if he had had the chance to explore the medium in any depth, but no one was indispensable and Fry's stubborn directness made producers think twice before inviting him to take part in programmes.

An idea for C.B. to figure prominently in a series called 'Sportsman's Diary' was shelved because of the outbreak of war and he declined an invitiation to take part in the early 'Any Questions?' programmes because he lacked the 'necessary leisure'. However, he was delighted to be asked to join the Brains Trust in 1944, and his only fear, patently unfounded, was that he might not be able to get a word in edgeways alongside seasoned performers like the philosopher C.E.M. Joad.

Producer Peter Bax had decided to get together a panel of unquenchable Englishness on a St George's Day theme, but C.B. made it clear that he wished to be referred to in the introduction as 'commanding the best pre-service naval training establishment in the world', rather than as 'the cricketer'.

This earnest desire to be recognised as a true all-rounder was reflected in a piece of rare humour from Denzil Batchelor. He and Fry were at a dinner together a few years after the war and Batchelor was surprised to hear C.B. say that he was sick of cricket and had decided to nurture an active interest in horse-racing. He would find out how trainers operated and when he thought he had got the hang of it he would branch out on his own. 'What as?' asked Batchelor. 'Trainer, jockey or horse?' Just after the war, in fact, C.B. went in for a spot of sedate equine competition, acquiring a show ring cob which he took delight in putting into the ring at Reading and Windsor.

Fry's hopes of a stirring debut on the Brains Trust in 1944 were lifted when Sir John Simon, a friend since Wadham days and Chancellor of the Exchequer in the War Cabinet, agreed to send in a teasing question. It was to read: 'Does a dog know when he is wagging his tail? What is the physical process which causes his tail to wag, and how is it actuated?' Fry purred at the prospect of tackling the question. However, the cautious Simon got cold feet and asked that the question should be used under a pseudonym. He wrote to C.B.: 'I feel, on reflection, that it is not seemly for the Lord Chancellor in war time to send a question to the Brains Trust. He has to devote such brains as he has to a continuous series of war questions, and I do not think my playful query would be well received in all quarters.' Fry groaned at such lack of adventure and in suggesting the pseudonym of Simple Simon from Tetbury told Peter Bax: 'That's why he will never be P.M.–or hold a popular audience–want of dash.'

C.B. compared his first appearance on the Brains Trust to a Test Match debut, but he was a definite hit and totted up half-a-dozen performances on the programme during the last year of the war. In March 1945 Fry coincided with Bertrand Russell on the panel of experts and wrote to Peter Bax before the programme, hoping that he might be given the opportunity to express his theories on relativity alongside those of the great philosopher.

He had great affection for the Brains Trust as a programme and his own eclectic talents were ideally suited to the format. His arguments were fluent and natural, if a little implausible at times, and he could improvise effectively on themes with which he was not so familiar. Curiously, though, he was not conventionally well-read. After one Brains Trust programme a woman wrote asking if he could suggest 100 books in the English language which might form the basis for her son's literary education. He felt unqualified for this task and referred it to Denzil Batchelor, who produced a highly conventional list. Fry perused it with casual interest before sending the reply and confessed that he had only read one of the selection, *The Pickwick Papers*, which he had not enjoyed much.

Fry's chosen reading was along more esoteric lines. He once accompanied Batchelor to a lecture based on a textbook on government written by a Pole in Latin during the reign of Queen Elizabeth I. The lecturer was baffled by Fry's ability to discuss the work knowledgeably, since there were believed to be only two copies of the book extant. C.B. explained that he had read the one in Oxford's Bodleian Library. The key to the book's appeal was clearly the language in which it was written: his tastes remained very much those of the classical scholar.

After the war C.B. was invited to do summaries for the Test series between England and India, but although he was a marvellous attribute to the commentary team, quibbles about fees and expenses decided the BBC that he was not a good long-term prospect, quite apart from his obvious seniority.

Age caught up reluctantly with C.B. Once he was past the age of seventy-five his limbs slowed and his health became more vulnerable, but his mind had lost none of its sparkle and he was inclined to volunteer for impractical duties. The exhausting schedule of an Australian tour, especially in the days before high-speed air travel, taxed even youthful spirits, but Fry would not have turned down a billet for the 1954–5 tour–when he was coming up to eighty-three.

He was underused as an authority on cricket, but in a sense that suited C.B.'s opinion of himself as a rounded performer. He was asked to do a series of talks for the Pacific Service under the banner 'As I See It'. One of these was about physical skill and it was a broadcast along similar lines in March 1948 which was marred by an unfortunate incident. In the course of his talk about Physical Prowess to Eastern Service listeners he referred to the 'American darkie athlete Jesse Owens'. At this point the broadcast was interrupted and Fry was told that darkie would have to be replaced with negro. He was severely displeased and pointed out that the BBC had been given five days to censor the script if they so wished. He described the jamming of the broadcast as 'impudence' and 'gross stupidity', and his anger was only equalled by the BBC's embarrassment. The producer faced with making the decision was none other than John Arlott, who had simply reflected the Corporation's concern with not causing offence. However, Fry maintained that the Indians who listened to the talk, possibly numbering several million, were less offended by the term darkie than negro, which was too similar to nigger. The recriminations endured.

It was not the only time Fry felt cause to berate Arlott. During the Fourth Test at Leeds between England and Australia in 1953 he telegraphed Rex Alston with the terse message: 'Please restrain Arlott from quacking nonsense.' On the other hand he was much in favour of the lyrical qualities which John Arlott brought to broadcasting and described a talk of his about cricket soon after the war as one of the best he had ever heard.

It was also in 1953 when C.B. was asked to appear on 'Frankly Speaking', where famous people were invited to bare their auto-biographical souls under the promptings of a panel of interview-ers. Interestingly, when he was first written to about the possi-bility of appearing on the programme, he replied: You might persuade me, but I'm shy-er than you'd think.' There was an element of truth in this, but that reticence failed to surface when the programme was recorded on 6 August. Allowing for brief interjections Fry talked non-stop for three hours and he was so pleased by the prospect of the broadcast, which somehow had to be reduced to thirty minutes, that he wrote asking for the date and time of the programme so he could tell Prince Philip to listen!

In the event C.B.'s life story was not told until the start of November, but there was plenty to entertain the listeners as Fry reflected on his time in India, his meeting with Hitler and his status as a minor poet.

When he was invited on to 'Personal Call' a couple of years later he took the trouble to send the BBC a curriculum vitae, which, in Fry's case, made rather impressive reading. Again he made a delightful interviewee. For instance his views on women: 'Oh well, they're a necessary good, for one thing, and they're very ornamen-tal, and I like them when they entertain you—when you take them out to dinner, instead of you having to entertain them. But I'm bound to say I think some of the French and Austrian girls are

rather better at it than most of our English would-be entertainers.'
This was a revealing assessment: C.B. was so much the dominant
figure in male company that it was hard to imagine that the roles
could be comfortably reversed when ladies were present.

22
MAN OF LETTERS

At the beginning of 1953 Charles Fry pleaded with *The Times* for help, but it was hardly a conventional appeal. He wrote: 'Several distinguished authors, including Mr Neville Cardus and Mr R.C. Robertson-Glasgow, have accused me (in print) of having successfully dumped on your newspaper Latin elegiac versions of hymns in the English Hymnal. This is not true. The only verses of mine you have published are in the English language, one called "Jai Hind", the other "From Agincourt to Alamein." One of the above critics remarked that Latin versification is the most "psittacine" and "simian" of all arts. Yes, perhaps; but I regard it as good as doing crosswords.'

His career as a 'minor poet' came to the fore again near the end of his life when he was asked in a television interview which of his many and varied achievements had given him most pleasure. Even allowing for a certain impish contrariness there was significance in his reply. The appearance of his poems in *The Times* ranked above all else, he said, because it was an honour generally reserved for Poet Laureates.

On the strength of a poem of C.B.'s which appeared in *Fry's Magazine* at the end of 1907 it was an unlikely honour. I would not wish to sully his reputation as a poet by quoting 'The Whitest Game' in its entirety (three verses), so the final four lines will suffice:

> We will sing for cricket,
> Sing its woes and joys;
> The whitest game for Englishmen –
> And for English boys.

The romantic side of Fry's character was clearly nurtured and flattered by a colourful meeting of minds with artists, writers and poets. In his active sporting days there was more of a battle waged between logic and impulse.

The confusion was already evident when he was at Repton and more so at Oxford. 'Apart from scheduled reading', wrote Wallis Myers, 'he hunted literature off the beaten track. The modern English fictionists did not appeal to him, and for the Society novel he had a genuine dislike; but the works of certain French authors, especially of George Sand and Alphonse Daudet, were conspicuous on his shelves. Madame Dudevant probably appealed to him, because, like Wordsworth, she had the inward eye and could demonstrate the mystical influences emanating from the world of sense, the witchery of the sky, and the soul of the river.'

Appearing for the opposition was John Stuart Mill, required reading for Greats and dry as the Sahara Desert. Maurice Bowra, later Warden of Wadham College, was led to understand that C.B. felt no affinity with Mill's arguments, but there was a different impression given by Harold Begbie's perceptive profile in the *Westminster Gazette* in 1904. Begbie said of Fry: 'From one subject to another he flies with the swiftness of light, and in every subject he discusses he reveals to you some fresh point in his personality. It would be difficult to decide at what point that personality most truly represents itself, and I doubt if he has ever stopped to consider in what single direction it is most vigorously trying to express itself. It is, I think, unfortunate that logic should be his favourite study and that he should have allowed his mind to be so powerfully dominated by John Stuart Mill . . . One might almost fancy him on some occasions to be a statesman bowed down by the cares of office, while at other times he seems like a jolly schoolboy with his hands full of pocket-money bent only on "standing tuck" to his friends.'

The radical split in his personality was always evident and almost twenty years after Begbie's piece Col. Philip Trevor wrote in the *Daily Telegraph*: 'What does surprise me, and will, I fear, always surprise me, is the way in which Fry has got his hundreds. By temperament Fry is an artist, and I am not quite sure that he is not a poet. The man is a mass of baffling contradictions—a most antithetical person. At Oxford he was a classic, but his mind is the mind of a ruthless logician . . . Had Fry as a boy been allowed to give the reins to his imagination I believe the artist in him would have predominated.'

Much of the spontaneity was reserved for the last twenty years of Charles Fry's life when the sparkle was reflected in his perky column for the *Evening Standard*; and nowhere was the heady combination of bright conversation, up-market refreshments and cultured wines more evident than in Fry's box at Lord's.

Legends were built and destroyed in this inner sanctum by the clock tower. C.B. had no divine right to élite accommodation during Test matches, but Lord's was denied vitality when he had to accept less exclusive seating arrangements. In 1938 he wrote, 'I have toured the swell boxes down by the clock tower in search of news for you—and the swell boxes have, all but two, fallen by ballot to members of the committee. Quite rightly, I say, remembering the worthy work of the MCC committee for the world of cricket, and for the well-being of their fellow members.'

When Fry was able to take his rightful place the guest-list was formidable. Poets, ancient and modern, were always welcome, so John Drinkwater, Edmund Blunden and G.K. Chesterton might join C.B. in discussion of the merits of anyone from Herodotus to Keats. There were writers, musicians, composers, critics and politicians—Clifford and Arnold Bax, James Agate, E.V. Lucas, Dr Hugh Dalton—and the names etched on cricket's roll of immortality like Jack Hobbs and Pelham Warner. The aesthetic quality of the occasion was always enhanced if a young actress like Peggy Ashcroft could be persuaded to lend glamour to the scene.

But fame, or budding notoriety, was not a prerequisite for admittance. Clifford Bax in *Some I Knew Well* recalled a day at Lord's when he asked Fry: ' "By the way, who are these two lean men at the back of the box?" "I have no idea," he answered. "I suppose you would call them box-crashers." ' Bax alternated between calling C.B. Charlemagne and d'Artagnan and saw him as a contemporary equivalent of Prince Rupert. He said it was more of a privilege for the artists to gaze upon the cricketing gods than vice versa.

The atmospheric opening to Denzil Batchelor's *Life of Fry* has been reproduced elsewhere, but it is still worth including here as an illustration of the scatty laissez-faire attitude which gave everyone the chance to dine with the stars:

It is half-past ten: time for the caravan to start from Brown's Hotel. The Bentley is at the door; Mr Brooks, the chauffeur, is wise-cracking out of the side of his guttapercha mouth. Aboard are writing pads and binoculars and travelling rugs, a copy of Herodotus, a box of Henry Clay cigars, and reserve hampers of hock and chicken sandwiches in case there has been a strike of caterers in North-West London. A monocle glitters. A silver crest pauses, high and haughty, above the cities of the plain. C.B. Fry is off to Lord's.

When the car is held up by the queue milling round the W.G. Gates, a greeting comes through the open window. It is uttered by a thin grey Colonel with the neatly folded look Soames Forsyte wore before he grew up to be imperious and hectoring like Errol Flynn. 'Excuse me, sir, but aren't you C.B. Fry?' It is probably the only time in his life the Colonel has ever spoken to a complete stranger. He does not blush, but he grows a richer grey with sheer embarrassment.

Charles Fry holds up a benevolent finger. 'I know exactly what you're going to tell me. You saw me bat in 1909 at Southampton. I made two.'

These shock tactics rattle the Colonel, who has expected nothing more than a little harmless long-distance trench warfare. 'As a matter of fact it was Southampton in 1909. But you only made one.'

By rights that should round off the campaign, but it doesn't. The Colonel is taken aboard and transported to Charles's box. Here he sits, day after day. At twelve he is given the cocktail a visitor from Mars had introduced into the box: a straight-forward tumbler filled with equal measures of gin and whisky which as soon as it has been christened a Bamboo-shoot is somehow accepted by the company as innocent to the point of being non-alcoholic. He eats lobsters for lunch with that fine Traminer '26 and has strawberries for tea and . . .

It has been a source of astonishment ever since that Charles Fry, always the focal point of these glittering proceedings and egocentric in the literal sense, could combine his duties as host with his responsibilities as columnist for the *Evening Standard*. He had the remarkable gift for addressing his mind to the conversation of the moment—and it was generally him doing the talking—while apparently giving the cricket his full attention and writing about it simultaneously. His reports stretched to a staggering 2,000 words a day during the 1938 Test matches with Australia.

The guests found it all pure delight. Clifford Bax said 'the experience was like a dream', while John Drinkwater confessed: 'To sit here watching a Test Match equates with my requirements in heaven.' Just occasionally a participant would find the rapid-fire exchanges a touch esoteric, like Bob Crisp in 1945, who said that he found it difficult to engage in a conversation which was often conducted in Latin and classical Greek. He was baffled by frequent mention of *duo et sex* between Clifford Bax and Sir John Squire, former editor of the *London Mercury*, until it dawned on him that this translated as two and six and referred to a bet about the size of England's total. Crisp then wondered about Fry's assertion that pools and gambling would never be associated with cricket.

Even when there was no box available Fry dealt out royal hospitality. He met Batchelor and an unimpressed lady friend on a boxless day at Lord's and promptly despatched a boy to the Langham Hotel, where he had dined the previous evening, to fetch a bottle of Liebfraumilch of appropriate vintage. The messenger was given precise instructions to return in a taxi and ensure that the driver did not exceed fifteen miles an hour.

These *bon viveurs* did not return home to an evening with their feet up in front of the fire. They ate at plush and fashionable establishments and talked some more, then danced into the early hours of the morning, resplendent in white tie and tails.

The provinces, too, were able to sample the urbanity of Fry and cronies. In 1938, when *Mercury* old boy Reg Sinfield made his one and only appearance for England, at Trent Bridge, the party checked in at The George at Grantham. C.B. had a rival in conversational gymnastics in the orientalist, Sir Denison Ross, while the audience was made up of Sir C. Aubrey Smith, Gerry Weigall and Denzil Batchelor, whose recollections of one particular evening at The George were on these lines:

In no time the talk turned metaphysical and took wings. If Einstein had dropped in to join us no doubt he would have interjected an occasional comment, but without him we fell back on silent admiration for the glimpses we got of that conversation sparkling above the mountains of the moon or zooming beyond suns that light up other universes. I say 'we fell back on silent admiration': in fact one of us just fell back, and fell asleep. At ten minutes to two, when the question of immortality was being debated against that kink in space which seemed to suggest that eternity has its limits, Gerry Weigall stirred, rubbed his eyes and rejoined us. 'That's it, Charles. That's what it all boils down to—playing a straight bat.'

The economically written letters became a vital part of C.B.'s communication with the outside world. When John Arlott and R.C. Robertson-Glasgow wrote appreciations of Fry in recognition of his eightieth birthday in 1952, both remarked how the flow of brief epistles had dried up two years earlier in deference to illness and had only just been resumed. These letters, often no more than three or four lines long, commented, advised and corrected. They also recommended: there was nothing that pleased Fry more in his later years than using his influence to advance the careers of promising sportsmen, writers, journalists and musicians.

He pleaded the case for much-abused cricketers, and in 1947, when the English side were taking a pasting Down Under, he quoted the notice which was prominently displayed for reporters on the *Westminster Gazette* when J.A. Spender was editor: 'Failure to make runs or take wickets or hold catches must not be imputed to cricketers as proof of moral obliquity.'

The Times, presumably innocently, relayed the same message via C.B. when England were playing in the West Indies in 1954, but he involved himself in a host of other discussions in both *The Times* and the *Daily Telegraph*. He wondered whether compositors could still handle Greek characters; he pleaded the case for teachers; and he suggested that a combination of full swing and precise timing would enable a girl to hit a cricket ball from the centre of Lord's to the top of the pavilion.

In the final few years of his life Fry was forced, a little

reluctantly, to take a minor role in the Lord's productions. The *Daily Telegraph* wrote on his eightieth birthday: 'Of recent years his extraordinary vitality has given place to a mood of philosophic calm. He is still to be seen at Lord's, but no longer as the focus of a crowd, demonstrating strokes with his walking stick in the Long Room. He is generally to be found outside the pavilion, sitting with a friend in the members' enclosure.'

23
THE FINAL SESSION

There was a marvellous generosity of spirit about Fry and when his days as an athlete were over he took altruistic delight in the promotion of protégés. Optimism was the key to his outlook and when he felt unable to praise his criticism was generally constructive: he never sought to score cheap points off someone with whom he did not agree. He would argue from dawn to dusk on a matter of principle, and reel off classical antecedents, but it would not occur to him to be sidetracked by an opportunity for personal abuse.

As a journalist he had sung the praises of his fellow-cricketers and footballers, moderate performers though some of them may have been, and later he became something of a fairy godfather. For the most part it was a service rendered gratis–C.B. wanted neither agent's reward nor thanks–but the chosen ones could sense the impetus to their careers and often learned secondhand that the legendary C.B. Fry had put in a good word for them.

There was nothing forced about his kindness. He was employed by the BBC to provide expert comment on the first Test series after the Second World War, when India were the visitors. Rex Alston made his debut as a commentator for the Corporation in the First Test at Lord's, a nervous occasion which he remembered in *Taking the Air*: 'I was even more honoured when I heard that the great C.B. Fry was to sit beside me during the morning and sum up play at the luncheon interval. I had never met him, and was nervous of performing in his presence, but he set my mind at rest with his opening remarks on the air, "You've just had a map of the play put before you and a very good, clear map too." '

Fry thought himself 'too impertinent' to be acceptable as a

commentator, but if he was not the man for the job he was only too willing to suggest alternative candidates. Included among these were two men who made a considerable impression on the world of broadcasting and are still well-known names. One was E.W. Swanton, whose early days on the *Evening Standard* had coincided with Fry's, and the other was Peter West. C.B. wrote to the BBC in May 1946 describing Swanton as their 'blue-eyed boy' and although they had already engaged him for commentary on county cricket his international prospects were powerfully endorsed. West says he owes 'an eternal debt' to Fry, recalling:

> I first met him when I was a young agency reporter in the early part of the 1947 season. It was at Taunton. Imagine my pleasure and excitement at sitting next to God in the press box. On the second day his telephonist failed to materialise. So the sycophantic West volunteered to do the job for him. It simply seemed a great honour! Shortly after I had done this, but I suppose not wholly on account of it, he asked me if I had done any radio commentary. No, sir. Would you like to? Well, I suppose we all would (a year or more before I had dismally failed a test as a would-be BBC announcer). Right, then, I'll suggest it.
>
> Heavens above. I don't think I really believed him—not knowing at that stage how he had dedicated much of his life to helping young people up the ladder.
>
> Well, he was a man of his word. He wrote to S.J. de Lotbinière, head of outside broadcasts, who must have been averse to receiving suggestions from all and sundry but listened to CBF, and, what is more, gave me an interview.

West was eventually telephoned by Rex Alston and invited to commentate on the game between Warwickshire and the touring South Africans. He was lacking a little in confidence and polish, but largely on the strength of C.B.'s introduction had got his foot in the door and went on to become a highly natural performer on both radio and television.

Someone else who had cause to remember Charles Fry in the summer of 1946 was one of the Indian tourists, Abdul Hafeez Kardar, later a leading figure in Pakistan cricket, both as a player and an administrator. He was keen to get into Oxford, but this was at a time when places were having to be found for members of the armed forces after demobilisation. However, Kardar was introduced to Fry during the Second Test at Old Trafford by the Indian captain, the Nawab of Pataudi. C.B.'s influence with the university was demonstrated by a choice of six colleges with which Kardar was presented.

He had dinner with C.B. in Manchester and was impressed with his polished recital of passages from the Omar Khayyam. There was also a nice illustration of Fry's natural flamboyance: 'He found something wrong with the dinner service and instead of calling the steward in attendance, who was a few feet away from our table, Fry chose to go to the house telephone, yards away from our table and got the steward summoned on the phone to lodge his complaint to him.'

Much of C.B.'s correspondence with the BBC concerned the inadequacy of his fees, but he also found time to toss a few names into the melting pot. There were personalities like Dame Rachel Crowdy, whom he saw as ideal for profile pieces, and artists of all kinds, either picked out by Fry himself or suggested to him as worthy of encouragement. He also took a healthy interest in the development of young cricketers, and not just the ones who passed under his expert eye at the *Mercury*. Fry's standards were high and youngsters lacking in talent tended to feel overawed, but he had an uncanny knack for assessing a player's strengths and weaknesses.

When Ronny Aird was Secretary of the MCC he recalled taking C.B. round the nets at Lord's during the Easter coaching classes:

We walked behind the nets and he watched the boys batting each for a short time but he stopped behind one net for quite a long time taking a particular interest in the boy who was batting.

He said to me, 'There is something wrong with this boy but I can't make out what it is.' Then he said, 'I believe he ought to be round the other way and batting left handed.' He told the boy to turn round and bat left handed and the result was a complete success and the boy played very much better that way. What I cannot remember is whether he asked the boy first if he had ever played left handed but I think he may have done. That does not matter very much but it seemed extra-ordinary to me that he could have thought the way he did. It must have required a very special brain.'

On another youth-watching brief at Lord's he was asked if he had particular interest in any of the young players on show: 'Interested in all of 'em,' he replied. 'Interested in everything. *Homo sum; humani nil a me alienum puto.*' This translates as: 'I'm a man; and I don't consider anything outside my province.' That was Charles Fry, both as practitioner and spectator.

In the final few years of his life C.B. found it difficult to accept that he was becoming an old man. He was asked to resign as director of the training ship *Mercury* and he was no longer in demand as a journalist. However, he was still a fair draw as a public speaker and when Plum Warner was uniquely honoured by having a celebration dinner in the Long Room at Lord's to mark his eightieth birthday, Fry was asked to propose Warner's health. They had not been particularly close, but their careers had moved in parallel lines from the time that Warner went up to Oxford a year after Fry. Cricket's voices of authority were all gathered at Lord's for that momentous occasion at the end of 1953. C.B. was a sprightly eighty-one. He had lost a little of the physical and mental agility which accompanied his every word and deed in the early part of the century, but he still cut a formidable figure.

Gubby Allen, who was similarly honoured almost thirty years later, remembers the occasion: 'He made a brilliant start and I remember thinking this is going to be a wonderful speech. The first seven or eight minutes were wonderful, but then he began to drivel on and people started talking.' This impression was confirmed by E.W. Swanton in *Sort of a Cricket Person*: 'If he had sat down after ten minutes it would have been perfect, but he tired and his voice weakened and the end was an anti-climax.'

Fry was never quite able to translate his mastery of the conversational stage onto a more formal platform. At the time when he was addressing himself to readers' queries in *The Captain* and venting his spleen in *Fry's Magazine* he was in great demand as a speaker before a tremendous variety of organisations. He could be superb, but when the adrenalin flowed erratically the results were equally unpredictable. Ian Peebles's theory, as expounded in

Spinner's Yarn, was this: 'On the several occasions upon which I heard him, Charles Fry was, surprisingly, an indifferent speaker for the reason that he usually was patently unrehearsed. As he was also very lengthy, his addresses were inclined to become increasingly rambled.'

There is a comparison to be drawn here between Plum Warner, the titled elder statesman, and Charles Fry, the outsider, who constantly had his sights set on the establishment, driven on by the proud assertion that he was a rebel. Warner settled comfortably into his MCC committee chair, but C.B. was carefully bypassed. His wise perspective would have made him an ideal president, but he was not even invited to sit on the committee. 'He said and did what came natural and uppermost,' said R.C. Robertson-Glasgow in *46 Not Out*, 'thus making silent but important enemies in influential snuggeries; enemies who, when they could, excluded, when they couldn't, belittled him. Thus, though for years he stood without rival in the combined theory and practice of batsmanship, Fry was never elected to the Committee of the Marylebone Cricket Club, where birth and convention have always ranked higher than originality and knowledge.'

Gubby Allen had a period of disenchantment with the MCC after the Second World War, when he thought the old guard were clinging jealously to their positions and the younger voices were being gagged. He was not surprised by the uneasy relationship between the cricket authorities and C.B.: 'Charles could be a very awkward chap—he was very self-opinionated and he did tend to rub a lot of people up the wrong way. He had some enemies, but I don't know who they were and why.'

There was some small sign that he had been given the nod of approval by those in authority when a statuette of Fry was introduced to the hallowed surroundings of the Long Room at Lord's in November 1953. It had been languishing sadly in the cellars of the pavilion. C.B. came up with a typically wry comment on his unexpected promotion when asked about it by the *Evening Standard*: 'I spent 20 years in the cellar and now I am on the shelf.'

As an eighty-three-year-old Charles Fry was still quite capable of stealing headlines. In deference to failing agility he had tempered his athletic excesses, but his tongue was as active as ever and his perspective just as contrary. He told the world that polo was definitely the best of all games—for those who could afford it—and gave up two seats at the 1955 FA Cup Final between Newcastle and Manchester City in order to attend the annual lunch of the Poetry Society. 'I think so much more of poetry than I do of football,' he explained. 'Anybody can kick a ball around.'

This recalls a piece of 'Straight Talk' in *Fry's Magazine* at the start of 1905 when the editor wrote: 'Sports and games are of very little importance compared with the serious business of life, but that does not mean they have no importance of their own. It is a matter of perspective. Sports and games should be taken for what they are worth, and for no more, and it is not a little.' Money has tended to blur the distinction between sport and 'the serious business of life', but the players of today would do well to mark the words written eighty years ago.

C.B. may have turned down his invitation to football's major domestic showpiece, but he was happy enough to be asked to attend the Speech Day celebrations at Repton on 10 June that year. By delightful coincidence his seventeen-year-old grandson, Jonathan, had won Classics prizes which C.B. himself had carried off almost seventy years earlier. Lord Hives had been asked to present the prizes, but the school could not resist the nostalgic temptation to invite Repton's star pupil of the 1880s to offer formal congratulations to his grandson.

A month later he brought about minor controversy with this letter to the *Evening Standard*: 'Next time I see females undressed in bikinis in P and Q block (of all places) at Lord's I will go there in pyjamas and parade in front of the Pavilion of which I am a part owner.' He elaborated a little the following day: 'Perhaps I am wrong in describing these garments as bikinis. But certainly there has been the regrettable sight of young ladies, presumably invited by members, divesting themselves of outer garments and sitting, uncomfortably I should think, on the iron seats in P and Q blocks in bathing costumes. I suggest that these young ladies should mind their P's and Q's and remember that Lord's is as much a private club as the Athenaeum'. C.B. even confessed that he had a pair of pyjamas which would 'knock them for six'.

There was less good-natured disagreement at London's other cricketing centre, the Oval, in August when England played South Africa in the Fifth Test. As a former captain of England, indeed the oldest surviving one, C.B. was accustomed to receiving a pair of complimentary tickets for Tests. This was no exception, but after Fry had been dropped off at the ground he discovered that he had left the tickets at home. He wanted to go to the Surrey office to pick up the duplicates, but to his great chagrin the turnstile man, gate man and a policeman all refused to let him into the ground. C.B. eventually got in, but he was none too pleased about the incident: 'There were a few words. Someone said, "Shove him out!" and I replied "You had better not try anything of the kind.". . . The maddening thing was, they all knew I was entitled to be there. It was a piece of silliness.'

There was equal silliness in an impromptu Mr World competition thought up by the *Daily Express* just after the 1955 Miss World event in October. Fry was not included among the original 'nominations', but he was selected all the same by Sir Gerald Kelly, one of the judges at Miss World, who explained his reasons: 'He's around 90 and still looks magnificent. I remember him when he was young. He looked like a piece of the Parthenon frieze come to life–a beautiful man.' C.B. was not suitably flattered by the description and complained that he had been 'deluged with letters chipping me and calling me Mr World'.

Fry's continuing concern for Oxbridge sport was reflected in an unusual offer prior to the soccer match between Oxford and Cambridge at Wembley on 7 December 1955. He requested permission to present two trophies at the 'Varsity game–one to the winners and one to the losers.

The Times reported: 'Although the presence of a cup in a University contest is unique it is probable that the joint committee formed by representatives of the F.A., Oxford, Cambridge and Wembley Stadium, will accept this kindly offer from one of the heroic figures in British sport, who himself continues to show a deep interest in games, especially those at the Universities.'

C.B.'s plan was to have the two trophies inscribed Happy Winner and Good Loser–'a good loser is as good as a good winner', he explained–but the football authorities were forced to opt for just one trophy, as an annual presentation to both sides would have infringed their amateur status. Fry modestly declined a suggestion that the trophy should be called the Fry Cup, in case it was confused with a bedtime drink!

A win for Oxford would have enabled them to draw level at 29 wins apiece in the 72nd match of the series, but it was Cambridge who won 4–2 and claimed the coveted trophy at the after-match dinner at the Public Schools Club.

It was less than a fortnight later, on 18 December, when C.B. was chosen as the subject for *This Is Your Life*. It was the BBC's property at this time and presenter Eamonn Andrews selected his victim from the studio audience. Fry was accompanied by Denzil Batchelor and soon found himself on the familiar lightning trip along the dim corridors of a life-time.

They brought on William Clarry, who had been an office boy on *Fry's Magazine*, Eric McGavin, who was in charge of musical instruction on the *Mercury*, and Dame Rachel Crowdy, C.B.'s fellow-mover at the League of Nations and dancing partner. Then there was Josephine Bradley, his gifted dancing instructor and friend, and Reg Sinfield, the *Mercury* boy who had gone on to play cricket for England. For the grand finale the surviving members of the 1912 England side which Fry had led to victory in the Triangular series were reunited with their skipper—legendary names like Jack Hobbs, Sydney Barnes, Jack Hearne, Tiger Smith and Wilfred Rhodes—and the fond reminiscing went on deep into the night. C.B's only slip was in confusing Reg Sinfield's voice with that of Jack Hobbs. 'How could I forget my chief hand', he said to Sinfield behind the scenes afterwards.

Fry was in the public eye right to the end. On 16 June 1956 he opened the new sports pavilion of the London Hospital Clubs Union at Walthamstow and a few days later he was among the crowd for the Second Test between England and Australia at Lord's. However, his health was gradually failing and on 28 June he was admitted to the Middlesex Hospital suffering from neuritis. His condition that evening was given as 'comfortable', but in effect it was the beginning of the end. He remained in hospital until 1 September and six days later died at his flat in Moreland Court. The cause of death was given as kidney failure due to infection of the urinary tract and prostatex.

The tributes were many and glowing. A minute's silence was observed before the match at the Oval between the champions, Surrey, and the Rest of England. The great deeds were recalled and if the plaudits tended to gush rather than flow it was only to be expected.

The Times preceded its obituary with the appropriate classical reference *mens sana in corpore sano* and the *News Chronicle*, whose readers had chosen C.B. as the greatest sportsman of the age, called him a 'perfect human being'. Gerald Walters wrote: 'The pattern of his whole life was devoid of ignoble ambition or mean jealousy. C.B. Fry is gone to Olympus. We and our world are the poorer. He was the Englishman of tradition. The Englishman we would all of us like to be.' The *Southern Daily Echo* described him as 'a gracious personality in spite of his occasional hauteur, a standard bearer of sport and an exemplar of fine and social service to his generation. We are entitled to look upon his life with awe.'

Frank Rostron, writing in the *Daily Express*, gave Fry's all-round qualities a modern perspective: 'If Charles Fry were in his prime today, this would be the tussle between the MCC and the British Olympic Association: should he go to South Africa to captain the cricket tourists and head the Test batsmen, or go to Melbourne for the Olympic Games as a sprinter, hurdler, or long jumper–and probably captain too? 'And the Football Association would be wanting him to winter at home.'

Plum Warner, Jack Hobbs, Len Hutton and Frank Woolley all added their personal appreciations, but there was no finer tribute than that of Neville Cardus in *The Guardian*, a piece which was reproduced in the 1957 *Wisden*. Cardus wrote:

Fry must be counted among the most fully developed and representative Englishmen of his period; and the question arises whether, had fortune allowed him to concentrate on the things of the mind, not distracted by the lure of cricket, a lure intensified by his increasing mastery over the game, he would not have reached a high altitude in politics or critical literature. But he belonged–and it was his glory–to an age not obsessed by specialism; he was one of the last of the English tradition of the amateur, the connoisseur, and, in the most delightful sense of the word, the dilettante.'

On 11 September a private funeral service was held at Golders Green Crematorium, with the Sussex and England cricketer, David Sheppard, officiating. A week later there was a well-attended memorial service at St. Martin-in-the-Fields, part of the proceedings being conducted by the Archbishop of Canterbury, Geoffrey Fisher, whose wife was daughter of the Rev. Arthur Forman, C.B.'s housemaster at Repton. An address was given by Harry Altham and the lesson was read by Jonathan Fry. Among those present at the service were the then president of the MCC, Field-Marshal Earl Alexander of Tunis, and three former England captains, Douglas Jardine, Freddie Brown and George Mann.

On 28 September C.B.'s ashes were interred at Repton Parish Church, next to the school and near the grave of Arthur Forman. Mr T.L. Thomas, the headmaster of Repton at the time, referred to Fry as 'a writer of great distinction and originality', and went on: 'This is not an occasion for sorrow and mourning. I can assure his family that we are proud to be entrusted with the task of preserving the memory of such an outstanding son of the school. His life will remain as an example, an inspiration, not only to us, but for many generations who will follow afterwards.'

He certainly did not die a wealthy man—he left just under £9,000 in his will. As mentioned earlier, Anne Bradley received £200 and the rest was shared between his two spinster daughters, Charis and Faith.

C.B. was not forgotten: two years after his death the C.B. Fry Memorial Fund was formed, friends and admirers having begun a trust to provide an annual prize at Repton in his memory. It was to be awarded, at the headmaster's discretion, to the boy who had best served the school as an athlete and scholar during the school year. He was not forgotten in his London home either. On 4 June 1959 a plaque was unveiled by the Mayor of Hendon at Moreland Court to mark C.B.'s six years in residence at Golders Green.

It is now nearly thirty years since Fry's death, but his name and achievements live on. An immortal figure, representing all that is admirable and valuable about amateur sport, in an age where money has consumed sport, his qualities are the finest testimony to the Olympic ideal.

CAREER RECORD

Season	Innings	Not Out	Runs	Average	Highest Score
1892	18	0	356	19.77	110
1893	21	0	398	18.95	59
1894	29	2	713	26.40	119
1895	30	0	894	29.30	125
1895–6	3	0	122	40.66	64
(in South Africa)					
1896	17	0	496	29.17	92
1897	16	1	449	29.93	122
1898	37	4	1788	54.18	179*
1899	55	1	2366	43.81	181
1900	41	3	2325	61.18	229
1901	43	3	3147	78.67	244
1902	48	2	1625	35.32	159*
1903	40	7	2683	81.30	234
1904	42	2	2824	70.60	229
1905	44	4	2801	70.02	233
1906	4	0	108	27.00	67
1907	34	3	1449	46.74	187
1908	20	1	1000	52.63	214
1909	25	3	834	37.90	132
1910	3	0	126	42.00	115
1911	26	2	1728	72.00	258*
1912	31	3	1592	56.85	203*
1914	13	1	411	34.25	112
1920	3	1	210	105.00	137*
1921	13	0	397	30.53	96
1921–2	2	0	44	22.00	44
(in India)					
Total	658	43	30886	50.22	258*

Test cricket (England v Australia)

Season	Tests	Innings	Not out	Runs	Average	Highest score
1899	5	8	0	187	23.37	60
1902	3	4	0	5	1.25	4
1905	4	7	1	348	58.00	144
1909	3	6	2	140	35.00	62
1912	3	4	0	145	36.25	79
	18	29	3	825	31.73	144

England v South Africa

1895–6	2	3	0	122	40.66	64
1907	3	5	0	221	44.20	129
1912	3	4	0	55	13.75	29
	8	12	0	398	33.16	129
TOTAL	26	41	3	1223	32.18	144

CENTURIES

The following are C.B. Fry's ninety-four first-class centuries:

Season

1892	110	Oxford University v Somerset (Oxford)
1894	119	Oxford University v Sussex (Hove)
	100*	Oxford University v Cambridge University (Lord's)
	109	Sussex v Gloucestershire (Bristol)
1895	125	Oxford University v Sussex (Hove)
1897	122	Sussex v Kent (Hove)
1898	104*	Sussex v Middlesex (Lord's)
	⎰108	Sussex v Middlesex (Hove)
	⎱123	Sussex v Middlesex (Hove)
	110	Sussex v Somerset (Taunton)
	133	Sussex v Hampshire (Hove)
	179*	Sussex v Yorkshire (Hove)
1899	162*	Sussex v Yorkshire (Harrogate)
	104	Gentlemen v Players (Lord's)
	181	Sussex v Australians (Hove)
	162	Sussex v Somerset (Taunton)
	157	Sussex v Hampshire (Portsmouth)
1900	145	Sussex v Surrey (Oval)
	101*	Sussex v Essex (Leyton)
	110	Sussex v Kent (Tonbridge)
	135	Sussex v Leicestershire (Leicester)
	⎰125	Sussex v Surrey (Hove)
	⎱229	Sussex v Surrey (Hove)
	110	Sussex v Middlesex (Hove)
	105	Sussex v Gloucestershire (Bristol)
	145	Sussex v Leicestershire (Hove)

271

1901	170*	Sussex v Nottinghamshire (Nottingham)
	244	Sussex v Leicestershire (Leicester)
	241	Sussex v Cambridge University (Hove)
	219*	Sussex v Oxford University (Eastbourne)
	126	Gentlemen v Players (Lord's)
	116	Sussex v Middlesex (Lord's)
	119*	Sussex v Somerset (Taunton)
	106	Sussex v Hampshire (Portsmouth)
	209	Sussex v Yorkshire (Hove)
	149	Sussex v Middlesex (Hove)
	105	Sussex v Surrey (Oval)
	140	Sussex v Kent (Hove)
	105	Rest of England v Yorkshire (Lord's)
1902	122	Sussex v Middlesex (Lord's)
	159	Sussex v Surrey (Hastings)
	159*	Sussex v Middlesex (Eastbourne)
1903	174	Sussex v Worcestershire (Hove)
	181	Sussex v Lancashire (Manchester)
	124	Sussex v Yorkshire (Bradford)
	200	Sussex v Surrey (Hove)
	232*	Gentlemen v Players (Lord's)
	160	Sussex v Hampshire (Hove)
	127*	Sussex v Leicestershire (Hove)
	⎧138	Sussex v Kent (Hove)
	⎩101*	Sussex v Kent (Hove)
1904	120	Sussex v Somerset (Hove)
	191*	Sussex v Leicestershire (Leicester)
	226	Sussex v Derbyshire (Hove)
	177	Sussex v Yorkshire (Sheffield)
	105*	Sussex v Lancashire (Manchester)
	150	Sussex v Cambridge University (Hove)
	191	Sussex v Leicestershire (Hove)
	181	Sussex v Surrey (Hove)
	211	Sussex v Hampshire (Hove)
	229	Sussex v Yorkshire (Hove)
1905	⎧156	Sussex v M.C.C. (Lord's)
	⎩106	Sussex v M.C.C. (Lord's)
	201*	Sussex v Nottinghamshire (Hove)
	233	Sussex v Nottinghamshire (Nottingham)

	175	Sussex v Kent (Tonbridge)
	111	Sussex v Yorkshire (Leeds)
	100	Sussex v Warwickshire (Hove)
	144	England v Australia (Oval)
	127	Sussex v Hampshire (Hastings)
	155	Sussex v Kent (Hastings)
1907	102*	Sussex v Lancashire (Eastbourne)
	125	Sussex v Worcestershire (Hove)
	187	Sussex v Derbyshire (Hove)
	129	England v South Africa (Oval)
1908	120	Sussex v Lancashire (Manchester)
	119	Sussex v Somerset (Hove)
	214	Sussex v Worcestershire (Hove)
1909	132	Hampshire v Warwickshire (Bournemouth)
1910	115	Hampshire v Worcestershire (Bournemouth)
1911	150	Hampshire v Derbyshire (Southampton)
	104	Hampshire v Kent (Southampton)
	121	Hampshire v Worcestershire (Southampton)
	{123	Hampshire v Kent (Canterbury)
	{112	Hampshire v Kent (Canterbury)
	258*	Hampshire v Gloucestershire (Southampton)
	102*	Rest of England v Warwickshire (Oval)
1912	152*	Hampshire v Somerset (Southampton)
	143	Hampshire v Kent (Southampton)
	203*	Hampshire v Oxford University (Southampton)
	101	Gentlemen v Players (Oval)
	186	Hampshire v Yorkshire (Southampton)
1914	112	Hampshire v Gloucestershire (Portsmouth)
1920	137	Hampshire v Nottinghamshire (Southampton)

MISCELLANEOUS RECORDS

Six Centuries in Successive Innings
1901   106   Sussex v Hampshire (Portsmouth)
           209   Sussex v Yorkshire (Hove)
           149   Sussex v Middlesex (Hove)
           105   Sussex v Surrey (Oval)
           140   Sussex v Essex (Hove)
           105   Rest of England v Yorkshire (Lord's)

Four Centuries in Successive Innings
1911   123 and 112   Hampshire v Kent (Canterbury)
           258* Hampshire v Gloucestershire (Southampton)
           102* Rest of England v Warwickshire (Oval)
(In between the games against Gloucestershire and Warwickshire Fry made three successive hundreds for the *Mercury* and the *Mercury* officers, thus compiling seven successive centuries in all cricket)

Century in Each Innings
1898   108 and 123* Sussex v Middlesex (Hove)
1900   125 and 229 Sussex v Surrey (Hove)
1903   138 and 101* Sussex v Kent (Hove)
1905   156 and 106 Sussex v M.C.C. (Lord's)
1911   123 and 112 Hampshire v Kent (Canterbury)

Ten or More Centuries in a Season
1901   13 Centuries
1904   10 Centuries
1905   10 Centuries
(Fry's 13 centuries in 1901 created a new record, unsurpassed until Jack Hobbs hit 16 in 1925)

Four Double Centuries in a Season
1901   241   Sussex v Cambridge University (Hove)
           219* Sussex v Oxford University (Eastbourne)
           244   Sussex v Leicestershire (Leicester)
           209   Sussex v Yorkshire (Hove)

Carrying the Bat
1898   104* (out of 197)   Sussex v Middlesex (Lord's)
1898   179* (out of 311)   Sussex v Yorkshire (Hove)
1901   170* (out of 254)   Sussex v Nottinghamshire
           (Nottingham)

Thousand Runs in a Month
1901 June   1130 Runs (average 125.55)
1901 August   1116 Runs (average 101.45)

Three Thousand Runs in a Season
1901   3147 Runs (average 78.67)

Top of Batting Averages
On the basis of a minimum of 20 innings being played Fry came
first in the batting averages in 1901, 1903, 1905, 1907, 1911 and
1912.

Big Partnerships
1904   (1st wicket) 287   with J. Vine, Sussex v Hampshire
           (Hove)
1901   (2nd wicket) 349   with E.H. Killick, Sussex v Yorkshire
           (Hove)
1901   (2nd wicket) 292* with K.S. Ranjitsinhji, Sussex v
           Somerset (Taunton)
1903   (3rd wicket) 309* with A.C. MacLaren, Gentlemen v
           Players (Lord's)
1912   (3rd wicket) 264*
                              with E.I.M. Barrett, Hampshire v
           Oxford University (Southampton)
1904   (3rd wicket) 255   with K.S. Ranjitsinhji, Sussex v
           Yorkshire (Sheffield)
1911   (5th wicket) 234   with P.F. Warner, Rest of England v
           Warwickshire (Oval)

Century Partnerships in Both Innings
1899   135 and 148   with G. Brann, Sussex v Middlesex (Lord's)
1903   170 and 179   with J. Vine, Sussex v Leicestershire (Hove)
           (Fry and Vine compiled 33 century stands together)

Fifty per cent Share of Both Innings in Match
1901   88 out of 159 and 106 out of 212, Sussex v Hampshire
           (Portsmouth)

Hundred Runs and Ten Wickets in Match
1896   89 and 65, 5–81 and 5–66, Sussex v Nottinghamshire
           (Nottingham)

Ten Wickets in Match
1895   5–75 and 5–102, Gentlemen of England v I. Zingari
           (Lord's)

Hat-Trick
1894   Oxford University v M.C.C. (Lord's)

BIBLIOGRAPHY

Many of the periodicals and books which I have consulted are mentioned in the course of the text. C.B. Fry's autobiography, *Life Worth Living, Some Phases of an Englishman* (Eyre and Spottiswoode), has been of particular value, as has A. Wallis Myers' book, *C.B. Fry: The Man and his Methods* (Arrowsmith), and Denzil Batchelor's *C.B. Fry* (Phoenix).

The newspapers and magazines which have been of most assistance are: *Daily Chronicle, Daily Express, Daily Telegraph, The Times, Westminster Gazette, Evening Standard, Sunday Express, Banbury Advertiser, Oxford Chronicle, Oxford Times, Southern Daily Echo, Sussex Daily News, Athletic News, Badminton Magazine, The Captain, C.B. Fry's Magazine, The Field, Isis, Oxford Magazine, Reptonian, Strand Magazine.*

Numerous volumes of *Wisden* have also been exceptionally useful. Included among other books consulted are:

Agate, James. *The Selective Ego* (Harrap)

Alston, Rex. *Taking the Air* (Stanley Paul)

Batchelor, Denzil. *Babbled of Green Fields* (Hutchinson)

   (ed.) *Great Cricketers* (Eyre and Spottiswoode)

Bax, Clifford. *Some I Knew Well* (Phoenix)

Bowra, Maurice. *Memories 1898–1939* (Weidenfeld and Nicolson)

Bradley, Josephine. *Dancing Through Life* (Hollis and Carter)

Cardus, Neville. *Autobiography* (Collins)

   Full Score (Cassell)

Catton, J.A.H. *Wickets and Goals* (Chapman and Hall)

Fenby, Charles. *The Other Oxford* (Lund Humphries)

Fingleton, Jack. *Cricket Crisis* (Cassell)

Frindall, Bill. *The Kaye Book of Cricket Records* (Kaye and Ward)

Fry, Charles. (ed.) *The Book of Cricket* (Newnes)

   Real Diabolo (Newnes)

   Batsmanship (Eveleigh Nash)

   Key-Book of the League of Nations (Hodder and Stoughton)

   (with George Beldam) *Great Batsmen* (Macmillan)

   (with George Beldam) *Great Bowlers and Fielders* (Macmillan)

   (with Beatrice Fry) *A Mother's Son* (Methuen)

Gibson, Alan. *The Cricket Captains of England* (Cassell)

Gilligan, Arthur. *Sussex Cricket* (Chapman and Hall)

Hammond, Wally. *Cricket My World* (Stanley Paul)

   Cricketer's School (Stanley Paul)

Harris, Bruce. *Australian Test Tour* (Hutchinson)

Hill, Alan. *The Family Fortune—A Saga of Sussex Cricket* (Scan Books)

Hollis, Christopher. *Oxford in the Twenties* (Heinemann)

Jessop, Gilbert. (ed.) *Cricket*, including 'Training for Cricket' by C.B. Fry (C. Arthur Pearson)
A Cricketer's Log (Hodder and Stoughton)

Knight, Albert. *The Complete Cricketer* (Methuen)

Lucas, Laddie. *Five Up* (Sidgwick and Jackson)

Mackinnon, Alan. *The Oxford Amateurs* (Chapman and Hall)

Marshall, John. *Sussex Cricket—A History* (Heinemann)

Miller, K. and Whitington, R.S. *Cricket Tycoon*, including guest chapter by C.B. Fry (MacDonald)

Pawson, Tony. *100 Years of the FA Cup* (Heinemann)

Peebles, Ian. *Spinner's Yarn* (Collins)
Straight From the Shoulder (Hutchinson)

Ranjitsinhji, Prince. *The Jubilee Book of Cricket* (Blackwood)

Robertson-Glasgow, R.C. *46 Not Out* (Hollis and Carter)

Rosenwater, Irving. *Sir Don Bradman—A Biography* (Batsford)

Ross, Alan. *Ranji, Prince of Cricketers* (Collins)

Shah, Maneklal. *Jam the Great* (Gujrat Times Press)

Smith, F.W. (Second Earl of Birkenhead). *F.E.; The Life of F.E. Smith First Earl of Birkenhead* (Eyre and Spottiswoode)

Swanton, E.W. *Cricket from All Angles* (Michael Joseph)
Sort of a Cricket Person (Collins)

Tennyson, Lionel Lord. *Sticky Wickets* (Christopher Johnson)

Thomas, Ivor. *Our Lord Birkenhead: An Oxford Appreciation* (Putnam)

Travers, Ben. *94 Declared* (Elm Tree Books)

Trevor, Col. Philip. *Cricket and Cricketers* (Chapman and Hall)

Turner, Ernest Sackville. *Boys Will be Boys*, introduction by C.B. Fry (Michael Joseph)

Various writers. *Cricket Heroes* (Phoenix)

Warner, Pelham. *My Cricketing Life* (Hodder and Stoughton)

Wells, Joseph. *History of Wadham* (Robinson)

Woods, Sammy. *My Reminiscences* (Chapman and Hall)

Woolley, Frank. *The King of Games.* (Stanley Paul)

Young, R.S. *Cricket on the Green*, prologue and epilogue by C.B. Fry (Hollis and Carter)

INDEX